# BICYCLING THROUGH PARADISE

# BICYCLING THROUGH PARADISE

Historical Tours around Cincinnati

Kathleen Smythe and Chris Hanlin

University of
CINCINNATI | PRESS

*About the University of Cincinnati Press*

The University of Cincinnati Press is committed to publishing rigorous, peer-reviewed, leading scholarship accessibly to stimulate dialog among the academy, public intellectuals, and lay practitioners. The Press endeavors to erase disciplinary boundaries in order to cast fresh light on common problems in our global community. Building on the university's long-standing tradition of social responsibility to the citizens of Cincinnati, state of Ohio, and the world, the Press publishes books on topics that expose and resolve disparities at every level of society and have local, national, and global impact.

University of Cincinnati Press
Copyright © 2021

Published in 2021

ISBN (paperback) 978-1-947602-75-5
ISBN (e-book, PDF) 978-1-947602-77-9
ISBN (e-book, EPUB) 978-1-947602-76-2

Smythe, Kathleen R., 1966- author. | Hanlin, Chris, author.
Bicycling through paradise : historical tours around Cincinnati / by
    Kathleen Smythe and Chris Hanlin.
Cincinnati : University of Cincinnati Press, 2021. | Includes
    index.
LCCN 2020020375 | ISBN 9781947602755 (paperback) | ISBN
    9781947602762 (epub) | ISBN 9781947602779 (pdf)
LCSH: Cycling--Ohio--Cinncinnati--Guidebooks. | Cinncinnati
    (Ohio)--Guidebooks. | Cinncinnati (Ohio)--Tours.
LCC GV1045.5.O32 C567 2021 | DDC 796.6309771/77--dc23
LC record available at https://lccn.loc.gov/2020020375

Designed and produced for UC Press by Jennifer Flint
Typeset in FreightText Pro
Printed in the United States of America
First Printing

# Dedication

KRS: To idealists past and present. You help me find paradise in this place I live.

CH: For Dawn

Creating a cycling guide book in the twenty-first century requires publishers to move beyond the boundaries of a traditional book, while still retaining the permanence of print. Rather than create a website or a print book, we have integrated the two to provide the richest experience possible. The website invites authors, cyclists, and readers to share details and feedback of their rides. Updates to the tours can be easily incorporated online, allowing the print book to focus on more timeless information—the history and culture behind the tours—to enhance the cyclist experience.

Our goal at the University of Cincinnati Press is to provide readers with a richer, more engaging experience with all the books we publish. We are excited to present online turn-by-turn tours on the open-access *Bicycling through Paradise Community Page*. The platform allows readers to view wayfinding directions, and download and export a specific tour. Each online tour combines a map with additional photographs of each stop to guide cyclists through the area. Together with the book, cyclists get personal and comprehensive guided navigation of the local landscape like never before.

The open- access *Bicycling through Paradise Community Page* hosts nineteen tours for each chapter in the print book. From the *Community Page,* when you can click on a specific tour (listed under the heading "Resources"), you will be navigated to a page that directs to you that tour. That page is also a place for cyclists to comment on and communicate about the tour. We hope readers will frequently engage through the annotations to provide feedback on the tours. Nature is evolving, construction crops up, and restaurants and hotels open and close regularly. As these tours need to adapt to the current environment, we hope cyclists will use the comment section to providers other readers and cyclists with updates, tips, and new ideas. From the print book, you can use the QR code with each chapter to navigate directly to the related tour. The QR code at the bottom of this page will direct to the online *Community Page* for the book.

Our mission at the University of Cincinnati Press is to build a community around content, in this instance, engaging cyclists and authors with one another. Our open access platform serves as a jumping off point for exploration of and connection with the tristate area. By including the maps and tours in an online environment, the book remains evergreen for any adventurer who wants to develop a sense of place in this paradise we call home.

Happy riding,
Elizabeth Scarpelli
Director, University of Cincinnati Press

Scan to visit the *Bicycling through Paradise Community Page*

# TABLE OF CONTENTS

# Acknowledgements

## Kathleen Smythe

For me, this book has a long gestation. It began in 2012 in a hotel room at an Association of Jesuit Colleges and Universities conference on sustainability as I proposed a new kind of history course to a colleague at home via email—a course involving readings, discussions, and bike rides, combining history and sustainability. I needed the encouragement of my colleague at the beginning and the encouragement of so many others along the way to pursue this project.

At Xavier University, where I teach, students who have taken my course "Bicycling Our Bioregion" over the last seven years have shared with me the ways the course changed them and have encouraged me to keep teaching it. To help inform them about what we were seeing and doing, I wrote what came to be chapter 1, "Path Dependency," to use in the course.

I chose to write about the Mill Creek because of the time spent there with Stan Hedeen and others he inspired.

Joe Humpert came to my aid in the fall of 2016 to ride along on my class sessions, helping with any mechanical trouble with the bikes and helping the students learn how to ride safely. Since then, he has co-taught the course with me every fall and a few summers for less than adequate pay. His passion for cycling and sharing it with all kinds of people with all kinds of interest has been inspiring.

My deep gratitude goes to my co-author and project visionary, Chris Hanlin. His passion and gift for expressing the way individuals' dreams make their marks on our landscape, combined with his love of getting to such places via bicycle, can be seen in every aspect of this book.

Shortly after we started working together, Chris created maps of many possible routes. He envisioned the scope of the book and the structure of the segments and tours. Chris is endlessly inquisitive and has an innate sense of what makes a good story and where to sniff one out. And he came up with this book's title. Chris and I rode all of the tours together, often with variations and alternates. We spent hours discussing ideas, sharing our personal journeys, and trading drafts of chapters. Chris has helped me, and hopefully other readers and riders, to realize that we are bicycling through paradise.

Danny Korman encouraged me to reach out to a local editor who might be interested in the manuscript.

Karen F. Zeller read versions of many of these chapters and made them much, much better. Darryl Smith helped with some fine points of military history.

Friend and editor Beth Norton read the entire manuscript, correcting errors and helping to make my voice and Chris's voice more consistent.

My cycling friends, the BABES, have listened to me talk about the book for years now and have joined me on several of the tours. Their support has helped me though ups and downs in the landscape and in the writing process.

# BICYCLING THROUGH PARADISE

# INTRODUCTION

## Cycling Advice

*Bicycling through Paradise* is more than a collection of directions and maps for bike rides in and around Cincinnati, Ohio. These bike tours will visit towns idyllically named Edenton, Loveland, and Utopia. Riders will visit the tiny dairy house called Harmony Hill, which is the oldest standing structure in Clermont County, Ohio. We will see the view from the top of a two-thousand-year-old, seventy-five-foot-tall, conical mound at Miamisburg and the Ohio River from Rising Sun on the Indiana side and Rabbit Hash on the Kentucky side. We will imagine Mary Ingles's journey through the Ohio River Valley. Cyclers are also reminded of the history of the Shawnee, Miami, Adena, and Hopewell peoples who called this place home, and who's connection to and removal from the land is part of the history we will discuss.

Riders will travel along the Little Miami Scenic Trail and then take a detour to see a castle on the banks of the Little Miami River. We will tour the Mill Creek Valley and gaze down into it from Greenhills. There are a number of Underground Railroad sites along the Ohio River and on its bluffs, affording views of it in a variety of places. On one tour, riders visit a full-scale replica of Jesus's tomb in northern Kentucky while overlooking downtown Cincinnati. And we can trace the route of the old Whitewater Canal in eastern Indiana. Finally, riders can experience the small pleasures of public parks, covered bridges, and one-room schoolhouses.

Discovering and writing about our area's rich history in a thematic and integrated way has been a joy, especially at the slow pace of travel permitted by a bicycle. Each chapter describes one tour, featuring information about the

Kathleen Smythe and Chris Hanlin in Utopia, Ohio

area's history, geography, settlement and industry, and more recent sustainability enterprises.

There are stops along these routes to look at historical markers, buildings, take a break in a park or hike in the woods, or spend the night. These routes wind through a varied landscape while offering stories and information about the region's religious history, the history of inclines or canal-building, or flood control, and more.

Paradise is inherent in cycling, whether on quiet country roads or through downtown Cincinnati. As any cyclist, hiker, or runner knows, the act of moving through space releases endorphins and makes one feel happier. Experiencing all the ways one's life journey intersects with those of people who came before while enjoying the rocks, hills, animals, plants, and rivers that first attracted people to this region is another form of paradise.

Most of all, with *Bicycling through Paradise* as guide, we can develop a deeper appreciation of this place we call home.

## The Tours

*Bicycling through Paradise* encompasses nineteen historically themed bike tours in Ohio, northern Kentucky, and eastern Indiana. The tours range in length from ten miles to about eighty miles, one-way. Each tour is composed of shorter, connected segments. A single segment is usually around ten or twelve miles long and can be ridden independently. Each segment contains something that is historically, ecologically, or culturally interesting. The segments start and stop in places with food, restrooms, and parking.

There is something here for all levels of cyclists. This is Cincinnati, so we cannot eliminate hills or traffic. But there is fair warning of stretches with more traffic or long climbs.

At the beginning of each chapter is a brief sketch of the suggested cycling route. Detailed maps and route information are available on the *Bicycling through Paradise* community page for this book. There is also current (as of 2020) advice about places to eat. And for those who want to plan a weekend or long-weekend trip, there are places to stay overnight. We recognize that over time, these establishments will change, and we invite you to keep the information updated for our fellow cyclists using the *Community Page.*

## Historical Visions and Ambitions

As it turns out, many who have come before us have sought both internal and external paradise in this area. The particular places they chose, buildings they erected, and communities they formed can still speak to us today, even in fragments. Those who lived in this area, whether thousands of years ago or just a few hundred years ago, all found the river-saturated landscape to be a kind of promised land. They sought to carve out settlements and lifestyles with high ideals in mind, whether ideal communities or places safe from the practice of slavery.

The first inhabitants of this land, Adena, Hopewell, Fort Ancient, and then the Miami and Shawnee made use of the nut trees (hickory, beech, and black walnut) as well as game and fish and the landscape of river valleys and hilltops for growing crops and collecting food and for safe places to build burial mounds and ceremonial or gathering centers, respectively.

European settlers not only had to find a way to quickly make a living on the landscape by clearing forests but also ways to attract more settlers for their own security and prosperity, and this involved building mills, distilleries, and other industrial enterprises along the Mill Creek and Little Miami Rivers. All of these activities have left traces on the landscape.

Early settlers left writings that express their appreciation of the land. Christopher Gist, a land surveyor and fur trader, traveled through Ohio from 1750 to 1751 and kept an account of his journey. In March 1751 he noted that he "went to the South Westward down the little Miamee River or Creek, where I had fine traveling thro rich Land and beautiful Meadows."[1] In 1872 W. H. Venable wrote a poem titled "June of the Miami":

> But here the valley loveliest
> Of all within the blooming West,
> In morning light before me lies,
> A second earthly Paradise;
> And here Ohio's fairest stream,
> Miami glides,—my chosen theme.[2]

In 1841 the city and setting were described thus by Charles Cist:

> The city is almost in the eastern extremity of a valley of about twelve miles in circumference, perhaps the most delightful and extensive on the borders of the Ohio...The hills which surround this extensive valley ... are always beautiful and picturesque...they present gentle and varying slopes, which are mostly covered with native forest trees. The aspect of the valley from the surrounding hills is highly beautiful.[3]

Not only did those who came before us find potential prosperity in the environment around them, they also had internal values and visions they sought to bring to life. For a number of decades, the Ohio River was a sacred boundary for those who were enslaved and those who fought against the institution of slavery in the early 1800s. John P. Parker—a former slave who bought his freedom after a failed escape attempt, Underground Railroad conductor, foundry owner, inventor, and author from Ripley, Ohio—and Harriet Beecher Stowe both found voice and home for their anti-slavery work and humanitarian values north of the Ohio River.

This book highlights towns such as Felicity and Utopia and a bygone Shaker village, all denoting a sense of bold vision and hope in the collective enterprise of village settlement. Other towns, such as the planned green space community of Mariemont and the trail town of Milford, offer visions of dignified living. Certain individuals also made their mark. Some are better known than others, such as William Henry Harrison, onetime soldier, governor of Indiana, and later president of the United States. Some remain more obscure but no less fascinating, including Harry Delos Andrews, who built Loveland Castle and led a group of boys who practiced medieval forms of combat. Then there was George Washington Williams, the first race historian in the United States, who preached from a pulpit in Cincinnati in the 1870s. There are also the usual firsts that any region can claim as people sought to innovate, create, and make a better world; ours stretch from the first reinforced concrete bridge in Ohio (in Eden Park) to the oldest Jewish congregation west of the Allegheny Mountains, K. K. Bene Israel. More recently, Cincinnati citizens and government officials have created a nationally recognized park system and bike trail system, all of which are included in multiple tours in this book.

## A Sense of Place

These essays and tours, either alone or combined, aim to inculcate a sense of place, a second kind of paradise. A sense of place is an appreciation for the landscape and history that shapes residents on a daily basis. Preindustrial cultures moved through the landscape more slowly, first on foot, at about three to four miles per hour. Riding on horseback or behind horses in carriages and stagecoaches at four miles per hour still allowed for intimate contact with passengers, horses, and the landscape. Frequent stops gave people a chance to talk with locals and appreciate the smells and sights.[4]

Trains, and later, automobiles, carry travelers through landscapes at much greater speeds. Nineteenth-century observers noted that traveling via railroad was disorienting for some, as distances that had been marked by particularity and a certain time scale were now more abstract and compressed. The French writer Victor Hugo commented about train travel: "The flowers by the side of the road are no longer flowers but flecks, or rather streaks, of red or white;

they are no longer any points, everything becomes a streak."[5] The in-between is of little consequence, only the beginning and ending points matter. Higher speeds are accompanied by the homogeneity of highway medians, gas stations, and airports.[6]

Many find this freedom and opportunity liberating and, of course, it is. But we pay a price for this freedom. The English essayist, soldier, singer, and poet Edward Thomas writes that "one of modernity's most distinctive tensions" is between "mobility and displacement on the one hand, and dwelling and belonging on the other."[7] Each successive increase in the speed of travel has deprived us of connections to a deep network of history and culture. Humans are hardwired to learn a place well enough to gain our livelihood and our social rootedness from it. But today many of us do not experience such a phenomenon in our childhoods or early adulthoods.

The hope is that after a ride or two (or ten), landscape and history will seem as one, and readers and riders will feel a deep sense of connectedness, of belonging, to not only the river valleys, hilltops, and parks but also to the people whose work, ideas, and actions have left their mark on this region in important ways.

For example, in the *Path Dependency* tour, cyclists will ride the Mill Creek corridor, which the ecologist Stan Hedeen has called "the mother of Cincinnati."[8] Yet the Mill Creek flows in an ancient wide riverbed. Because of its width, industrialists, like the founders of Procter & Gamble, and planners, who first built a canal, then a railroad, and then highways in the same valley. The I-75 corridor will never be the same again after traversing it by bike and learning about the layers of history upon which so many travel.

## The Stories We Tell

This sense of place is something all human communities used to have and is likely an important part of our success as a species. Fortunately, history and culture leave their mark on the landscapes, evoking events and characters.

The writer Robert McFarlane speaks of English naturalist Finlay MacLeod and his dedication to historicizing the land:

> One of the many reasons I enjoy being with Finlay is his ability to read landscapes back into being, and to hold multiple eras of history in plain sight simultaneously. To each feature and place name he can attach a story—geological, folkloric, historical, and gossipy. He moves easily between different knowledge systems and historical eras, in awareness of their discrepancies but stimulated by their overlaps and rhymes...To Finlay, geography and history are consubstantial. Placeless events are inconceivable, in that everything that happens must happen somewhere, and so history issues from geography in the same way that water issues from a spring: unpredictably but site-specifically.[9]

Due to more rapid travel and other forms of technology, however, many people have lost a sense of remoteness and locality. These rides visit locations that are not technically remote but will seem so since they are beyond normal paths of travel. But they illuminate stories and characters that are interesting and inspiring and will be memorable long after the riding is done. And talking to the people encountered on a journey is another way to learn about connections to places that might otherwise be overlooked.

## Sustainability and Health

Finally, being outside, getting exercise, and making connections are beneficial to personal and communal well-being. In *A Sense of Wonder*, the environmentalist Rachel Carson expresses the wish that all children should gain: "A sense of wonder so indestructible that it would last throughout life, as an unfailing antidote against the boredom and disenchantments of later years, the sterile preoccupation with things that are artificial, the alienation from the sources of our strength."[10] Carson also notes that as adults, "Those who dwell... among the beauties and mysteries of the earth are never alone or weary of life."[11] People who feel a sense of wonder, Carson argues, will love the places where they live and seek to ensure their integrity. For those who cycle, part of what draws us out is our sense of wonder both at the natural world that beautifies our every ride but also the human-built world in all its contradictions and awesomeness.

Being outside, particularly surrounded by trees and greenery, can be a natural antidepressant. Japanese researchers have demonstrated that forest bathing reduces psychological stress, depressive symptoms, and hostility, while improving sleep and increasing vigor and liveliness.[12] Each of the bike tours described in this book has some exposure to a park or other green space. Get off the bike once in a while. Have a drink or snack. Take a walk. Talk to the locals. It's time to reconnect.

Our region, like all of those across the United States, needs to make significant changes to ensure that there will be clean air, water, good soil, and healthy ecosystems to support human communities. The goal is that *Bicycling through Paradise* will help create and refresh a group of citizens who love this region and want to ensure its best possible future.

## The Structure of the Book

The tours in this book are laid out in three parts. In part 1, "Waterways," all the tours follow a river for most, if not all, of the tour, highlighting the opportunities and challenges such landscapes offered and continue to offer, such as transportation corridors, flooding, and boundary making and breaking. Part 2, "Paradise," examines various places and people who found elements of paradise in our region over the centuries, whether through planned, religious, or ethnic communities. Part 3, "Big Ideas," investigates a variety of ways in which inhabitants of the land strove to enact substantial ideas of freedom, inclusion, education, nation-building, and industry.

Alms Park Pavilion

## Cycling Advice

### Getting Your Bike Ready

There is something in this book for cyclists of all levels. If you haven't had your bike out for a while, take it to a bike shop for a tune-up. They will adjust the brakes and shifters, clean and oil the chain, and adjust the tire pressure. If you do not have a headlight and a flashing taillight, get them. If you ride often, you will eventually get a flat tire, so look into getting a travel pump, a spare inner tube or patch kit, and a couple of small plastic tire tools to help get the tire off the rim. If you do not know how to change a tire, the folks at the bike shop will be happy to show you. You may also want to look at other accessories, such as a rearview mirror, or a storage bag. And, of course, you'll need a bike lock and a helmet.

### Getting on the Road

The Cincinnati region has some great bike trails, but you will also want to get comfortable riding on regular roads. By law, Ohio roads are open to all traffic, including farm vehicles, Amish buggies, and you. In general, cyclists have the same rights as drivers—and the same responsibilities. Obey all traffic laws, including stopping at stop signs. You should ride toward the right of the lane, but in general, it's not a great idea to ride on the shoulder: you may be sending a subtle visual clue to a driver behind you that it's okay to pass close by you. It's better to ride inside the white lines and let drivers take account of your presence. You belong here, so ride with confidence!

### You Can Ride Further Than You Think

If you haven't ridden much in the past, twenty miles may sound like a lot. For most people, it's a piece of cake. Thirty miles is not too hard, after some practice rides. Forty miles is something that you can build up to. And plenty of people ride much, much further.

Mill Creek Greenway

*Change Gears Frequently*

You should change gears every time there is a minor change in the terrain, so that you maintain a light, even pressure on the pedals. Don't work too hard. Gear down and relax.

*Don't Just Push Down on the Pedals*

Think about making small circles with your feet, not just pushing down on the pedals. On the upstroke, don't rest your leg on the back pedal—that would make you work harder on the downstroke to lift your back leg. You might consider using toe clips: cages you slide your feet into, keeping your feet better attached to the pedals. Toe clips take some getting used to, but they allow you to pull the pedals up on the upstroke as well as pushing down on the downstroke. This spreads the same effort over more muscles. (Specialized cycling shoes do the same thing better.) As you find your natural cadence—the rhythm at which you pedal—you will be able to go further with less effort.

*Stay Well Hydrated*

Carry water or sports drinks with you, and do not let yourself get dehydrated. Stop every five miles or so to drink, maybe eat a snack, maybe stretch a little. That way, you can ride forever.

## Planning Your Ride

Evaluate your route for the level of traffic that you are comfortable with. Avoid heavily traveled commuter routes during rush hour. A number of our routes use roads that are lightly traveled most of the time but could become busy in the morning and evening. Sundays are great, because traffic is generally lighter. Also consider that riding in a small group can help improve your visibility to drivers.

Check the weather forecast and dress accordingly, always in bright colors, so that drivers can see you. (Bright colors on your feet and legs are especially helpful, since drivers perceive the movement better.) Wear a helmet. Also, on longer rides, you may want to carry a small first aid kit in your bike bag. A kit could include pain medication, antiseptic wipes, bandages, gauze, bandage tape, an antihistamine, and sunscreen. And of course, carry a cell phone.

## Dealing with Problems

Every experienced cyclist has had a few rides that were absolutely miserable. A wrong turn, a flat tire, a sudden change in the weather—there are plenty of potential difficulties. Put safety first. Then relax, take it easy, and remember that the difficult rides are the price of admission to the good ones. You're going to have lots of good ones.

### Traffic

Ride predictably, so that drivers know what to expect of you. Signal your turns, and do not weave in and out of a parking lane. Be cautious about riding too close to a line of parked cars: if someone opens a car door suddenly into your path, you might not have much time to react. On a busy road, it can be tricky to merge left to make a left turn; sometimes it is better to dismount and walk your bike through the crosswalks. And if you end up someplace where you do not feel safe, reconsider your route. You can lock up your bike and call for a lift.

## Riding Downtown

Some riders feel anxious about the idea of riding in downtown traffic. Really, it is pretty safe. Vehicle speeds are relatively slow in the heart of downtown, and drivers are already watching out for pedestrians, so they'll see you, too. Keep checking behind you, signal your turns, and go ahead. One special note about riding in downtown Cincinnati: the streetcar tracks have grooves in the pavement alongside them. If your tire gets caught in the groove, you could fall. Cross the tracks at a sharp angle, as close to ninety degrees as possible, and you'll be fine.

## Hills

Going uphill, gear down and take it easy. Relax your arms and shoulders. Breathe. In a hilly area, some people coast on the downhill and work hard on the uphill. Sometimes it's better to pedal down the hill and use your momentum to help carry you up the next. And remember, when the hill gets a little too steep, there is no shame in walking. On the downhills, do not let your speed get out of control, and be aware of what might be at the bottom of the hill or around the next turn.

## Sidewalks

It's not a great idea to ride on the sidewalk. Bikes and pedestrians don't always mix well. Drivers are not always expecting a bike to suddenly drop into the roadway at a crosswalk. And in more remote areas, it's likelier that there will be broken glass on the sidewalk than in the roadway. Furthermore, in the City of Cincinnati it's illegal for a cyclist over fourteen years of age to ride on the sidewalk. Ohio law allows—and even encourages—cyclists to ride on the sidewalk, and there are places where it might be a good idea. But in general, sidewalks should probably be avoided.

## Saddle Soreness

Make sure you have a comfortable bike seat, and you might consider padded cycling shorts. After that, there is exactly one cure for soreness: ride more. Over time, the more you ride, the less sore you will get.

*Mechanical Trouble*

Bike shops provide courses in bicycle maintenance, and over time you will get better at changing a tire or putting a slipped chain back on the gears. Note also that if you get stuck with mechanical difficulty, and you are a member of AAA, they will provide roadside assistance by "towing" (in a pickup truck) your bike to a location you designate.

## Planning a Weekend Trip

A cycling weekend, or a long weekend, can be a wonderful experience, so our tour descriptions include notes on overnight accommodations. To carry extra clothing, you'll need a set of saddlebags, called panniers, which attach to the rear rack. (Panniers are better than a backpack, which would raise your center of gravity.) Pack light. On longer trips, plan to carry a small travel clothesline and wash a few things out in the sink to avoid carrying duplicate clothing. At your starting point, note that not every public parking lot allows parking overnight, so check the rules.

Staying in a hotel or a bed and breakfast is nice, but bicycle camping can be a lot of fun as well. For a bike camping trip, you'll need to select your gear with care and do a short test ride with packed panniers ahead of time, to make sure you are comfortable carrying what you need. When you're ready to go, just relax into the ride and find your natural cycling cadence. Your trip is going to be great.

# Part I

## Waterways

# PATH DEPENDENCY

## Layers of History along the Mill Creek

*Northside, Ivorydale, Elmwood Place, and Lockland*

> It is possible to think of the degradation of the creek as the price that
> Cincinnati chose to pay for prosperity. A more truthful analogy: the sac-
> rifice of the Mill Creek was not a payment, but a loan, one that is now
> coming due.
>
> –Robin Corathers, *The Mill Creek*[1]

Many, but certainly not all, of the tours in this book follow a river valley for
some or all of the way, either the Great Miami, the Little Miami, or the Ohio.
In addition to providing a relatively level grade and the serenity of moving
water, these rivers contribute to a sense of place in a variety of ways. Each of
these waterways is part of a much bigger watershed. A watershed describes
an area of land that contains a set of streams and rivers that feed into a larger
body of water, a river, a lake, or an ocean. As the Mill Creek Alliance website
explains, "Any drop of water that falls in the Mill Creek watershed will make
its way to the Mill Creek."[2]

The idea of the watershed is one way to think about where we live. Riding
along the Mill Creek in this tour, think about all the water that comes to these
waterways from nearby areas and then, in turn, how all that water dumps into
the Ohio River, then into the Mississippi River, and eventually the Gulf of
Mexico. There are historical and contemporary, social and economic, and ecological meanings behind the idea of a watershed. Before roads and railroads,
the greater Cincinnati region was marked by the boundaries of the Little
Miami River on the east and the Great Miami River on the west. This was

the area within the Northwest Territory, some three hundred thousand acres, originally claimed by New Jersey congressman John Cleve Symmes in 1794 and called Symmes's Purchase.[3] In between those two much longer rivers lay the Mill Creek, what the ecologist Stan Hedeen calls the "mother of Cincinnati." Much of the account that follows is drawn from Stan Hedeen's 1994 history of the Mill Creek, *The Mill Creek: An Unnatural History of an Urban Stream*.

The Little Miami River is 111 miles long and its watershed covers 1,757 square miles.[4] The Mill Creek watershed covers 166 square miles.[5] The Ohio River watershed is a thousand times bigger than the Little Miami watershed and drains over 200,000 square miles and parts of eleven states.[6]

## The Tour

More detailed information on the route is available on the *Bicycling through Paradise* community page. We invite you to leave additional information on route updates, detours, and establishments that will be helpful to future cyclists of this route. Here's a general idea of the route.

This tour is ten miles one-way, downhill and then gradually uphill. The tour begins in Clifton at a public parking lot behind the Clifton Market and ends in Reading. Restaurants and stores are located up and down Ludlow Avenue. Turn-by-turn directions are on our website. From Clifton to Elmwood Place is about six miles, and from there to Reading is about four miles.

We begin at the top of a long, graceful hill that will take us down into the Mill Creek Valley. We will cross the Mill Creek on a large bridge over I-75. Hop up on the sidewalk and observe the Mill Creek and the valley and all the different activities going on in it from the bridge. Once in the valley, we will cycle along or near the creek for the rest of the tour. In Northside, we pass by the site of Ludlow Station (with historical marker) and then will cycle along the Mill Creek Greenway, then back onto Vine Street into Ivorydale and through the Procter & Gamble industrial corridor. In Elmwood Place, there are a number of restaurants and convenience stores.

From Elmwood Place, just after Vine Street, and on and Anthony Wayne Avenue, we will cross the Mill Creek at another spot where early settlers lived, called White's Station. Once on Cooper, look for a small park with a historical marker about Lockland on the right. As we enter Reading, we will cross the Mill Creek yet again and enter the wedding district of Reading, where there is something to eat (or wear) and places to park.

## Imagining Early Settlement of Cincinnati

In the late 1700s, one did not have to imagine the watershed because the most efficient means of entering the land beyond the Appalachian Mountains was by river, slowly drifting downstream past tributary after tributary of the mighty Ohio River. On a boat on the Ohio River in the area where Cincinnati now lies, if you looked to the south to the Kentucky side and then to the north to the Ohio side, the Kentucky hills rise much more quickly out of the Ohio River Valley than do those of Ohio. On the Ohio side, there is a low shelf near the river before the hills begin. That is why early settlers chose to settle in what became Ohio. But if one had traveled as far as the mouth to the Mill Creek, one would see that the Mill Creek Valley is deep and broad, broader than the shelf on the north side of the Ohio River. With such a valley, it would be possible to settle large numbers of people, develop farms and businesses, and use the Mill Creek and adjoining area for transportation.

The reason this small creek, only about twenty-eight miles long, had such a wide basin, one and a half miles wide, is because it lay in an old path carved first by two larger rivers—the Licking River more than two million years ago and then by the Ohio River more than a million years ago. Four hundred thousand years ago, successive ice sheets had pushed the Ohio River into its current configuration near Cincinnati.[7] When John Cleve Symmes first saw it, the wide, broad Mill Creek Valley invited human settlement. Symmes saw fertile, flat farmland, forests for timber and food, and plenty of water.

Europeans were not the first to admire and settle here, of course. They were invading land that Native tribes were already inhabiting. By the middle of the eighteenth century, the land on which Cincinnati sits was part of one of the "most contested regions in the world" according to the environmental researcher Uwe Lubken. The recently arrived (since 1400) Shawnee considered it the "center of the earth"; both the French and the British had sought control of it, and American immigrants were eager to explore and settle it.[8] The

Shawnee called the stream that came to be known as the Mill Creek *Maketewa*; Symmes called it *Mill Creek* to leave no doubt that it would be possible for new residents to set up mills for grain and lumber. But early settlers also fished the creek, swam, and canoed in it.[9]

In the late 1700s, the region was densely forested. Stan Hedeen often tells students that in the late 1700s a squirrel could have traveled from treetop to treetop from the Ohio River to where Dayton is today without touching the ground once. The writer Scott Russell Sanders recalls accounts of early settlers along the Ohio River who marveled at the enormous size of the trees, particularly the sycamore trees, some of which, after hollowing out at the bottom (a natural occurrence), could become a temporary house for a family.[10] There are some things we would like to travel back in time to see, and a sycamore tree that size is certainly one of them. The first European settler in what became Mount Adams above Eden Park was a woman who lived in a sycamore tree! For more on that, see the *Floodplains and Hilltops* tour. The forests were home to a wide variety of animals, including deer, buffalo, and elk. These are the kinds of things readers and riders can imagine as you walk and cycle through this landscape.

In 1997 the American Rivers organization called the Mill Creek the "most endangered urban river in North America."[11] That is some feat for such a small body of water. It was mostly deforested, mostly devoid of the animal life that used to inhabit its shores and waters, and, in many places, an urban blight. Its relatively short length, combined with intensive economic activity, were the cause of its demise. This activity had been growing and ongoing since the earliest European settlers arrived in the region. There were early settlements in other parts of what has become Cincinnati, such as at Turkey Bottoms (where Lunken Airport is now) and what has become the East End and California.[12] But the significant concentration of industry along the Mill Creek was much greater. Now no one swims in it or fishes in it, but as you will learn, they do canoe it.

Early European settlers set up stations, or fortifications, along the Mill Creek. These were often at natural stream crossings, as the creeks and rivers provide a wide variety of resources to early settlers, but they also posed a barrier to travel between the two sides of the Ohio River. Therefore, places where it was easy to cross, or ford, became natural sights of settlement. These stations had blockhouses that the settlers used as protection. These were thick-walled buildings, much like small forts. The stone for the buildings was taken from the Mill Creek. Sometimes there were a few soldiers placed at the blockhouse as well. In 1789 James Cunningham made the first settlement along the creek some distance from the Ohio River (where Evendale is today). This intrusion of Shawnee land, however, led to hostilities and Cunningham and his family returned to Cincinnati a year later.[13]

The next station, built by Israel Ludlow, a land surveyor throughout Ohio, was built in what is now Northside, at the corner of Knowlton and Mad Anthony Wayne in 1790.[14] In 1792 Jacob White built a station at the third crossing at the north end of Carthage, not far from the Hamilton County Fairgrounds. It consisted of a blockhouse and cabins for multiple families.[15] Both of these sites are on this tour.

The stations operated with a certain level of organization. An early settler at another location in the area noted:

> The system of starting a station was, by a mutual contract to agree to stand by each other in difficulty—to obey the principal man after whom the station was named—to share equally—the dangers of defence—and perform the double duty of soldier and laborer. In addition to these written articles of compact there were inexorable customs prevailing among the stations, which required prompt assistance to be given in case of attack, amounting to a sort of warlike alliance between separate communities. There were also rules relating to capture and recapture of property, as well understood as the system of prize cases of the Admiralty Court.[16]

In the late 1700s, American pioneers sent three expeditions to try to break Native resistance to White settlement in the Northwest Territory. These expeditions used the trails that lay along the Mill Creek Valley. The first, led by General Josiah Harmar, met defeat in Fort Wayne, Indiana, in 1790. The second, led by General Arthur St. Clair, with a badly trained army, left Cincinnati via the Mill Creek Valley, camping at Ludlow Station for six weeks.

They reached what is now called Fort Recovery in west central Ohio. There, a Native force, led by Chief Little Turtle and aided by the British, surrounded them in the night and forced a retreat. General St. Clair left nine hundred dead American soldiers, the most disastrous defeat (given the size of the original army) that had ever befallen an American army.[17]

In 1792 President George Washington appointed General Anthony Wayne to replace General St. Clair as commander of the Western Army. In 1794 General Wayne trained three thousand soldiers, also camped at Ludlow Station, and moved north in 1793. He chose to build a fort at the site of General St. Clair's defeat, and at the end of 1793 named it Fort Recovery. At Fallen Timbers in August 1794, U.S. forces destroyed Shawnee villages and fields, creating a "fifty-mile swath of devastation," giving General Wayne a more decisive victory. Native Americans were forced to sign the Treaty of Greenville, allowing White settlement in much of the Northwest Territory.[18] The Treaty of Greenville opened up all of southern Ohio for settlement, driving Native Americans to the swampy northwest corner of Ohio. As a result of increased military presence, Cunningham was able to return to his home site in 1793, where he established a sawmill and a flourmill. Settlers to Cincinnati developed two roads using Native American trails. Hamilton Avenue follows St. Clair's Trace, and Spring Grove Avenue follows Wayne's Trace.[19]

## Four Sources of Pollution

European settlers cut down trees to build houses, fences, other buildings, and to clear land for farming (barley, wheat, and corn). Clearing land for farming required the destruction of much of the forest; building needs were quite small in comparison. Many of the trees were so large that felling them would have taken a tremendous amount of time, so settlers girdled them. Girdling required cutting a four-inch belt of bark off the tree. This killed the tree, as nutrients could no longer flow to the branches and leaves. In the following year, the tree was set on fire. By 1881, forest coverage in the Mill Creek Township was 15 percent of what it had been a century earlier. With the trees went the large mammals, such as black bears, gray wolves, mountain lions, and birds, such as the Carolina parakeet and passenger pigeon. In the absence of trees, more soil was able to wash into the Mill Creek, increasing sedimentation, changing, among other things, the character of the creek bottom and the amount of light that could penetrate to the creek bottom. Fish, invertebrates, and other species declined as a result. Without tree cover, water temperatures increased. In addition to soil erosion and sedimentation into the creek, manure from animal farms was also dumped into the creek. Without tree roots and litter to retain rainwater, the creek was prone to higher floods and longer periods of low water.[20]

The second impact on the Mill Creek in the early decades of the 1800s was the development of various industries, such as pork slaughterhouses, paper mills, and breweries. The first slaughterhouse was opened in the 1830s. The waste of pork processing, including blood, was dumped into the creek. From the 1830s to the 1860s, Cincinnati was the chief pork-processing city in the United States. Even after this time, pork processing continued to be an important industry. In 1881 all the slaughterhouses that were nearer the city center, and were dumping the offal into the Deer Creek, were moved to the Mill Creek Valley. Many also combined slaughter and packing operations so that not just blood but also inedible grease and salting and curing solutions were produced. These by-products were dumped into the Mill Creek as well. Additionally, a massive stockyard, located along the Mill Creek after 1871, disposed of the animal waste in the creek. By 1913, one cup of every gallon of water flowing through the Mill Creek contained alcohol or animal by-products.[21]

Pork processing produced all sorts of waste, some of which could be turned into soap. The soapmaker James Gamble and his business partner and wife's brother-in-law, the candlemaker William Procter, founded Procter & Gamble in 1837. In 1885 they moved their operations from downtown Cincinnati to what is now Ivorydale. It was named, of course, for the inexpensive high-quality soap Procter & Gamble started making in the 1880s on the Mill Creek. Today the area is still known as Ivorydale. The Procter & Gamble industrial campus expanded over the years from 11 acres to 243 acres with ten buildings, including a fire station, dining rooms, and recreational facilities, in addition to the factory buildings and smokestacks. The campus was an example of a factory community, seeking to provide for many of the needs of its workers.[22]

By the mid-nineteenth century, both soil and industrial waste were being deposited into the Mill Creek.

Industrial development depended on reliable transportation. Construction of the Miami to Erie Canal began in 1825 and finished in Toledo in 1845, and a portion of it ran right along the Mill Creek.[23] This tour ends near Lockland, named for four locks along the canal in this area. Before construction of the canal, there was no formal settlement. Within a short period of time, however, the forty-two-foot waterfall from the locks brought industry to the canal.[24] According to a historical marker in Lockland, when the canal was in demand, twelve boats would pass through in a twenty-four-hour period, some carrying people, and others carrying coal, grain sand, ice, and pigs, among many other things. The Erie Canal was also a place for recreation: picnics, fishing in the summer, ice skating in the winter, and romantic outings. The last boat trip was in July 1912.

Railroad construction began in 1848 on the west side of the Mill Creek. The first two railroads to connect Cincinnati to other points were built in river valleys in order to minimize costs. Eventually, by the early twentieth century, nine rail lines used the Mill Creek Valley to enter Cincinnati. A significant number of the 220 passenger and mail trains that entered the city

Mill Creek at Ivorydale

on a weekday in 1889 traveled this corridor. The Mill Creek had become an industrial corridor, home to industry, rail, and intensive settlement.[25]

All of those people produced a lot of waste, a third source of pollution for the Mill Creek. Initially, many people had outhouses or septic systems, which kept the human waste largely in place, but as more people lived in the same amount of area, it was impossible to maintain sanitation with such systems. In 1863 the Cincinnati City Council allowed sanitary waste to be discharged into underground storm drains. With this move, combined sewers carried sanitary sewage on a regular basis and excess rainwater after strong rains. Combined sewers were cheaper to build than separate sewers, of course. In 1934 a ten-mile-long interceptor sewer, a combined sewer system, was built along the Mill Creek. The chief reason was to take human waste from homes and other buildings and collect it in pipes that would then take it to a treatment plant. In 1959 a wastewater treatment plant was built near the mouth of the Ohio River to treat water before it entered that waterway.[26]

The secondary purpose of a combined sewer system, to divert rainwater from residential areas to prevent flooding and allow it to be channeled into the sewers as well, meant that, as populations increased, the sewers could not handle the primary and a secondary load. When overtaxed, they would open and empty into the Mill Creek. By 1910, Cincinnati's population was about 350,000, and the Mill Creek received about half of the city's sewage. The organic waste and heat pollution of the postindustrial water that were dumped into the creek destroyed all fish and insect life. A 1903 article noted that the Mill Creek was "an open sewer." In 1940 about 8 percent of the time that it rained, the sewers overflowed and dumped into the creek.[27]

By the 1970s, residents alongside the Mill Creek knew that not only was the creek gross both in terms of sight and smell but that it endangered their health. In 1989 a hepatitis A outbreak in Mt. Airy and South Cumminsville was linked to children playing in the creek. Vapors from the creek exceeded healthy levels; one resident recorded that the stench was so bad, you gagged while outside. Others saw pieces of toilet paper float by from time to time.[28]

A combined sewer system is still in use in Cincinnati. Every time the area gets more than a tenth of an inch of rain per hour, the sewers flood with rainwater and end up overflowing into the Mill Creek, dumping raw sewage into the creek and eventually into the Ohio River. On the tour, you will see a number of combined sewer overflow (CSO) pipes. They open into the Mill Creek with a flexible door that gets pushed open with a surge of water during the storm. The water carries raw sewage into the Mill Creek. The farther downstream one travels, the larger the overflow pipes become. According to the writer John Tallmadge, there are 158 combined overflow ports on the Mill Creek watershed.[29]

Most eastern cities suffer from similar problems. The US government has required all cities to take care of the problem, but has not offered funding to assist with rectifying the situation. This is called an unfunded mandate. The problem is that the cities and counties that have the faulty sewer systems do not have the funding necessary to fix the problem. If they were to fix it, it would mean charging water users an extraordinarily high fee for decades to come in order to cover the cost. Cincinnati and other US cities are in a difficult situation, not wanting to continue polluting their waterways and downstream neighbors' water source but also not having the funds to take care of the problem through large infrastructure fixes.[30]

The final contributor to Mill Creek contamination is non-point-source pollution. This is pollution that runs off from parking lots, lawns, etc. It can contain salts from wintertime road salting, fertilizers and pesticides from lawn treatments, and an array of other chemicals that result from washing cars, to pouring old liquids into a suburban yard.[31]

## Path Dependency in History

These visible layers are illustrations of an important concept: *path dependency*. The Mill Creek lay in the very old basin created by the former Ohio River. Native Americans were drawn to the broad valley and created trails. European settlers and US generals and, eventually, motor vehicles, followed the same trails. In the early 1800s, a canal was built in the same channel, then a few decades later, the railroad was built there, and eventually in the 1960s, I-75. This transportation corridor in Cincinnati has a tremendously long history.

Those in a passenger car along I-75 are figuratively traveling in the multiple layers—geological/glacial, Native American, and early settler—of history.

The term path dependency can be applied to both the natural environment as well as the human built environment and means a situation of constrained development unfolds along a certain path with no clear way back. As the infrastructure of homes, businesses, roads, canals, bridges, mills, etc., built up along the Mill Creek, residents became increasingly tied to the location and susceptible to flooding. As settlement and industry increased, the potential risk from flooding increased as well.

As Uwe Lubken argues, from the perspective of the Ohio River and the water in the river (a hydrological perspective), the floodplain (part of the broad valley that was so attractive) of the river is a natural part of it. It is the area that during low or average flow is not covered by water but that has been and likely will again be flooded when the water level rises. Settlers in the Ohio River Valley were eager to recognize the benefits of the floodplain—fertile soil, level ground, access to the river—but far less willing to accept the historical and ecological reasons the floodplain was there to begin with, that it was a part of the river itself. Lubken refers to settlements, like those along the Mill Creek, as "floodplain invasions."[32]

One response to the combination of floodplain invasion, path dependency, and river dynamics was that engineers sought to contain rivers to control their flow in order to prevent flooding. The Mill Creek suffered from a number of floods in the 1800 and 1900s. Hedeen notes that newspaper accounts report flooding of the Mill Creek from an overflowing Ohio River every other year between the nineteenth century and the first half of the twentieth century.[33] The first flood of record is in 1805. Another flood occurred the following year. The Ohio River flood of 1937 was, Lubken writes, "At that time, the most devastating river flood in U.S. history (in terms of economic damage)."[34] The normally twelve-foot-high river crested at more than seventy-seven feet and an oil spill caused a fire on top of the flooding.[35]

The United States Army Corps of Engineers was charged with taking care of the flooding problems. There was simply too much invested in the valley to even consider defaulting to the natural inclinations of the Mill Creek and to relocating human settlement and industry. Instead, the decision was made to take steps to ensure that the Mill Creek never flooded again. The first step was to build a barrier dam across the mouth of the Mill Creek. Such a dam would seal off the Ohio River floodwaters and provide an outlet for water from the Mill Creek through a water gate. The barrier dam was completed in 1948.[36] In the first decades of the twenty-first century, at least $10 million worth of repair is needed for the Mill Creek Barrier Dam to ensure that it continues to protect $3 billion worth of public and private investment.[37] This money has to come out of the city of Cincinnati's budget, and some of it will likely be passed on to residents, who produce wastewater and sewage and benefit from the dam's effective operation.

The next problem was preventing flooding on the Mill Creek. Two solutions were implemented, both determined by cost effectiveness. Dams were built on upper tributaries of the Mill Creek, one creating Sharon Lake (1937), and the other creating Winton Lake (1952), both to be visited on the *Town and Country* tour. After that, the Mill Creek was channelized. In this process, the Army Corps of Engineers widened the stream to double or triple its normal size, stripped out all the trees, and put riprap (old broken rocks or old

West Fork of the Mill Creek at Lockland

pavement) up the banks. In some places along the Mill Creek, such as where it runs through the Procter & Gamble complex, concrete lines the bottom and sides of the creek. The goal was to allow more water to move more quickly through the channel during peak times. The result was total loss of vegetation along the creek and within the creek in the areas with the most intense channelization. As Hedeen writes, "Channelization forecloses any possibility of restoring a natural stream community."[38] The channelization project was never completed due to a lack of funds, so there are stretches close to downtown Cincinnati and further upstream that were never channelized and are more natural-looking, with trees, grasses, fish, birds, and other animals enjoying the clearer water and the shade from the tree canopy.[39]

## Cleaning up the Creek and Raising Awareness

Where does all of this leave us? It is now clear to many that the pollution of the Mill Creek is a loan that is coming due, as Robin Corather's statement at the beginning of this chapter notes. But that awareness has been gained through the efforts of many over the last three decades, including those involved with the Mill Creek Alliance and this organization's prior incarnations. The Mill Creek Valley could provide recreation, food, rest, and biological diversity if it were not treated as a waste receptacle.

Remember that some people canoe the Mill Creek? They do so with the leadership and inspiration of the Mill Creek Yacht Club. The name alone should suggest grand inspiration (or delusion). The Mill Creek Yacht Club, though the name is said tongue in cheek, has a serious purpose, and that is to raise awareness both of the creek's current degraded state but also of some of the areas where nature is making a comeback. They also do so to remind us that this is our city's waterway and it should be our jewel—a recreational and biological wonder rather than a toxic dump.

The Mill Creek Yacht Club runs organized canoe and kayak trips down the entire length of the twenty-eight-mile creek. On one of their trips a few summers ago, both channelized and nonchannelized parts of the creek were on display. A tree-lined stretch that ran almost to the Ohio River looked healthy, while a channelized, degraded wide urban waterway totally exposed to the sun made up the other portion. But even in this section, trees, shrubs, and grasses were poking through cement and through riprap, and the stream was still doing its meandering thing. Of course, the same polluted water than ran through both sections. The day of this particular trip was not long after a significant rain, so the leaders made it clear that canoers were likely traveling through sewage.

The Mill Creek Yacht Club is part of a much larger effort to restore the creek to a healthier state. Part of that solution, of course, is to reduce and eventually eliminate the disposal of any kind of waste into the stream. Federal environmental regulations, such as the Clean Water Act, have helped to regulate industrial waste. But there are other sources of the creek's pollution, and in order to take care of those, a number of steps have been taken to help lessen the amount of rainwater that reaches the storm sewers and to bring back some of the biological diversity to the banks of the creek, including providing spaces for people who dwell near it to use it for recreation and enjoyment. The Mill Creek Alliance has undertaken thirty-three ecological restoration projects along the Mill Creek and its tributaries, including bank stabilization, streambed stabilization, wetland restoration, and wildlife habitat restoration. In 2013 a thirty-acre stream restoration project was finished where the east fork of the Mill Creek flows into the main stem. The goals of the project were to improve the water quality, wildlife and aquatic habitat, reduce flooding, and provide recreational and educational opportunities. The Mill Creek Alliance created meandering stream banks, a five-acre floodplain wetland, man-made riffles, and planted stream sides with native plants. A decade or so before that, a significant demonstration project was opened at Salway Park, across from Spring Grove Cemetery. There, a series of rain gardens, a few solar panels, pervious pavement, and a sculpture convey how people can become stewards and protectors of the environment and restore the Mill Creek instead of degrading it. Since the opening, fruit trees (as part of an edible forest project) and other plantings and rain gardens have been planted in other places. Thanks to these efforts, turtles, salamanders, beavers, and birds are all returning to the Mill Creek corridor.[40]

Another vision of how the Mill Creek corridor might be used with less of a damaging footprint is as a bikeway. Small sections of bike path dot the lower half of the creek. The goal is a bike path run from what used to be White's Station down beyond Ludlow Station. A region-wide bike trail plan calls for connecting the entire city area with a fifty-mile loop path, and in the center of it would run the Mill Creek bike path.[41]

The *Path Dependency* tour provides a chance to ride through layers of history, but they are only visible if you know what to look for: a broad valley carved by glaciers long ago on the descent to Ludlow Avenue; creeks that supported the Shawnee, whose name for the Mill Creek, *Maketewa*, is carved in a stone block resting by the bicycle pathway; historical markers that denote the sites of early European stations at creek fords; Army Corps of Engineers concrete embankments that are giving way to plants and trees; and edible forests and rain gardens, which seek to restore the creek to a more natural state as site of food, recreation, and spiritual renewal.

Scan to visit the "William Henry Harrison and the Shawnee Nation" route

CHAPTER 2

# WILLIAM HENRY HARRISON
# AND THE SHAWNEE NATION

## The Ohio River Valley West to Harrison's Tomb, Shawnee Lookout, and Indiana

Beginning in the 1780s, White settlers and their armies gradually pushed Indigenous people out of Ohio through a cycle of encroachments, battles, treaties, and betrayals.[1]

This colonization by U.S. forces was commanded principally by five generals, more or less in succession: George Rogers Clark, Josiah Harmer, Arthur St. Clair, Anthony Wayne, and William Henry Harrison. Harmer and St. Clair both suffered major defeats, and substantial Native resistance continued until 1813, when the great Shawnee leader Tecumseh was defeated and killed in battle by U.S. forces under William Henry Harrison.

After the death of Tecumseh, William Henry Harrison retired to North Bend, Ohio, just west of Cincinnati. Harrison would eventually be elected president, in 1840.

"Tecumseh" statue at Sayler Park

But in the meantime, he farmed and was active in local affairs. And he developed a fascination with the people he had helped to displace. Harrison examined the remains of an abandoned Shawnee village at what is now Shawnee Lookout Park, and he published an article about his observations. He had thoroughly misunderstood what he had seen.

## The Tour

More detailed information on this route is available on the *Bicycling through Paradise* community page. We invite you to leave additional information on route updates, detours, and establishments that will be helpful to future cyclists of this route. Here is the general idea.

This is an easy tour, tracing the Ohio River Valley west of Cincinnati. The tour starts at Gilday Recreation Complex in Cincinnati's Riverside neighborhood and ends in Aurora, Indiana.

The tour is composed of three segments. Total distance is a little over thirty-five miles one-way, but each segment is fun to ride independently. Each segment starts and stops in places where you can find parking, food, and bathrooms. For anyone planning a weekend trip, there are overnight accommodations in Lawrenceburg.

The tour runs mostly along quiet roads, with some stretches of dedicated bike lane, plus a few miles of bike path in the last segment. There is only one serious climb, in the middle segment, and it's an optional spur. If you don't take the climb, you won't see Shawnee Lookout Park, but you'll see everything else.

**Segment 1** goes from Gilday Riverside Park to Cleves (12.5 miles, flat to rolling). We'll head west on Hillside Avenue to the Victorian neighborhood of Sayler Park, where we'll see an Adena culture mound and the "Indian Chief" Statue. For generations, people assumed that the statue represented Tecumseh, but the truth is that the statue was bought out of an 1893 ironworks catalog, which only calls it, "#53, Indian Chief," further evidence of a whitewashing and caricaturing of Native life.[2] We'll then head west on Highway 50. Approaching North Bend, we'll head up Miami Avenue until we get to the historical marker describing William Henry Harrison's role in the development of the Cincinnati and Whitewater Canal. (There, you can tie up your bike and take a very short footpath to see the remains of an old canal tunnel in the hillside.) Just north of here, at Cleves, there is an outstanding restaurant: Nick's American Café. Try the pie.

**Segment 2** goes from Cleves to Lawrenceberg (18.6 miles, including an optional climb into Shawnee Lookout Park). This area is a cyclist's paradise, with low traffic and beautiful scenery. We'll head back south on Miami Avenue and then west on Brower Road to the tomb of William Henry Harrison. From there, a very short spur up Cliff Road goes to Harrison's home site. We'll continue west on Brower Road. At the entrance to the Duke Energy plant, there's a small monument to Fort Finney, site of a 1786 treaty between the United States and the Shawnee. We'll continue on Brower Road/Lawrenceburg Road to the entrance of Shawnee Lookout Park. An optional long climb into the park will take us to the 1795 Micajah Dunn log cabin, a stone schoolhouse built circa 1800, and another small Native American mound. We'll then retrace our steps, descending back to Lawrenceburg Road and continuing to Highway 50. Approaching Greendale, Indiana, we'll turn right onto Oberting Road and then left onto Ridge Avenue. We'll continue on Ridge Avenue, then jog over to enter Lawrenceburg on Walnut Street. Lawrenceburg has places to eat, and several hotels.

**Segment 3** goes from Lawrenceburg to Aurora (4.0 miles, flat). From Lawrenceburg, we'll take the Dearborn Bike Trail, which starts on top of the floodwall and continues all the way into Aurora. At Aurora, check out the Hillforest House Museum, built in 1855 for the industrialist Thomas Gaff.

## Fort Finney

In 1785 U.S. forces built a small fort, Fort Finney, on the Ohio River, near the mouth of the Great Miami. The fort was built to protect US commissioners who intended to negotiate a treaty with the Shawnee Nation.

The Shawnee had lived in what is now Ohio since the late 1600s. They were an Algonquian-speaking people, skilled at farming and hunting. They'd first encountered White people as fur traders—French, Spanish, and British.[3]

During the Revolutionary War, the Shawnee had allied themselves with the British. The U.S. victory against the British put the Shawnee in a weaker position to negotiate, as White settlers increasingly pushed into Shawnee territory.

At Fort Finney, one of the US commissioners was George Rogers Clark. In Vincennes, Indiana, in 1779, Clark had tomahawked Native American prisoners and had thrown their still-moving bodies into the river. Clark had also led vicious attacks on Shawnee villages in 1780 and 1782. "To excel them in barbarity," Clark explained, "is the only way to make war upon Indians."[4]

Another of the commissioners was Richard Butler. Butler had two children by a Shawnee woman, and he was able to speak the Shawnee language. This did not stop him, however, from committing atrocities against the Shawnee.

About 150 Shawnee men and 80 Shawnee women came to meet the US delegation at Fort Finney. After some preliminaries—welcome speeches, smoking peace pipes, dining—the US commissioners demanded that the Shawnee should give up all their land in southern and eastern Ohio. The commissioners vowed that northwestern Ohio would continue to belong to the Shawnee.

The Shawnee refused the offer. One of their leaders, Kekewepellethe, took out a black wampum belt, symbolizing war, and held it out for the commissioners to take. The commissioners would not take it, so Kekewepellethe laid it on the table. George Rogers Clark took his cane, knocked the wampum

belt onto the floor, and ground it under his boot. There were tense discussions, including US threats against the well-being of Shawnee women and children. The Shawnee were forced to accept the terms the U.S. commissioners put forth, and the treaty was signed on January 31, 1786.[5]

After Fort Finney, most Shawnees moved northwest to the Auglaize and Maumee Rivers, near present-day Toledo. White settlers continued encroaching, and the US Army backed the settlers. In 1790 General Josiah Harmer took an

Fort Finney monument

expeditionary force of 1,500 US soldiers from Fort Washington in Cincinnati to the Maumee River. Harmer was soundly defeated in battle by Native American forces, led by Shawnee chief Blue Jacket and Miami chief Little Turtle. The following year, U.S. forces under General Arthur St. Clair marched out again from Fort Washington to northwestern Ohio, only to be thrashed once more.[6]

## The Rise of William Henry Harrison

In the autumn of 1791, William Henry Harrison was commissioned as an ensign in the US Army. Fortunately for him, he arrived at Fort Washington just a bit too late to join St. Clair's disastrous expedition. Harrison was there just in time to see what was left of St. Clair's forces dragging back to the fort.

Harrison was young, aristocratic, and studious. He had no military experience. He was not interested in the carousing that was common at Fort Washington. Ensign Harrison was not immediately popular with the enlisted men.[7]

With St. Clair now discredited, the forces were put under the command of the Revolutionary War hero "Mad" Anthony Wayne. Despite his nickname, Wayne was a methodical and disciplined leader. Wayne took three full years to recruit and train his troops before he marched out to engage the Shawnee again.

This time, the U.S. forces won. In August 1794, at the Battle of Fallen Timbers, near Toledo, Wayne defeated the Shawnee and Delaware under Blue Jacket. William Henry Harrison served as aide-de-camp to Wayne during the battle, and Wayne recognized Harrison in his report.[8]

The following year, White and Native leaders met at Greenville, Ohio, to discuss a new treaty. Anthony Wayne was the lead negotiator, and Harrison was there as well. During the negotiations, Wayne made effective use of spies, bribes, gifts, and threats. When the Treaty of Greenville was finally signed, the Shawnee had relinquished nearly all of their lands in Ohio.[9] (The Shawnee held on to parts of Indiana, and on the *Whitewater Canal* tour, we'll ride by a boundary hill marker for the Treaty of Greenville line near Brookville, Indiana.)

Soon afterward, Harrison resigned from the army and accepted a political position as secretary of the Northwest Territory, later becoming governor of the Indiana Territory.[10] Harrison had studied Anthony Wayne's negotiating tactics carefully, and he would spend the next twenty years whittling away at the remaining Native American lands.

Harrison's brilliant yet manipulative tactic was in playing Native tribes against each other. He would, for example, sometimes bribe and bully a tribe into ceding land they didn't really own, only afterward approaching the actual inhabitants with an agreement that appeared as a fait accompli. During Harrison's time as governor of Indiana, he negotiated coercive treaties with the Delaware (1803), the Kasakiawa (1803), the Sauk and Fox (1804), and the Miami, Delaware, and Potawatomi (Treaty of Fort Wayne, 1809).[11]

Harrison was also a pro-slavery advocate, and he had at least one enslaved man with him during his time in Indiana. The Northwest Ordinance of 1786 outlawed slavery anywhere in the Northwest Territory, including Indiana and Ohio. But Harrison, manipulated the ordinance, creating a cruel loophole. He believed that this rule was not retroactive, and that slaves who'd been brought into the territory prior to the 1786—and their progeny—could be held in bondage indefinitely.[12]

## The Open Door

For all Harrison's diplomatic clout, even he would have a difficult time dealing with an emerging Shawnee leader named Tecumseh. Tecumseh was a brilliant and charismatic soldier and politician. And Tecumseh had a younger brother, a spiritual leader who claimed prophetic powers.

In 1805 Tecumseh's brother fell into a trance and had a vision. He saw the Master of Life, who told him that the Native Americans must renounce all of the White men's ways. They must hold property in common. They must abstain from alcohol and stick to a diet of traditional Native foods—corn, beans, maple sugar, and deer meat—rather than eating White man's food such as bread. They could keep their guns for self-defense but should hunt with bow and arrow. They should be monogamous and not lead promiscuous lives. They should pray, morning and evening, to the Master of Life. Only in this way could the White intruders be driven from the land.

Up to this time, Tecumseh's brother had been named Lalawithika, which means "the noise maker." But now he gave himself a new name: Tenskwatawa, which means "the open door." The name suggested a possible, alternative future. And after this time, many people called Tenskwatawa something else, too: they called him "the Shawnee Prophet."[13]

Tenskwatawa began to attract followers. He established a new village, called Prophetstown, at Greenville, in western Ohio. As the movement grew, members of other tribes—Delawares, Potawatomis, Wyandots, Miamis, Sauks, and others—came to hear the Prophet's teachings. A new Native confederation began to emerge, with Tecumseh standing by as a potential military leader.

William Henry Harrison was alarmed and threatened by the developments at Prophetstown. So Harrison wrote an infantilizing open letter to the Shawnee and their associated tribes:

> My Children: My heart is filled with grief, and my eyes are dissolved in tears at the news which has reached me. You have been celebrated for your wisdom above all the tribes of the red people...But who is this pretend prophet who dares to speak in the name of the great Creator?... If he is really a prophet, ask of him to cause the sun to stand still, the moon to alter its course, the rivers to cease to flow, or the dead to rise from their graves. If he does these things, you may believe he has been sent from God.[14]

Harrison must have felt that his letter was a masterstroke. Until, that is, Tenskwatawa responded by correctly predicting the solar eclipse of 1806.

Tenskwatawa named the day and hour at which he would cause darkness to fall across the sun. And at the appointed hour, a full solar eclipse crossed North America in a swath that covered nearly all of the area of the Prophet's influence. At Prophetstown, the eclipse was 99 percent complete.[15] It is possible that Tenskwatawa had simply gotten his information from a farmer's almanac. But at the time, few of his followers would have been aware of this possibility. The Prophet's credibility soared.[16]

In 1810 Harrison and Tecumseh arranged to meet in Vincennes, Indiana, for negotiations. Tecumseh brought four hundred warriors with him. Tecumseh demanded the retraction of treaties that had been forced on the Shawnee. Harrison refused. The two sides parted with no agreement.

Frustrated with diplomacy, Harrison rejoined the army. Leading U.S. forces, he attacked Prophetstown in 1811. Tecumseh was away, and the Native forces were scattered. This came to be known as the Battle of Tippecanoe. Years later, when Harrison was campaigning for president, he and his running mate John Tyler would make much of this victory.[17]

During the War of 1812, the Shawnee allied themselves, once again, with the British, and in 1813 Harrison attacked British and Shawnee forces in Ontario, Canada, in the Battle of the Thames. It was a decisive American victory. Tecumseh was killed in the battle. Tenskwatawa remained alive, but with without his elder brother, the Prophet's power was broken. Shawnee resistance collapsed.[18]

## North Bend and Shawnee Lookout

After the death of Tecumseh, William Henry Harrison retired from the army and moved with his family to a farm in North Bend, Ohio. In 1795 Harrison had married Anna Symmes, a daughter of Judge John Cleves Symmes, and Judge Symmes sold Harrison the property. During Harrison's time in North Bend, he cultivated the land and enlarged the existing log farmhouse.[19]

Harrison was also a major supporter of the construction of a new canal, the Cincinnati-Whitewater, to bring agricultural produce from southern Indiana to markets in Cincinnati. Harrison was a stockholder in the canal company, and he sold land to the company where the route crossed his farm.[20] In 1836 there was a large celebration for the groundbreaking, and many people came from Cincinnati to Harrison's farm to observe the festivities.[21] (They came on the ill-fated steamboat *Moselle*—a ship whose story will be told in the chapter "Bicycling Through Paradise".)

Also during his tenure in North Bend, Harrison spent time examining the remains of a long-abandoned Shawnee village at what is now Shawnee Lookout Park. Shawnee Lookout is a high ridge just north of the Ohio River. It had been occupied by Indigenous peoples for perhaps ten thousand years before the arrival of White settlers. There are dozens of archaeological sites scattered across what is now a thousand-acre park. Excavations have uncovered arti-facts from many cultures, including Archaic peoples, the Hopewell, and other Woodland period groups. There are still mounds and other earthworks, but some were more visible in Harrison's day.

Harrison had previously studied the elaborate earthworks at Circleville and at Newark, Ohio, constructed by the people we now call the Hopewell and Adena. Harrison admitted that these Mound Builders must have had a rela-tively advanced civilization. He believed that the Circleville earthworks were purely ceremonial and were "never intended for military defences."[22]

Based on the existence of similar earthworks in Mexico, Harrison also believed that the original Mound Builders had eventually moved south, becoming the people we know as the Aztecs. (This was a standard belief at the time, though one that we now know is wrong.)

Harrison also visited earthworks along the Ohio River, including those at Marietta and at Cincinnati (which no longer exist), and then Shawnee Lookout. Harrison believed that the Ohio River earthworks had been constructed by the same Mound Building people, but later and for a different purpose. These earthworks along the river, Harrison stated, "Have a military character stamped on them which can not be mistaken," showing a proper appreciation of flank defenses and with bastions placed "precisely as they should be."[23]

Then Harrison drew a sweeping conclusion. He decided that the original, relatively civilized Mound Builders had been forced out of Ohio by more warlike tribes, after a string of dramatic battles along the Ohio River. Harrison decided that the Mound Builders had evacuated to Mexico only as a last resort.

Who were these warlike tribes who had so violently dispossessed the Mound Builders? Harrison believed it to be the Shawnee, and other current tribes like them. And where had the Mound Builders made their last stand? He assumed at Shawnee Lookout, the southernmost fortified position on the Ohio River. Harrison wrote:

> The interest which everyone feels who visits this beautiful and com-manding spot, would be greatly heightened if he could persuade himself of the reasonableness of my deductions...That this elevated ridge...once presented a scene of war, and war in its most horrid form...It was here

that a feeble band was collected, "remnant of mighty battles fought in vain," to make a last effort for the country of their birth, the ashes of their ancestors, and the altars of their gods.[24]

Harrison was mostly wrong. It was true, of course, that there had been many previous conflicts between tribes in the Ohio Valley. And it was true that Shawnee Lookout was a naturally defensive location. But Harrison's vivid and romantic description of a "last battle" was pure fantasy. And there was a reason why this fantasy was attractive. As Robert Silverberg explains in *The Mound Builders*, "The myth of the Mound Builders was a satisfying one: it was splendid to dream of a lost prehistoric race." Silverberg continues:

> The United States was then busy fighting an undeclared war against the Indians ... and as this century-long campaign of genocide proceeded, it may have been comforting to the conquerors to imagine that there had once been another race that these Indians had pushed out the same way. Consciences might ache a bit over the uprooting of the Indians, but not if it could be shown that the Indians, far from being long-established settlers in the land, were themselves mere intruders who had brutally shattered the glorious old Mound Builder civilization.[25]

This is exactly the game that Harrison was playing. And as archaeological excavations continue at Shawnee Lookout, the error and harm of Harrison's theories becomes increasingly visible.

## Archaeology at Shawnee Lookout

Kenneth Tankersley, assistant professor of archaeology at the University of Cincinnati, has conducted fieldwork at Shawnee Lookout, especially with student groups working in the summer of 2009. Preliminary results have been described by Carey Hoffman, who interviewed Tankersley about his work.

Tankersley stated, "This site was originally described by William Henry Harrison as a great military fort. What we've discovered this summer is that it is not in any way, shape or form a military fort." What Harrison thought were wooden "gates" in the "fortifications" turned out to be fired logs and clay bricks that were used as small dams and channels to control the flow of water.

Tankersley and his students sunk drill cores into the earth, which turned out to contain ponded water sediments and clay minerals, "Exactly what you ought to find on an area where water was being captured." Artesian springs on the hillsides were the source of the water, which was captured and distributed for agriculture.

Tankersley thinks he knows why an irrigation system was needed: the system appears to have been constructed in the five-hundred-year period leading up to CE 500—a period that was unusually cold and dry. Droughts would have been common, and Native Americans would have needed reliable ways to cultivate crops, in order to supplement meat from hunting. According to Tankersley: "It makes you rethink the stereotype for indigenous people. It was thought they were war-like. But they were sophisticated. As the climate was changing, they could adapt. Instead of engaging in warfare, these people were working in harmony."[26]

Interestingly, some of the irrigation earthworks are carbon dated to a later period, during the time of Shawnee habitation, suggesting that the Shawnee were doing the kind of work previously attributed only to the Hopewell and Adena. Tankersley believes that this argues for some form of cultural continuity between the various groups who have occupied Shawnee Lookout. If Tankersley is right, many previous ideas about relationships between Native American tribes will need to be rethought.[27] Assumptions like those Harrison held are harmful and rest on incredibly problematic stereotypes. Work like Tankersley's helps to highlight the flaws in such assumptions and contextualizes the truths of the Native peoples in this area.

## President Harrison and President Tyler

The last part of Harrison's story is the part that many have heard before. William Henry Harrison, "Old Tippecanoe," ran for president in 1840, on the Whig ticket, and he won. At his inauguration, Harrison spoke for an hour and forty-five minutes: the longest inaugural address in US history. He gave that speech outside on a chilly day, caught cold, then contracted pneumonia, and died after thirty-one days in office: the shortest US presidency.

Less familiar is what came next. Harrison's vice president, John Tyler, was sworn in as the tenth president of the United States. Tyler was a bland functionary, whom no one had expected to become president. "His Accidency," he was called, by his many detractors.[28]

Tyler was a pro-slavery Southerner, and as president, he became a champion of states' rights. After his time in Washington, DC, was over, Tyler went home to Virginia. As relations between the North and the South worsened, he advocated for secession. In 1861 he was elected to the Confederate House of Representatives.[29] John Tyler never became a major historical figure. But to the extent that he had any impact at all, it was to hasten the Civil War—a war that would define Ohio and the nation for generations to come.

Scan to visit the
"Visions and Dreams"
route

# VISIONS AND DREAMS ALONG THE LITTLE MIAMI SCENIC TRAIL

## Milford to Xenia via Loveland Castle, Kings Mills, and George Barrett's Concrete House

From its headwaters near Springfield, Ohio, the Little Miami River flows south for over a hundred miles until it empties into the Ohio River south of Milford. Over the last two centuries, the river valley landscape has been repeatedly reimagined and re-created by individuals with distinct visions of what should happen next. Today, the Little Miami Valley is home to one of the best bike-hike trails in the United States.

Bike station at Xenia

## The Tour

More detailed information on this route is available on the *Bicycling through Paradise* community page. We invite you to leave additional information on route updates, detours, and establishments that will be helpful to future cyclists of this route. Here is the general idea.

This tour runs mostly along the Little Miami Scenic Trail (part of the Ohio to Erie Trail), which is nice and flat. The tour starts at the Milford Trailhead and ends in Xenia. We'll take a few detours from the trail to see historic sites, taking some hills in the process, but we'll always return to the trail.

This tour is composed of four segments. The total one-way distance is over fifty-five miles, but each segment is fun to ride independently. Each segment starts and stops in places where you can find parking, food, and bathrooms. For anyone planning a weekend trip, there are overnight accommodations in Waynesville and Xenia.

**Segment 1** goes from Milford to Loveland (9.2 miles, mostly flat). We'll begin at the Milford Trailhead of the Little Miami Scenic Trail, just a short distance from downtown Milford. We'll head north on the trail, taking a brief detour through the town of Camp Dennison to see the Christian Waldschmidt Homestead Museum. Loveland is a charming spot with a variety of places to eat.

**Segment 2** goes from Loveland to Morrow (15.3 miles, flat except for a hilly detour to see Loveland Castle). We'll leave the trail, crossing the river on Loveland Avenue and heading north on Fallis Road. We'll climb up Rich Road and descend steeply back into the river valley on Mulberry Street until we reach Loveland Castle. Climbing back up, we'll continue north on Rich Road and Davis Road until we pass Jeremiah Morrow's barn and recross the river at Foster. We'll rejoin the trail and continue north, passing the ruins of the Peters Cartridge Company (Cartridge Brewing), until we reach Morrow.

**Segment 3** goes from Morrow to Waynesville (15.0 miles, flat). We'll head north on the Little Miami Scenic Trail, passing under the Jeremiah Morrow Bridge, then going through Oregonia and up to Corwin. We'll turn left on Corwin Avenue to go into Waynesville. Waynesville is a great place to visit, and it's also a stop on the *Schoolhouses and Scholars* tour. There are several restaurants, and for anyone staying overnight, Waynesville has both a bed-and-breakfast (the Hammel House Inn, which is nice) and a small motel (the Creekwood, which is inexpensive and clean).

**Segment 4** goes from Waynesville to Xenia (14.8 miles, mostly flat). We'll return to Corwin and continue north on an especially beautiful section of the bike trail. At Spring Valley, you can see George Barrett's Concrete House (not open to the public, but there's a marker, at 4 Main Street). The segment ends at Xenia Station, which is the nexus of several major bike trails. There are several restaurants in Xenia. And for anyone planning an overnight trip, you can stay at the Hampton Inn (avoid the Ramada) or Victoria's Bed and Breakfast.

## Christian Waldschmidt and His Mills

Christian Waldschmidt was born in Pennsylvania, the son of German immigrants. In 1796 he led a group of German settlers from Pennsylvania to the Little Miami Valley, where he purchased a thousand acres from Judge John Cleves Symmes. Within a few years, several dozen German families arrived. They called their community "New Germany."[1]

Any vision of the future carries within itself a vision of the past: a point of reference, or of departure. Many of the settlers in New Germany were Pietists, a sect who wanted to restore the vigor and vitality of primitive Christianity. Back in Germany, their movement was regarded with hostility by the authorities, who believed that the Pietists tended to generate an excess of fervor and to promote vague mysticism.[2]

Christian Waldschmidt (also spelled Waldsmith) saw the Little Miami Valley as a refuge from past religious persecution, and he saw the river itself as a source of future industrial power. In the summer of 1797, Waldschmidt built a dam across the Little Miami and put up the frame of a gristmill. By that autumn, the mill was in operation, starting with just one pair of millstones. That same year, Waldschmidt added two copper stills for making whiskey. In 1804 Waldschmidt built a fine stone house (now a museum), which included a store. By 1810, Waldschmidt was also running a paper mill, the first in the Northwest Territory, supplying paper to printers across the Cincinnati region.[3]

Like many other visionaries, Waldschmidt combined hard physical work with gentle persuasion. He sometimes preached in the local church, and he

Christian Waldschmidt House

taught children in the school. In 1811 he ran the following advertisement in the *Western Spy*: "C. Waldsmith will engage six or eight boys as apprentices to the paper-making business. From 15 to 16 years of age—of good moral character. He will give one hundred dollars in cash, and a suit of clothes worth twenty-five dollars when free, and nine months night schooling in the time."[4]

Christian Waldschmidt died unexpectedly in 1814, at the age of fifty-nine. His son-in-law Matthias Kugler took over the mills. By this time, others were already copying their success.

### Jeremiah Morrow and the Little Miami Railway

Prominent among early mill owners was Jeremiah Morrow. Morrow was born in Pennsylvania in 1771 and was raised in an area so heavily Scotch Presbyterian that Morrow grew up with a Scottish accent, which he retained for the entirety of his life. He was a small man with dark, expressive eyes, whose manner and dress, as described by a newspaper in 1830, were "delightfully quaint, simple, and puritanic."[5]

At his farm on the Little Miami River, Jeremiah Morrow and his wife, Mary Parkhill, kept sheep, and they grew flax. They built a barn, which is still standing (so obscured by renovation that it now looks like an ordinary house, though it has a historical marker). For years, the Morrows got their flour and meal from Waldschmidt's mill, ten miles south, but around 1813 they built a mill of their own.[6]

Jeremiah Morrow was also involved in politics. He helped write the Ohio constitution. He was Ohio's first representative to Congress. And in 1822 he was elected governor of Ohio. Morrow believed, however, that political involvement was secondary to life as a farmer and citizen. When a delegation came from Xenia to give Morrow the news that he had been elected governor, they found him "in the forebay of his mill, up to his middle in water, engaged in getting a piece of timber out of the water-gate," looking "like a drowned rat."[7]

During his two terms as governor, Morrow went to Columbus only once a month, and he spent the rest of his time on his farm. When the Duke of Saxe-Weimar came to pay his respects in 1826, he found Morrow wearing a red flannel shirt, his face smudged with soot from burning brush, and "engaged at our arrival in cutting a wagon pole."[8] Other important callers found Morrow rolling logs or pitching hay, and it sometimes took a bit for the governor to convince them that, yes, he was the man they were seeking.[9]

At the same time, Morrow was a master of persuasion. Henry Clay said of Morrow, "A few artless but sensible words pronounced in his plain Scotch-Irish dialect were always sufficient to insure the passage of any bill or resolution which he reported."[10]

As governor, Morrow championed the construction of roads, schools, and canals. These projects filled him with optimism. "The nations of antiquity," Morrow pointed out, had all eventually experienced "a decline and final extinction." But Morrow believed that now, and for an "indefinite period of duration...we may calculate on a continued course of improvement."[11]

Morrow left the governorship in 1826. From his mill, he continued supplying flour to the local area. He had his eye on the larger market in Cincinnati, but Morrow had to have his flour hauled by wagon along a rough dirt road.[12] By contrast, farmers and millers in the Great Miami River Valley could undercut

Morrow's prices, because there was now a canal running parallel to the Great Miami, allowing products to be shipped cheaply. (In 1817 a group of investors had explored the idea of building a similar canal along the Little Miami, and a canal company had been chartered, but construction never began.)[13]

And then Jeremiah Morrow had an idea. There should be a railroad. By this time, along the Little Miami River, there were fifty gristmills, twenty saw mills, six distilleries, three paper mills, and a cotton factory. A railroad could connect them all.[14]

When the Little Miami Railway was chartered in 1836, with Jeremiah Morrow as president, it was only the second railroad chartered in the state of Ohio. The route was surveyed in 1837 (by Ormsby Mitchel, later founder of the Cincinnati Observatory), and construction started later that same year.

Construction began at Fulton (near Columbia-Tusculum) and proceeded east toward Milford. By the end of 1841, only ten miles of track had been laid, but the first trains were beginning to run. A passenger on one of the first excursion trains remarked, "There were men with us who could tell the tales of Indian warfare...and yet in their day they have lived to see the power of science turning this wilderness into a garden."[15]

Construction crawled up the Little Miami Valley, reaching Fosters in 1842 and South Lebanon in 1844. When the tracks reached Todd's Fork, a new town sprang up. The town was named Morrow. In 1845 the railroad reached Xenia, and it was clear that it would soon reach its terminus at Springfield.[16] That same year, Morrow's wife died, and Jeremiah Morrow resigned his position as president of the railway. He spent his last years in a small house on the Little Miami River, close enough to his mill that he could hear the rumbling of his millstones.[17]

## George Barrett and His Concrete House

Even before the new railway was fully complete, people from outside areas were moving to the Little Miami Valley to take advantage of the new opportunities of small-scale industrialization and improved transportation. One of those people was George Barrett, who moved to Spring Valley in 1843, about a year before the Little Miami Railroad came to town.

George Barrett was a Quaker, an abolitionist, and "a man of decided ideas."[18] He was born in Vermont in 1796. Barrett was an expert in the construction of woolen mills, and in Spring Valley he erected a series of mills, powered at first by water and then by steam.[19] In the late 1840s, Barrett won prizes at the county fair in Xenia for his woolen blankets, flannel cloth, rag rugs, and cashmere.[20]

In the spring of 1853, Barrett's house caught fire. He watched it burn. Barrett, his wife Mary, and their six children were all safe, but the experience was a profound one. Barrett later wrote, "As I witnessed the appalling ravages of the devouring element, my mind received the indelible impress, never to rebuild with a material that could be licked up by the voracious flames."[21]

Barrett remembered an article he had seen the previous year in the *Xenia Torchlight*, written by a man named Orson Squire Fowler.[22] Fowler was a prodigious believer in human advancement, who wrote books about education, heredity, phrenology, sexuality, temperance, and architecture.[23] Fowler's article in the *Xenia Torchlight* was about the possibility of building with concrete—or as Fowler called it, "gravel wall construction."

The idea was this: once a wall was laid out, a formwork could be built from wood and then filled with a mixture of gravel, lime, water, and clay. The lime causes a chemical reaction, which makes the mixture harden. Afterward, the formwork could be removed. Wood beams could be placed on top, set in notches in the walls. The walls would be more fireproof than wood, or even brick or stone.

Barrett seized on the idea that concrete was the material of the future. He wrote to Fowler for details, didn't receive a reply, and forged ahead anyway. He experimented with concrete mixes and found a formula that he liked. He laid out the plan of a house forty-two feet long by twenty-two feet wide, with one interior cross wall. He planned two stories, each ten feet tall.

Barrett asked local brick masons for help, but they weren't interested, so he built the house by himself. Using gravel from the riverbed, Barrett poured the first floor walls fifteen inches thick, with openings for the windows and doors, and then he poured the second floor walls thirteen inches thick.[24]

Barrett wanted his house to be revolutionary, but he didn't want it to look revolutionary. So he covered the exterior with a coat of mortar, scored to resemble stone blocks. He added wood shutters and a wood front porch with a Greek pediment. (Today there is also a left side wing, which is wood frame.) Barrett was very proud of the results.

The Barrett family moved into their new home around the end of 1853. A year later, Barrett published a short book titled *The Poor Man's Home, and Rich Man's Palace; Or, the Application of the Gravel Wall Cement to the Purposes of Building*. In his book, Barrett extols the virtues of concrete and he states his desire to promote "good and comfortable dwellings...until the entire world of human kind shall be gathered and arranged into families consistent with the divine economy, and every family have its own happy home."[25]

Barrett also says that his house "is a prominent one in Spring Valley, and I would courteously extend the invitation to one and all...to come and see."[26] It's an invitation that, like the house, still stands.

## Gershom Peters and Kings Mills

Different people can look at the same landscape and see different things. Nineteenth-century settlers saw that the banks of the Little Miami were thickly wooded with willow trees—which can be partially burned to produce a very high grade of charcoal—which was an essential ingredient in the making of gunpowder. As a consequence, explosives manufacturing commenced on the banks of the Little Miami at least as early as 1846 and continued long after the willow trees were both gone and no longer necessary for the production of explosives.[27]

The first powder mill was north of Xenia, near the town of Goes Station, named after a local settler. You might think that manufacturing gunpowder would be dangerous, and you'd be right. There were so many explosions, people later joked that it must have been called Goes Station because "there it goes."[28]

Around 1850, a man named Joseph Warren King bought into the business at Goes Station, creating what would be known as the Miami Powder Company.

In the 1870s, King left the firm and started a rival operation just thirty miles downstream, near what is now called Kings Mills.

Joseph King needed help, so he brought his nephew Ahimaaz King into the business.[29] Then Joseph approached his son-in-law Gershom Peters. Peters was a graduate of the Rochester Theological Seminary and was pastor of a Baptist church in Buffalo, New York. Peters was also, however, a natural tinkerer and inventor. Peters was hesitant about leaving the ministry, but he felt some filial duty (and perhaps some financial pressure), so he and his wife, Mary Elizabeth King Peters, moved back to Ohio.[30]

As a pastor, Peters may have been good, but as a munitions manufacturer, he was a pure genius. He helped King get into the business of making smokeless powder, which did not require charcoal, easing operations. And he invented the first steam-power-driven machine for loading shotgun cartridges, drastically reducing labor costs. From that point forward, King made the powder, and Peters packed it into shells.[31]

Over the next quarter century, Gershom Peters registered dozens of patents, all of them for munitions: "Crimper for cartridge loading machines," "Means for orienting or guiding cartridges during the manufacturing process," "Apparatus for packing cartridges in boxes," and so on. He always insisted that he had never intended to leave the ministry permanently. But he thought, once he was at the powder mill, that "Providence seemed to require him to remain where he was."[32]

Today's it's easy to bicycle past the old Peters Cartridge Company (now Cartridge Brewing) without thinking about its founder, but Gershom Peters was a real and complex person, who had an ambiguous view of the future but a clear reference point in the past. In 1911, the year that he retired from the cartridge business, Gershom Peters finished writing a lengthy and lightly fictionalized account of the life of Jesus, which he titled *The Master*.

Peters had combined the four gospels into one and then invented scenes, details, and dialogue to flesh out and intensify the story. It was an approach whose value can be debated. But even the most scrupulous historian would do well to pay attention to Gershom Peters's objectives. Peters said that he wanted "to supply missing links, to recast scenes and circumstances, to trace motives and mental processes, to invest with personality many who have hitherto existed only in name."[33]

## Harry Andrews and Loveland Castle

As a medic in World War I, Harry Andrews had seen firsthand the effects of weapons of war, such as those produced at the Peters Cartridge Company. Andrews had been inducted into the army in 1917 and was sent overseas in July 1918, just a few months prior to the armistice. After a year in France, Andrews was honorably discharged. He returned to the United States, and a few years later, he moved to Cincinnati. He taught high school and Sunday school, and he worked for the Department of Immigration, writing a handbook on citizenship for new immigrants.[34]

In 1927 Andrews purchased some property on the Little Miami River near Loveland, to use as a camp where he and the boys in his Sunday school class could fish and swim. Andrews pulled limestone rocks up from the riverbank to form circles where they could sit, and he built two small stone rooms—"stone tents," he called them—where they could sleep.

On the riverbank with his Sunday school boys, Andrews found a vision of robust, manly purity—a vision in sharp contrast to the rest of society, which, Andrews was convinced, was in a period of moral decay. He believed that the country was being overrun by the "lower grades" of people: "puny weaklings" and "moral inferiors." "God intended us," Andrews wrote, "to fill and rule the earth, not to overflow it with semi-human beings and waste its resources."[35]

Harry Andrews had the solution: knighthood. Andrews was inspired by "the simple strength and rugged grandeur of the mighty men who lived when Knighthood was in flower."[36] So Andrews knew what he needed to do. He would establish a new chivalric order, which he would call the Knights of the Golden Trail. And for the centerpiece of his movement, Harry Andrews would build a castle.

On a slight ridge just above the river, Andrews laid the cornerstone of the castle in 1930. Work proceeded at a snail's pace for decades, until Andrews retired at age sixty-five, in 1955. After that, Andrews devoted his full energy to the castle. Most of the construction we see today dates from after 1955.

Andrews also issued an appeal: "Any man of high ideals who wishes to help save civilization is invited to become a member of the Knights of the Golden Trail, whose only vows are the Ten Commandments."[37] The recruits were male teenagers, drawn primarily from his Sunday school classes. The group resembled a Boy Scout troop. Andrews taught his knights that they must not smoke or drink, and he often cautioned them against premarital sex.[38]

Surprisingly, Andrews did not expect the knights to work on the castle; he did all the work himself. At the riverbank, Andrews filled five-gallon buckets with stones and carried them up to the building site. Each bucket weighed sixty-five pounds. It is estimated that the castle contains fifty-six thousand buckets of stones. Each year, during the spring rains, the creeks in the steep hillsides would bring more stones down to the riverbank. For some of the interior walls, Andrews used concrete bricks, which he made by filling one-quart milk cartons with mortar. The wax coating inside each carton made it possible to remove the cardboard, leaving a brick.

As the castle took shape, more and more people came out to have a look and to meet Andrews, now a sort of Don Quixote de Loveland. Andrews didn't charge admission, but he placed a donations bucket prominently by the front door. The contents of that bucket paid the full college tuition for around twenty of his knights.

By his own account, Andrews received over fifty proposals of marriage from "widows and old maids who wanted to live in a castle," but he steered clear of women.[39] A sense of male youth and vigor was central to Andrews's vision.

Andrews did his best to explain his vision. As the historian Thomas A. Michael points out, Andrews published a pamphlet about his work and beliefs, and he wrote an occasional newsletter. In each issue, he implored delinquent knights to write to him, or to come and visit.[40]

As beautiful as the castle is, there is more at work here than simple nostalgia. In his *Gardens of Revelation*, John Beardsley states:

> Andrews constructed an elaborate environment that resonates with his ideas about strength, manliness, and purity...Its thick walls and small windows express a powerful desire to shut out a world perceived as depraved...[It is] the representation of his wish to be sealed off from a threatening world in the company of his noble youths, the saviors of mankind.[41]

Harry Andrews was still working on his castle at the age of ninety-one. He was still strong, but slower, and the work was not yet complete. "If I can't finish it," he said, "some of the Knights will have to." In March 1981, Andrews lit a trash fire on the castle grounds. His clothing caught fire, and he was badly burned. He died a month later.[42]

Many of Harry's knights felt a deep connection to their former benefactor. They raised money and contributed labor to complete the construction. Today some of the knights, now in their eighties, still come regularly to volunteer as castle tour guides, and to explain the ideals of the order.

Loveland Castle

## Ed Honton and the Ohio to Erie Trail

By the early 1970s, the trains had ceased to run along most of the Little Miami Railroad, doomed by a decline in rail passengers and by the closing of some factories. The river was by this time badly polluted, and the riverbanks were littered with trash.

The Ohio Department of Natural Resources, together with the local governments of Xenia and Yellow Springs, started purchasing land along the river in 1973.[43] Two years later, the *Cincinnati Enquirer* began reporting on proposals to turn the old rail bed into a bike trail.[44] In 1984 the Loveland Bike Trail opened: a thirteen-mile stretch from Loveland to Morrow.[45] (The name would later be changed to Little Miami Scenic Trail.) The bike trail was extended south to Milford in 1991.[46]

Throughout this time, many groups and individuals championed environmental cleanup and trail construction. One individual stands out: Ed Honton. Honton was an avid cyclist and a trained civil engineer, who believed that the world could become a little less dependent on automobiles. As county engineer for Franklin County, Ohio, Honton advocated for bike lanes and bike trails. In 1985 he joined the Ohio Department of Transportation and created the Office of Bicycle Transportation Administration.[47]

Then Honton began to advance his most important idea: to extend the Little Miami Trail all the way from the Ohio River at Cincinnati to Lake Erie in Cleveland: a distance of well over three hundred miles. In 1991 Honton founded the nonprofit group Ohio to Erie Trail.[48]

It should have been impossible, but Honton, like the other visionaries of the Little Miami Valley, had great physical endurance: he biked, he led group rides, and he led hikes along proposed segments of trail. Also, like those other visionaries, he employed every available means of persuasion: he explained, he cajoled, he gave interviews, he solicited donations, and he nibbled away at the inevitable opposition. One short stretch at a time, the Ohio to Erie Trail began to take shape.

Not all of the trail sections are contiguous yet. Today around 280 miles of the Ohio to Erie route are on bike trails, and another fifty miles or so are on city streets and rural roads. Ed Honton died in 2005, so his vision wasn't fully realized during his lifetime. But someday, it will be. The group that he founded continues to acquire the needed right-of-way and to extend the trails. Thanks to other organizations, the river and the banks are cleaner than they used to be. And the willow trees, the kind of trees that the earliest White settlers saw, are coming back.

Edward Franklin Honton died at a hospice in Columbus. His obituary begins, "Ed Honton climbed his last hill on October 12, 2005 at Kobacker House. May the wind be at his back forever."[49]

# Floodplains and Hilltops

## Eden and Ault Parks, Cincinnati Observatory, Pioneer Settlement, and Lunken Airport

Three rivers—the Ohio, Little Miami, and Great Miami—demarcate the boundary of Judge John Cleves Symmes's original land purchase (the Miami Purchase) in 1788. Symmes purchased the land just one year after Congress adopted the Northwest Ordinance to open land between the Allegheny Mountains and the Mississippi River for settlement in an effort to raise funds for the struggling federal economy. Out of the Miami Purchase, subsequent settlers carved smaller areas for settlement.[1] The floodplains and hilltops that mark this riverine landscape, as many tours in this book demonstrate, have deeply shaped peoples' choices and opportunities. This tour travels for miles uphill from the Ohio River. In the 1800s, on its banks, one of America's wealthiest men, Nicholas Longworth, grew grapes. Many of the locations of his vineyard have become parks, including three we will see on this tour: Eden, Ault, and Alms. We will also cycle to the Little Miami and Ohio River floodplains and learn about Lunken Airport and the original settlement of Columbia.

Southwestern Ohio was at the bottom of a sea between 550 and 400 million years ago. After the sea receded, the Ohio River ran in the lower portion of the Little Miami River valley. The Illinois glacier (about 250 million years ago) reshaped the land as far as Florence, Kentucky, and the Ohio River was pushed south into its current location. The most recent glacier was the early Wisconsin glacier, 70,000–20,000 years ago. The Little Miami River formed after the retreat of this glacier and flows through many of the channels created by the meltwater of the glacier. The Little Miami River Valley, like that of

Overlook at Eden Park

the Mill Creek Valley, is broader than it would have been without prior river occupation. The Little Miami River runs narrow and broad in a number of places between the Ohio River and Springfield, Ohio, most notably cutting through gorges at Foster and just north of Yellow Springs. The Little Miami is a national and state scenic designated river and the only such river in the United States to pass through an urban area.[2]

## The Tour

More detailed information on the route is available on the *Bicycling through Paradise* community page. We invite you to leave additional information on route updates, detours, and establishments that will be helpful to future cyclists of this route. Here's a general idea of the route.

This tour is a single segment, 10.8 miles each way, and hilly. In just over ten miles, we will travel a stretch of the Ohio River, first on the hilltops and then into the floodplain. It will be hilly! But we will certainly get to experience the topography of the Ohio River Valley. The starting point is Eden Park, where we can park on Lake Drive and take in the view of the Ohio River (and to the east see Alms Park, where we are headed). There are bathrooms in the park and parking at the overlook. Nearby are restaurants in Mount Adams and Walnut Hills. The ending point is Lunken Airport. Parking is available at the Ohio River Trail trailhead across Wilmer Avenue. Bathrooms and a restaurant are available inside the old terminal building.

It is possible to add the Lunken Airport bike path to this tour for an additional five miles and a scenic tour of "Sunken Lunken." Between Eden Park and Lunken Airport, we will take in two other Cincinnati city parks, Ault and Alms, both overlooking the Little Miami River Valley. We will get to these parks via Madison Rd, Erie Ave, and the streets of Mt Lookout. Alms has a beautiful vista of the Ohio River as well from an attractive pergola. We will also stop at the Cincinnati Observatory, home to the oldest public telescope in the country.

## Pioneer Cemetery

In the late 1800s, there were three settlements started at about the same time in the area that became Cincinnati—Columbia, at the mouth of the Little Miami River; Losantiville, across the Ohio River from the Licking River; and North Bend, at the mouth of the Great Miami River.[3] The land that became the Columbia site was in the floodplains of both the Little Miami and Ohio Rivers.

Captain Benjamin Stites, a Revolutionary War major, and twenty-six other settlers came from New Jersey to Columbia. The story is that Stites discovered the area by accident while trading in Kentucky. After some Shawnee stole a few horses and crossed the Ohio River with them, Stites and his men followed them up the Little Miami River Valley all the way to what is present-day Xenia, fifty miles to the north. He and his men never recovered the horses, but the land he had passed through seemed ideal for settlement. After returning home, he made contact with John Cleves Symmes, a congressman from New Jersey, who in 1788 had purchased an enormous tract of land between the Little Miami and Great Miami Rivers. Symmes sold twenty thousand acres to Stites at the confluence of the Ohio and Little Miami Rivers at less than a dollar an acre.[4] You can read more about Symmes and the Symmes Purchase in the *Path Dependency* tour.

Stites, his son Benjamin, and his party left for Ohio in late 1788. They stopped in Limestone, Kentucky (what is now Maysville), in early November in order to ready as much as possible for landing in Ohio. Native peoples had been forced out of Northern Kentucky by this time, as the territory had been fought over for decades and the Shawnee had retreated north and the Cherokee south. This was not the case on the Ohio side of the river, where Stites knew that his new party would be vulnerable to attack and raid by Native Americans until they could build fortifications.

He and his party spent the time in Limestone, building the pieces they would need to erect a fort so that they could proceed as quickly as possible after landing. They left Limestone and sent a small scouting party to the area of what is now the Pioneer Cemetery to make sure that they would not be ambushed. They posted sentinels, cleared an area for gathering, prayed and sang, and then went to work. While they erected their own buildings, they stayed in Fort Miami.[5] *Stockades in the Wilderness* by John Steinle and Richard Scamyhorn notes:

> Fort Miami, the initial refuge of the Columbia settlers, was a well-planned rectangular fortification with a sturdy blockhouse at each of its four corners. The walls of Fort Miami were actually the outer walls of the log dwellings, which were built end-to-end between the blockhouses to form a protected compound.[6]

About six days later, an initial blockhouse was completed. Subsequently, other blockhouses were built and joined together to form a fort. Houses were built as well, though they, too, resembled forts in that they were built to ensure safety. Thick doors and very small windows were part of the design.[7] The community established the first Protestant congregation and school in Hamilton County in 1790. The cemetery there is the oldest in Hamilton County.[8]

Initial contact with the Native Americans was friendly. The Shawnee visited frequently and were invited to a Christmas feast, held outside on a warm day. On early maps, *Slaughterhouse* was written on the location at Columbia, recording the violence that followed as it became clear the newly arrived White settlers wanted control of the Native land upon which they were intruding.[9]

The floodplain was both gift and challenge to the settlers. It was ideal for cultivating corn, and the settlers had easy access to game, such as turkey. By 1790, there were fifty cabins, a mill, a church, and a school, according to Richard C. Wade.[10] Almost every year the rivers swelled and flooded the small establishment, forcing settlers to evacuate. Many left for the Losantiville site. Those that remained eventually moved to the current area of Columbia Tusculum, up against the Tusculum hill in the late 1700s and early 1800s, eventually abandoning the Columbia site altogether. There are two houses from this period that still survive: 3811 Eastern Avenue and the Stites's family house at 315 Stites Avenue.[11]

## "Sunken Lunken"

What has come to be known as the East End has played an important role in transportation history. Prior to 1815, most of the commerce in the region traveled from east to west and north to south following the flow of rivers, such as the Ohio and Mississippi. After the advent of the steamboat, it was possible to travel both directions on the rivers and with much greater speed. The steamboat revolutionized commerce and settlement beyond the mountains of the eastern United States. There was a vibrant steamboat building industry along Eastern Avenue in the mid-1800s.[12] Three-fifths of the steamboats built in the United States in the 1820s and 1830s came from Pittsburgh, Cincinnati, and Louisville.[13]

The next revolution in commerce was the railroad, and this section of the Ohio River was essential to rail development in the area and in Ohio. Rail development in the early 1800s was challenging. Few investors, public or private, were certain about this new technology and its future. At this time, many were investing in canals, as noted in nine other tours in this book. Despite this, the state of Ohio decided to invest in two railroads in the 1830s—the Little Miami, and one coming from the north, the Mad River and Lake Erie line. The Little Miami Railroad began in 1836 with the hopes of running to Springfield, Ohio, and from there joining with the Mad River and Lake Erie Railroad in order to connect shipping and trade between the Great Lakes and the Ohio River. At the time, goods traveled across the Allegheny Mountains, which were impassable in the winter, or south along the Ohio and Mississippi Rivers to New Orleans for shipment to the east. Such a connection did not materialize, though, until 1849. By that time, the Little Miami Railroad had connected to the Columbus and Xenia rail line. By the mid-1850s, railroads from the east were entering Ohio and provided an efficient means of getting goods to the east. The north-south orientation of the Little Miami Railroad was out of sync with the east-west direction of the other rail lines. In 1870 it leased most of its line to the Pennsylvania Railroad system. Traffic remained significant, though, and in the 1930s, twenty-four trains ran a day. After World War II, passenger service ended and freight traffic declined as well. All use ceased in the late 1970s, and the state of Ohio began converting it into a rail trail in the late 1980s. The rail trail is now poised to connect downtown Cincinnati to Cleveland, just as envisioned almost two hundred years ago. There is more about the Little Miami Railroad in the *Vision and Dreams* tour.[14]

Cincinnati has also been home to pioneering efforts in aviation and, of course, some great personalities. Meet one such pioneer from Lunken Airport, Martha Lunken. In her seventies but with the energy of someone much younger, Kathleen got to know her on a tour of the airport that she gave a small group of college students.

Martha Lunken stepped on the accelerator, even though not everyone had shut their car doors, to take us further down "the Road to Everywhere." The passenger yelped, leaned inward, reached for the door, and closed it as the car turned around. Martha Lunken was as excited about flying at the age of seventy as she had been decades earlier. She wanted to show us her Cessna 180 two-seater airplane, which she keeps in a hangar at the end of Airport Road, the road she called "the Road to Everywhere." This was the last stop on a tour of Lunken Airport. She had met us at the Pioneer Cemetery, taken us to see the fixed-base operator that sells fuel and caters to private and corporate pilots, and then to a national company based on the field with some very large and expensive private airplanes. What stood out was Martha's complete and utter passion for aviation. And this in a predominantly male field. As of 2019, approximately just 8 percent of pilots in the United States are women. The percentage of female commercial pilots is only 4 percent.[15] Given this statistic

Interior of Lunken Terminal

and the fact that the numbers were far smaller in the past, you won't be surprised to hear that Lunken is strong-willed and formidable.

As we walked into the old passenger terminal and control tower, Lunken gushed about what wonderful memories she had of being a teenager in Cincinnati and coming down to the airport for hours at a time and wandering freely through the terminal, onto the tarmac, mingling with pilots and passengers. She lamented the restricted access that now prevails, wondering how the next generation of pilots is going to be produced if they do not have the freedom to wander the facilities and fall in love the way she did. She had flown in one of the airplanes hanging from the ceiling of the lobby, met her husband, Edmund P. Lunken (the grandson of the airport's founder), and learned to fly herself at the airport. A priest who taught her religion in high school was a pilot, and learned quickly of Lunken's obsession with aviation. He and another pilot priest helped Lunken and her sister get their private pilots' licenses in 1962.

A gifted teacher, Lunken ran a flight school, the Midwest Flight Center, from 1966 to 1976. She then worked for the Federal Aviation Administration (FAA) until 2016. She was first trained to inspect Douglas DC-3s, originally used in World War II. Later they were used to haul cargo across the country. A 2015 *Cincinnati Magazine* article recounts Lunken's memories of those days:

> When she stumbled over a spittoon between the cockpit seats, 'I knew immediately that I had entered the FAA's "good ole boy" club,' she recalls. Most of her colleagues reacted to her arrival among their ranks with absolute incredulity. 'Some fellow inspectors—strangely, mostly airworthiness [mechanic] types—seemed to like and respect me,' she recalls. 'In fact, when I moved from Indianapolis, the guys formed a convoy of pickup trucks and moved my stuff.' But many on the operations side couldn't understand why she'd rather be out flying than in the office.[16]

For years Lunken wrote a column for *Flying Magazine* called "Unusual Attitudes" and now has a book by the same title.

Lunken learned to fly at one of the first commercial airports in the country. After World War I, a group of ex-army pilots leveled off a grain field in the floodplain of the Little Miami River and built a small barnstorming airport. In the 1920s, development of the airfield that is now Lunken began thanks to the donation of land to the city by a manufacturer by the name of Edmund H. Lunken. Scheduled passenger service began in 1928, and in 1929 the airport saw more than twenty-nine thousand flights, including one by Amelia Earhart. In 1930, when it officially opened, it was the biggest airport in the country in terms of land area. Seventy thousand people came for the opening. Lunken was the first home of Embry-Riddle Aeronautical University and American Airlines.[17] The terminal building that still stands today was set to open in 1937 when a flood hit and the entire building was under water. The just-finished plasterwork froze in the January cold and fell off. Murals by William Harry Gothard were saved and clearly demonstrate the sense of freedom and ease that airline travel promised. They were part of the New Deal projects, injecting art, literature, music, and history into the rebuilding of the United States.[18] Explore more on New Deal projects in the *People, Animals, Water, and Salt* tour.

The location was challenging. Both flooding and frequent fog made scheduled airline service difficult, earning the airport the name "Sunken Lunken." In 1947 an airport in northern Kentucky opened to serve the region. Lunken Airport remains an important piece of Cincinnati's aviation past and present, particularly after the closure of the Blue Ash Municipal Airport in 2012, housing corporate operations for Macy's, Kroger, American Financial, and Cintas, among others.

In the 1960s, a long runway was built to service the new Leer private jets. Building the runway required moving the course of the Little Miami River to provide the necessary space. The river and its floodplain lie at the heart of Cincinnati's history not just because of the airport but also because across Wilmer Avenue is the site of the first European settlement, Columbia, in Cincinnati. Martha's temerity in a male-dominated field is a fitting legacy to that of Benjamin Stites, founder of Columbia, his family members, and fellow settlers.

## Nicholas and Maria Longworth

Nicholas Longworth (1783–1863) was one of a dozen or so men who significantly shaped the early decades of Cincinnati's history. Much of the following comes from Clara Longworth's account. His sister wrote that he and his wife, Susan, whom he met at an artist's studio, were closely identified with the artistic and intellectual growth of Cincinnati. He grew up in poverty in New Jersey, mostly as a result of his father's Loyalist position during the Revolutionary War, for which the family's property was confiscated. Hoping to escape this past, he moved to Cincinnati in 1804. He was the first commercially successful winemaker in the United States, and thus the "Father of the American Wine Industry." This was how those in the wider United States knew of Longworth. He was a lawyer and banker by profession as well as a very successful real estate investor. In fact, in 1850 Longworth paid the second highest tax bill in the nation. He is also the founder of cultivated strawberries.

Curiosity and a passion for botany led Longworth to grape growing. Prior to Longworth's attempts, American grapes were deemed too musky for good wine or good raisins. When early settlers tried importing European vines, the vines died. They could not withstand the diseases and pests that attacked them. An accidental hybrid of European and American grapes, the Alexander grape, had a bit more success. It had a taste closer to the European varieties and some of the resistance of the American varieties. A Swiss immigrant started to grow this new variety in Vevay, Indiana ("New Switzerland"), in the early 1800s. The Revolutionary War major John Adlum also grew the new varietal in Maryland.

Longworth corresponded about viticulture with Adlum, who settled in Georgetown, Ohio, farther up the Ohio River, and it was Adlum who introduced Longworth to the Catawba grape, another accidental hybrid. The major thought Longworth particularly inquisitive. "If you threw him into the Ohio River, I bet he would at once begin to search for a rare species of fish and not come to the surface until he found it," his sister recorded.[19] Longworth's interest in wine came from multiple directions. Concerned about alcoholism and other problems associated with hard liquor drunk in large quantities by many Americans, he thought that wine, with its lower alcohol content, would provide an important alternative to his countrymen and women. After experimenting with many varieties, Longworth decided to grow Catawba grapes.

The wine that resulted was mostly appreciated by German immigrants to Cincinnati. When a batch of wine was accidentally subjected to a second fermentation, it produced a sparkling wine with a more widely appealing taste. Longworth hired Champagne makers from France to come show him how to produce the sparkling wine. The experiment was expensive. In one year, forty-two thousand bottles exploded in the cellars. But non-Germans and Easterners liked it. The sparkling wine became known around the country as Golden Wedding Champagne. By the 1850s, Longworth was producing one hundred thousand bottles a year. The wine inspired Henry Wadsworth Longfellow to write the poem "Ode to the Catawba Wine." An excerpt gives a flavor of both the poet and the setting:

> *For the richest and best*
> *Is the wine of the West,*
> *That grows by the Beautiful River,*
> *Whose sweet perfume*
> *Fills all the room*
> *With a benison on the giver.*
>
> *Very good in its way*
> *Is the Verzenay,*
> *Or the Sillery soft and creamy;*

*But Catawba wine*
*has a taste more divine,*
*More dulcet, delicious and dreamy.*

*While pure as a spring*
*Is the wine I sing,*
*And to praise it,*
*one needs but name it;*
*For Catawba wine*
*Has need of no sign,*
*No tavern-bush to proclaim it.*

*And this Song of the Vine,*
*This greeting of mine,*
*The winds and the birds shall deliver*
*To the Queen of the West,*
*In her garlands dressed,*
*On the banks of the Beautiful River.*

Longworth is also remembered for his philanthropy, particularly to individuals, including vagabonds, drunkards, and prostitutes, to whom he gave bread on a regular basis (300–800 loaves per week). Regular paupers, Longworth noted, would be able to find someone to help them, whereas those he referred to as "the devil's poor" would not. He sheltered and then freed by payment a runaway slave, Harvey Young. Young became a devoted servant in the family until Longworth died. He was generous with his family as well. Two daughters continued to live under his roof after marriage. Apparently, every day Longworth left a certain sum of money in a drawer of his desk and anyone could take what he or she needed, including sons-in-law.[20]

Longworth donated land in what was originally called Mount Ida to the Cincinnati Astronomical Society for an observatory. An elderly John Quincy Adams came to dedicate the observatory in 1843 and the hilltop community was renamed Mount Adams in his honor. In 1871 the observatory moved to its current location in Mount Lookout near Ault Park to avoid the smoke of downtown industries. The observatory is also on this tour and affords another magnificent hilltop view.[21] Prior to the Civil War there were a few industries in Mount Ida/Adams, including a limestone quarry (that would be influential in building Eden Park infrastructure), a wooden shoe shop, and a fireworks factory.[22]

The owner of the fireworks factory, Harrison Diehl, established a popular attraction—the Pyrotechnic Garden—composed of firework displays. In a fitting transition, the Rookwood Pottery Factory, founded by Maria Longworth Nichols Storer (1849–1932), Nicholas Longworth's granddaughter, was relocated to the site of the Pyro in 1892.[23]

Storer was one of two Cincinnati women in the last quarter of the nineteenth century who were important in the history of American ceramics. The other was M. Louise McLaughlin. Both were painters of china, or painting over the glaze, who achieved acclaim for their work. They began painting porcelain for their own homes and then took their work to shows as well. Both women exhibited their work at the 1876 Centennial Exhibition in Philadelphia. McLaughlin published a how-to book on china painting, which was very successful. In 1877 she discovered a technique for painting pottery before applying the glaze, requiring both an underglaze and an overglaze. As the first person to do so, McLaughlin was celebrated in New York and Paris. She then used the technique on a very large vase. In 1879 McLaughlin founded the Cincinnati Pottery Club. Not to be outdone, Storer also created a very large vessel and painted under the glaze (using McLaughlin's technique). Using her family wealth, Storer started the Rookwood Pottery Company in 1880. It was one of only a handful of companies worldwide that could paint under the glaze. Rookwood Pottery won the Grand Prix at the 1900 Paris Exposition Universelle.[24]

Storer, like her grandfather, had a strong personality, and one that is credited with shaping Rookwood Pottery into an exemplar of the kind of factory that the Arts and Crafts movement sought to create in the late nineteenth century. The Arts and Crafts movement—despairing of the lack of craft, independence, and art in industrial manufacture—sought to recapture all these facets in craft production of furniture, carpets, upholstery, ceramics, etc. One account of the movement highlights Rookwood Pottery as a factory that held beauty, worker cooperation, and integrity as its chief goals rather than production and thus achieved not only a strong quality reputation but also far-reaching influence.

Fountain steps at Ault Park

Storer's intelligence, ethics, and affection were stamped on the enterprise. Management was loose, providing freedom of experimentation and learning for the craftsmen and women, while maintaining a unity of design that became its hallmark. She sought just working conditions for those in her factory.[25] Storer was deeply influenced by Pope Leo XIII's views on worker's rights, so much so that in 1892 she converted to Catholicism after hearing the pope's beliefs espoused by Archbishop John Ireland.[26] The factory was also a place of apprenticeship and education and had an adoring public that came to the exhibition hall and sought its products. Storer and her husband were also founders of Cincinnati's long-standing May Music Festival and had a hand in creating the Cincinnati Art Museum and Music Hall.[27]

## Eden Park

Nicholas Longworth called the land that he owned on the top of the hill east of the city the "Garden of Eden." Cincinnati residents called the hill Mount Ida after its first recorded resident, a washerwoman, Ida Martin, who lived alone in the hollow of an old sycamore tree. In the early 1800s, the hillside was barren, stripped of trees to build homes. In 1831 Longworth purchased a mansion and much of the land at the top of the hill for a vineyard. His vineyard stretched across much of the distance on the tour, from what became Mount Adams, including Eden Park, to Alms Park, miles upriver.[28] Several times, starting in 1818, Longworth offered to sell it to the city for park space but the city was not interested and was forbidden by the state to acquire public land for parks until much later. Eventually, the city saw need of the land to build a reservoir for clean water for the city's residents. Prior to this, the city was taking water out of the river, the same source into which waste from Duck Creek industries were discharged. So, in 1865 Cincinnati began acquiring land from Longworth's relatives and other private landowners.[29]

Visitors to Eden Park today can see the remnants of one of the walls of the double-basin reservoir. Beneath Mirror Pond is another reservoir, which is still in use today. One can imagine the large expanse of land that was covered in water. A pumping station was built and remains standing in the park today. The Spring House Gazebo, near Mirror Pond, sits atop an old operating spring.

Eden Park became home to much more than the reservoirs. Eventually, an art museum, theater, and conservatory all became popular elements of the park. In addition, there are beautiful views of the Ohio River, and twin lakes where the old limestone quarry used to be, a popular destination for photographs. As one travels from the conservatory to the ponds, one bicycles under the oldest reinforced concrete bridge in Ohio. At the time of construction, it was an engineering marvel. Michael George, a naturalist for Cincinnati Parks, told Kathleen that Cincinnati residents used to come and stand near the bridge after it was first built at the end of the nineteenth century, waiting for it to fall down.

## Alms Park

Up above the Columbia settlement lies Alms Park, a small Cincinnati city park that provides overlooks of both the Little Miami and the Ohio Rivers as well as Longworth's well-preserved wine cellar, erected in 1859 as his vintner fortunes declined. The location was originally known as "Bald" Hill, possibly because it was cleared of trees by Native Americans, who sought a clear view of the European settlement below.[30] In addition to the wine cellar, look up the hill for the cement slide. Several other Cincinnati parks also have cement slides, thanks to the Civilian Conservation Corps. On the east side of the park, you are several hundred feet above the cemetery (Pioneer Cemetery), which is now located where the first European settlers built their houses in Columbia. It was also known as Turkey Bottoms.

# Following the River:
# The Story of Mary Ingles

## Bellevue, Oneonta, and Alexandria, Kentucky

This tour illuminates the strength and fortitude of two pioneer women, Mary Ingles and her companion, Ghetel Stumpf, who were caught in circumstances beyond their control in the Ohio River Valley. They found reservoirs of strength and courage that neither knew they possessed and that few could imagine when they recounted their stories. The account here is drawn from James Alexander Thom's, *Follow the River*, a story of historical fiction. It should also be noted, however, that the story of Mary Ingles was used frequently to paint an picture of the Shawnee, and Native peoples in general, as violent and savage-like. Ingles and her family, like other White settlers, were encroaching on already inhabited Indigenous land. Her capture and escape, though remarkable, also served as ammunition for further violence against Native peoples and to justify taking control of their land. Access to similar accounts from the Shawnee would give us a more complete picture of Indigenous history.

## The Tour

More detailed information on the route is available on the *Bicycling through Paradise* community page. We invite you to leave additional information on route updates, detours, and establishments that will be helpful to future cyclists of this route. Here's a general idea of the route.

The tour begins in Bellevue, Kentucky, and ends in Alexandria, Kentucky. There are two segments in the tour. We follow the Ohio River for most of the time, and then gently ascend to Alexandria. The ride along the Ohio River is lovely and is a route often used by cyclists. There is a wide shoulder and sparse traffic in the middle of the day and on the weekends. The road along the river, though, does suffer from buckling and landslides from time to time, so be prepared for patches of rough road.

Segment 1 goes from Bellevue to Melbourne (10.5 miles, flat). Begin in Bellevue Beach Park, where there is ample parking. In town, there is lodging, parking, and restaurants, including Elusive Cow, Siam Orchid, and Avenue Brew, all along Fairfield Avenue within a few blocks of each other. South and east along Mary Ingles Highway, also Highway 8, we will pass through Silver Grove, with a few services, such as convenience stories, dairy bars, and gas stations. Silver Grove is also home to St Anne's Convent, a landmark building that was a filming location for the film *Rainman*. (It's the institution where Dustin Hoffman's character was held until found by his brother, Tom Cruise.). The gates at St Anne's are typically open, and the cemetery behind or labyrinth in front are good places to get off the bike and stretch. There are porta-lets at Pendery Sports Park, and just east of Melbourne, there is parking. Melbourne has a Marathon convenience store.

Segment 2 goes from Melbourne to Alexandria (11.8 miles flat, then uphill). This section is mostly pastoral as we continue to ride along the Ohio River Valley and Mary Ingles Highway (Highway 8). The last "town" is the ghost town Oneonta, mostly washed away in a flood. The climb up out of the river valley on KY 1566 and then 1997 after Oneonta is not terribly steep and passes lovely scenery. In Alexandria, it is possible to park in front of the old courthouse in Alexandria.

## Mary Ingles

In July 1755 Mary Ingles was living in a small community in southwestern Virginia with her husband, William, and two young sons. Mary and her family were pioneers, leaving the safety of relative civilization and settling on land that was already inhabited by the Shawnee. They weighed the risk of attack with the benefit of relative "freedom." Native Americans, of course, did not take such intrusion on their lands lightly, and as American settlers moved further west, they continued to encounter both the interest and retaliation of various groups of Native Americans.

That summer, a Shawnee Nation party raided their village, scalped a number of settlers, and kidnapped Ingles, nine months pregnant, and her two young sons, while her husband was away from the village working with another man. Over the next several months, Ingles gave birth to a daughter, and walked or rode on horseback through West Virginia and Ohio into territory few White men or women had seen. The Shawnee followed the New River and then the Ohio River (referred to as "the beautiful river") until they came to their main settlement, Chillicothe, Ohio. There Ingles stayed for a while and was wooed by a Shawnee chief, Wildcat, who sought to take her as his wife, having been impressed by the strength of her character during the long ordeal.

She refused, wanting to return to her husband and the life she had with him. In retribution, Wildcat took both her sons from her. Just two days into her capture, Ingles began to count the days of their travel so that she had some crude estimate of distance. She also noted as many landmarks as she could so that she could find her way back to her husband. Thom explains Ingles's resolve to return to her husband:

> The reality was that she was here on this earth and her husband was on this same earth, four or five hundred miles away across a mountain range, at the far end of a wilderness river.[1]

In September some of the Shawnee traveled further west along the Ohio River, down to Big Bone Lick (highlighted in the *People, Animals, Water, and Salt* tour) to harvest salt. They brought Ingles with them. Thom explains her first impressions of the site:

> The setting sun's eerie light showed a basin of about ten acres looking more dead and bleached than any landscape Mary had ever seen. The flat ground was chalk-gray, pocked with thousands of hoofprints and foot-prints, and what appeared to be tree stumps and curved limbs jutted from the low ground. Smelly, murky water oozed up through the morass and dribbled down white rills into the creek.... They were in a vast graveyard of fantastic beasts.[2]

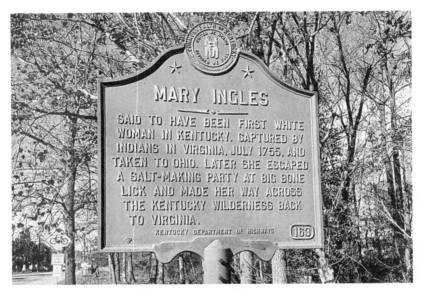

Mary Ingles historical marker in Silver Grove

There with another captive European woman, Ghetel Stumpf, Ingles made plans to escape. Stumpf had apparently been a cook and was very fond of German pastries and baking, and with Mary's help made delicacies for the Shawnee that were well-received. Their plan was to take a blanket each and a stolen knife and retrace the steps Ingles had taken to get there, first along the Ohio and then the New River. In order to do so, Ingles had to leave her baby girl behind. She went to say good-bye, finding the girl asleep near her Shawnee caretaker. She smelled her daughter, kissed her, and then, blinded by tears and in deep anguish, stumbled to the edge of camp and walked with Stumpf into the woods toward her home in Virginia.

The tour follows Ingles's journey along the Ohio River for about twenty miles between Bellevue and Oneonta along Mary Ingles Highway. The only possible way Ingles could return home was by following the rivers, the way she had come. She could not swim, and she had no idea what most of the interior of the country looked like. She left no trace of her journey; she could start no fires and dared not leave signs of where she spent the night, but the highway memorializes her courage and stamina.

The danger and immensity of Ingles's and Stumpf's journey are breathtaking. By day they would navigate the terrain alongside the river, and look for food (ever scanter as fall gave way to winter). Early on, they had pawpaws (a North American fruit resembling a mango) and hickory nuts but later needed to forage for roots and unsuccessfully tried to hunt small-game animals. On day twelve, they had a dinner of chestnut oak acorns, uncooked, and on day thirteen, nothing to eat.

Ingles and Stumpf camped at night, finding somewhat level, protected places to spend the night, using each other's bodies for added warmth. Thom describes the first night of their journey: after a heavy rain, they sought a level, well-drained spot with dry leaves from the previous year. Their dresses and wool blankets were soaked, and they began to shiver as soon as they stopped walking. They had eaten little, so were hungry as well. It was a long night.

The only way Native Americans, European settlers, and Ingles and Stumpf could move from one place to another in the vast stretches of the North American continent was to set up camp at night. Ingles and Stumpf did not dare to light a fire, so they spent a month and a half camping without the protection and warmth of fire.

Navigating by the river was not as easy as one might think. The land was more level by the river for the most part, unlike the interior. But, of course, there were no roads. More significantly, each tributary of the two mighty rivers had to be travelled upstream to a navigable crossing point and then back downstream. These tributaries added days and strenuous miles to the journey. As Thom writes:

> They emerged from a densely wooded downslope to find their way blocked by the mouth of a river that flowed into the O-y-o [Ohio]. Mary remembered this one. The word for buffalo [the Licking River]...It was far too wide and apparently too deep to try to cross here. Ghetel's face drooped in dismay and she sat down abruptly on the ground in a slumping posture of defeat...They were exhausted, scratched and bruised when on their fourth day out of the salt camp, they came to a riffle that indicated a shallows.[3]

These were necessary but energy-sapping detours. And one of them cost them a valuable asset. Ingles and Stumpf found a horse one day and took it so that they could take turns riding, thus saving themselves a great deal of energy. For several days, the horse lifted their spirits and was a great aid in their travels. But, upon reaching yet another tributary, Stumpf grew impatient with the circumnavigation and wanted to cross the river earlier than Ingles thought was safe. Stumpf thrust the horse into the river, where it broke a leg and was lost in the river.

As the days wore on, their clothing disintegrated and they were left with blankets to keep warm. Also, they were increasingly hungry and walking all day with less and less nutrition. Ingles's traveling companion also became more and more difficult, several times threatening to kill her out of fear, frustration, and desire for her flesh. Stumpf kept taunting herself and Ingles with images of foods, such as cakes, that could never be found in the Appalachian forests, let alone in the frontier territory to which they were hopefully headed. Out of fear for her life, Ingles took an abandoned canoe across the river and remained there for the rest of the journey. Stumpf ended up with the remaining blanket.

Ingles and Stumpf walked more than six hundred miles through territory that few would have willingly traversed with far more preparation and resources. The last days, Ingles spent climbing a three-hundred foot escarpment. Shortly thereafter, one of her neighbors found her crawling through his cornfield. Thom writes, "She was a skeleton covered with bruised and lacerated skin. Her hands and feet were bloody and swollen to a grotesque hugeness. Her knees were worn through to bone...Her hair, though matted and dirty, was white as snow."[4] The man who found Ingles, Mr. Harmon, was shocked by her condition and, in tears, carried her gently to his home, where he ordered his sons to slaughter a cow so that they might have a ready supply of beef broth to nourish her. Mr. Harmon's family restored Ingles to health. They also, on her instructions, went to find Stumpf and restored her to health as well.

The Harmons and Ingles's husband had a very hard time believing that she had walked more than five hundred miles, across terrain unknown to Americans and Europeans, and full of potential dangers, without horses, weapons, clothing, or food stores. It was beyond their fathoming. So enormous was the undertaking, Thom suggests, that for some time Ingles's husband felt inferior in her presence, unable to imagine that he would have held up in similar circumstances. He was also taken aback by the genuine affection Ingles demonstrated for the emaciated Stumpf when she was brought to the Harmons's for convalescence, another sign of the experiences she had had that her husband would never be able to fully understand. Ingles went on to live to an old age with her husband and the children they had together after she returned. But what happened to Stumpf after the ordeal, no one seems to know. To this day, children in northern Kentucky spook each other with the taunt that Stumpf is still roaming the woods looking for something to eat.

Mary Ingles was a pioneer, noting the terrain and the way home, in case she had an opportunity to return. Her memory and knowledge allowed her to eventually find her way back home. Every day and night she relied on the resources and terrain at hand, camping along the way. Keep her and Stumpf's journey in mind, and at tributaries, imagine having to walk uphill to skirt them as they did.

Bellevue Beach Park

## Oneonta

At the end of the tour along the Ohio River Valley lies the "town" of Oneonta. It used to be a small river town, much like Rabbit Hash or Bellevue, but suffered mightily in the flood of 1937. Now the only structure that remains in the town is the Inn at Oneonta, which mostly serves as a wedding venue. It is privately owned and visitors are not allowed in without prior permission. The grounds are beautiful and with permission ahead of time, it is worth a visit.

## Bellevue Beach

The tour begins in Bellevue Beach, the name of which, much like the Mill Creek Yacht Club (of the *Path Dependency* tour), makes one pause and hopefully ask a question or two. The answer this time is that yes, there was a beach here, almost directly across from Eden Park on the Ohio side, before the river became too polluted and locks and dams were built on the Ohio River in the 1960s. Bellevue (and nearby Dayton) was a spot where the riverbank was shallow for some distance out into the river. Families and children would come during the summer and set up blankets and umbrellas and swim in the Ohio River. After the dams, the average level of the river was higher than before and the beach disappeared.[5] There is still a lovely park, though, where one can contemplate both the ever-changing nature of the river and history.

Scan to visit the
"Ohio River and the
Search for Freedom"
route

CHAPTER 6

# THE OHIO RIVER
## AND THE SEARCH FOR FREEDOM

### Underground Railroad Sites in New Richmond, Moscow, Ripley, and Maysville

There was a time when the Ohio River was the dividing line between the slave states south of the river, and the "free" states, like Ohio, to the north. But Cincinnati and other river towns were crawling with bounty hunters, and a fugitive slave who managed to cross the river was not genuinely free until reaching Canada via the Underground Railroad.

Here in Ohio, we are proud of our historic role in the Underground Railroad. Sometimes, perhaps, a bit too proud. It was underground largely because

John Rankin House

Ohio was a border state where sympathy for slavery was widespread. Most White people favored the idea of some sort of "gradual end" to slavery but were vague about how that might be accomplished. The alternative to a "gradual end," of course, would be immediate abolition, but many White people were convinced that sudden abolition would be a chaotic disaster.

So when we read the stories and visit the historic homes of Ohio's committed abolitionists—John P. Parker, John Rankin, Thomas Fee, and others—it's important to realize that many ordinary Ohioans thought that these people were dangerous fanatics.

## The Tour

Detailed information on this route is available on the *Bicycling through Paradise* community page. We invite you to leave additional information on route updates, detours, and businesses that will be helpful to future cyclists of this route. Here is the general idea.

This tour runs mostly along the north side of the Ohio River, on US-52, east of Cincinnati, starting near Coney Island and eventually reaching Maysville, Kentucky. The route is mostly flat to rolling (except for some hills in the first segment), but note that US-52 carries a lot of traffic. Riders will want to consider what hours you will be on the road, and consider that riding in a small group may improve your visibility. The heavy traffic, the hills in segment 1, and the William H. Harsha Bridge over the Ohio River in segment 6 make this a very challenging tour.

There are six segments in this tour. The total one-way distance is a little over 60 miles, but each segment is fun to ride independently and has something historic to see. Each segment begins and ends in places where you can find parking, food, and bathrooms. For anyone planning a weekend trip, overnight accommodations are available at several points along the way.

**Segment 1** goes from Coney Island/Belterra Park to New Richmond, Ohio (14 miles, hilly). Just east of Coney Island, there's a trailhead for the Ohio River Trail, across Kellogg Road from the Belterra Park Casino. (The trailhead has a small parking lot, and this is a great place to begin or end a ride, because the casino has restaurants and bathrooms.) We'll ride a short stretch of trail and then take some hills on Five Mile Road and Asbury Road, before descending back into the river valley. We'll head southeast on Old Kellogg Road until it dead ends. Then we'll jog over to US-52 (which has marked bike lanes in this segment) and continue east until we can pick up the old highway again and head into New Richmond. We'll take a loop around town to see Underground Railroad sites, including the Ross-Gowdy House Museum and the Caleb Swan Walker House. In New Richmond, make sure to eat at the Front Street Café. There's a bed-and-breakfast for anyone staying overnight.

**Segment 2** goes from New Richmond to Moscow, Ohio (8.1 miles, mostly flat). From the center of New Richmond, we'll head out along the Ohio River, traveling southeast on US-52/Ohio River Scenic Byway. We will visit the Ulysses S. Grant Birthplace in Point Pleasant, and then we'll continue into Moscow, Ohio, where there is a large convenience store for drinks and snacks. Moscow is also home to Fee Villa (116 Broadway Street, now private property). This was the home of abolitionist Thomas Fee and a major stop on the Underground Railroad.[1]

**Segment 3** goes from Moscow to Chilo, Ohio (8 miles, mostly flat). We'll continue southeast on US-52/Ohio River Scenic Byway through Neville. Nearing Chilo, on the north side of the road, is the tombstone of Diana Whitney, who died at age sixteen, in 1823. The grave has become a sort of small roadside shrine, because what is now US-52 was once a wagon train route, and Diana Whitney is the only person known to have died in Ohio while on a wagon train, seeking the freedom of the west.[2] In Chilo there's a museum of the Ohio River lock-and-dam system.

**Segment 4** goes from Chilo, Ohio, to Augusta, Kentucky (7.7 miles, mostly flat). This is the quietest, easiest segment on this tour. We'll head east on US-52/Ohio River Scenic Byway, passing through Utopia, Ohio, which is also a stop on the *Bicycling through Paradise* tour. (There isn't much to see at this spot, but the sign saying *Utopia* is a great place to take a picture.) Then we'll reach the Augusta Ferry, where you can cross the river into Augusta, Kentucky. Augusta is a wonderful place to visit, and it's another stop on the *Bicycling through Paradise* tour. There are good places to eat, especially the Beehive Tavern, plus options for lodging.

**Segment 5** goes from Augusta, Kentucky, to Ripley, Ohio (11.8 miles, mostly flat, with an optional very steep climb to see the John Rankin House). From Augusta, we'll take the ferry to cross back to the Ohio side of the river. We'll then take US-52/Ohio River Scenic Byway east through Higginsport into Ripley. Note that there can be heavy traffic approaching Ripley. Ripley has two of the most important Underground Railroad sites anyplace: the John P. Parker House and the John Rankin House. Ripley has a charming downtown with lots of historic buildings and several restaurants. Don't miss Rockin' Robin's Soda Shoppe.

**Segment 6** goes from Ripley, Ohio, to Maysville, Kentucky (10.2 miles, mostly flat). From Ripley we'll continue east on US-52/Ohio River Scenic Parkway until we cross over the river at the William H. Harsha Bridge on US-62. On the Kentucky side of the river, we'll take KY-8 east into Maysville. Maysville is home to an Underground Railroad museum with exhibits including a tobacco press invented by John P. Parker, the great African American conductor. Maysville also has good places to eat, plus a nice hotel right on the riverfront.

## Slavery, Politics, and Protest

During the first half of the nineteenth century, people in the North understood that slavery was evil. They knew, at least in an abstract way, that the system of slavery was based on beatings, whippings, and rape. But it was easy to denounce slavery as evil and still adopt political positions that would tend to reinforce the status quo.

Typical among politicians of the day was Alexander Duncan, a US congressman from Cincinnati, elected in 1837. In Congress, Duncan opposed the expansion of slavery into western states. In 1838 Duncan wrote, "[Slavery] is not only a moral and political evil in itself...but in all its bearings and effects."[3]

Still, Duncan believed that Southern states had the right to continue the institution of slavery if they wanted to. In his speeches, Duncan makes a few mealymouthed comments about some sort of gradual end to slavery, such as colonization—the idea of sending African Americans "back to Africa"—but he never advanced any real policy ideas toward this end.

Duncan probably realized, as many people did, that colonization was a pipe dream. The American Colonization Society (ACS) had been founded by Quakers with high ideals. They did establish a new black colony at Liberia. But ACS existed for half a century and relocated a total of only thirteen thousand people, at a time when millions of enslaved people in the South were being bred like cattle. Eventually, some serious abolitionists began to see ACS as an essentially pro-slavery organization, dedicated to the indefinite postponement of meaningful action.[4] (There's more about this topic in the chapter "A Holy City.")

What Duncan wanted, mainly, was to forestall any serious talk of immediate abolition. In 1840 he wrote:

> The result, then [of abolition], would be to turn loose upon society, and overspread the country with three millions of ragamuffins, paupers, beggars, thieves, robbers, assassins, and desperadoes; all, or nearly so, penniless and destitute, without skill, means, industry, or perseverance to obtain a livelihood; each and all possessing, brooding, cherishing, and spreading, revenge for supposed or real wrongs...No man's fireside, no man's person, no man's family, no man's property would be safe by day or night...Sir, every man would have to make laws for his own defense; every man would be his own police...I know of no plan that could be adopted, which would be more likely to result in the extermination of the African race in America, than to restore them to immediate and unconditional freedom.[5]

Duncan believed in the right of individual states to set their own policies about slavery, "to move in the spheres and orbits in which their respective constitutions direct them."[6] Southerners played this same game. A letter published in 1837 in the *Maysville* (KY) *Eagle* states, "Kentucky is as much opposed to slavery as Ohio, but she cannot all at once get clear of it, with safety to herself or justice to other members of the confederation; it is an evil entailed upon her by her fathers, engrafted upon her constitution."[7]

In Cincinnati it could be dangerous to publicly proclaim a desire for swift abolition. In 1836 James G. Birney founded an abolitionist newspaper, the *Philanthropist*. Birney published his paper first in New Richmond, Ohio, but later that same year he moved the operation to Cincinnati. That July, an angry mob broke into Birney's print shop, destroyed the press, dragged all the press equipment down the riverbank, and threw it into the river. The men who did this were not slaveholders from Kentucky. They were well-to-do businessmen from Cincinnati.[8]

Even in a stronghold of anti-slavery sentiment, such as Cincinnati's Lane Seminary, there were differences of opinion about the wisdom of immediate abolition. When abolitionists got out into the Ohio countryside, things only got worse. According to the historian Anne Hagedorn, "One Lane Rebel was driven from a town by farmers with buggy whips. Another was dragged from his bed, stripped naked, tarred, feathered, and dumped ten miles outside a town where he had spoken the night before. Stones, eggs, even shards of glass were thrown in the faces of touring abolitionists."[9]

## Fugitive Slave Laws and Fugitive Slaves

Aiding a fugitive had been illegal in the United States ever since the Fugitive Slave Act of 1793. Ohio passed its own fugitive slave law in 1839, further weakening the rights of fugitives. The situation got even worse with the enactment of the Fugitive Slave Act of 1850, which imposed a $1,000 fine on anyone who assisted a fugitive slave, along with other, draconian provisions.[10] Then there were the rewards paid for the capture of fugitives, which could be up to $500 for a fugitive captured on the Ohio side of the river.[11]

These policies shaped local attitudes toward fugitives, as can be seen in the case of John Tibbets. Around 1840, Tibbets was working on his farm in Clermont County, Ohio, when he was approached by a neighbor, John Butler. Butler said that he was harboring two fugitive slaves. They'd been skulking in the woods for days until hunger forced them to come to Butler's house. Butler knew that Tibbets was an abolitionist, so Butler asked for help. Tibbets later wrote:

> I told him I thought I could take them to a place of safety but I did not know of any underground stations at that time except Deacon Barwood of Cincinnati but I told Mr. Butler I could not furnish a team as we had hands at work for us that could not be trusted and I could not go away with our team without being suspected.[12]

Butler offered his own light buggy and a horse for the trip. Tibbets agreed and said he would start after dark, but he still felt anxious:

> I was to drive to Cincinnati, a distance of twenty-two miles and it must be driven before daylight. I had three toll gates to go through, which made it very risky business as almost every man at that time was an enemy to the poor fugitive.[13]

Tibbets nearly got caught. At the Withamsville tollgate, the tollkeeper tried to look behind the curtains in the back of the buggy. Tibbets wrote, "I caused my horse to jump against him which caused him to run and open the gate and let me through."[14] Tibbets delivered his passengers, said good-bye, and returned home without further trouble. No one knows what happened to those passengers.

## New Richmond

With this background, it's possible to see how remarkable a place New Richmond, Ohio, really was. It was home to several abolitionist churches, plus a prominent anti-slavery society that had a membership of around three hundred. It was the sort of town where abolitionists might, at least sometimes, find strength in numbers.

In 1862 a fugitive slave named Leroy Lee crossed the river into Ohio but was captured by slave hunters. Lee was marched toward New Richmond. His captors intended to take him back across the river from the public landing.

As Lee was paraded down Main Street toward the public landing, people along the street started shouting at the bounty hunters in disapproval. According to an article in the *Clermont Sun*, the local citizens "presently swelled to crowds, and crowds presently became an army standing in solid phalanx across the street, barring the passage of the slave drivers."[15] The bounty hunters drew their guns and demanded to be allowed to pass, but the New Richmonders shouted at them, "Release your man."[16]

Badly outnumbered, the bounty hunters let the man go. A few weeks later, Lee enlisted in the Union Army, as part of what was called the United States Colored Troops. After the Civil War, Lee returned to New Richmond and stayed there for twenty years. Then he retired to Indiana. He drew a Union veteran's pension to the end of his life.[17]

Today, New Richmond is home to a number of important historic sites. The 1853 Ross-Gowdy House Museum is at 125 George Street. Thomas Gowdy lived here during the 1870s. In 1856 Gowdy was a defendant, along with a former slave named Henry Poindexter, in a famous court case that upheld Poindexter's rights as a free man. The museum has exhibits about the Underground Railroad and the Gowdy/Poindexter court case.

The Caleb Walker House (208 Susanna Way) was home to the Methodist circuit-riding preacher Caleb Swan Walker. In 1837 Walker was president of the New Richmond Anti-Slavery Society. He owned several small, frame dwellings built on lots behind his home so that he could provide low- or no-cost housing to former slaves. For many years, local people called these the "slave houses." The last of these was demolished after the flood of 1964, but the Reverend Walker's home still stands (now on private property).[18]

The Cranston Presbyterian Church is at 200 Union Street. The current chapel dates to 1856, but the congregation is older, and the New Richmond Anti-Slavery Society was meeting here as early as 1836. James G. Birney, John Rankin, and Calvin Stowe (husband to Harriet Beecher Stowe) all preached here. Amos Dresser was appointed pastor in 1842. Dresser was famous because several years earlier, he'd gotten caught in Nashville carrying anti-slavery pamphlets and had been punished with twenty bullwhip lashes.[19]

The Second Baptist Church (513 Market Street) is a historically black church, built in 1861. By 1880, the church had a congregation of 125. One of the members was Howell Boone, a successful African American businessman, who in 1857 was a founder of the Union Association for the Advancement of the Colored Men of New Richmond—an organization that predated the National Association for the Advancement of Colored People (NAACP) by more than fifty years.[20]

## Ripley and John P. Parker

Like New Richmond, Ripley, Ohio, was considered by slaveholders to be a "damned abolitionist hellhole." One of the most important figures in town was a Black man named John P. Parker. Parker was born into slavery in Virginia in 1827. After being sold to a doctor in Mobile, Alabama, Parker worked as an iron molder in a foundry. He eventually earned enough money to purchase his own freedom.[21]

Parker moved north, married a woman named Amanda Boulden, and settled in Ripley. He invented and patented several pieces of farm machinery, including a soil pulverizer and a tobacco press. Eventually he purchased a small foundry.

Parker was also a fearless conductor on the Underground Railroad, guiding hundreds of enslaved men and women toward freedom. Unlike most other conductors, Parker was willing, almost nightly, to cross the Ohio River into Kentucky, to help bring fugitives out, at the risk of his own life.[22]

Parker even wrote an autobiography, *His Promised Land*, which is probably the best account of American slavery ever written by someone who'd experienced the institution firsthand. Parker describes a typical night in Ripley when an enslaved man arrived, having rowed across the Ohio River in a stolen boat. The man brought news of a party of refugees hiding in the woods in Kentucky, twenty miles south of the river. Parker and another conductor, Tom Collins, heard this man's story, and Parker volunteered to go with the man back into Kentucky.

The following night, Parker and his guide found the group in the midst of the deep woods. There were ten in all, including two women and their husbands. It was impossible to travel by road because of the patrols of slave catchers. But traveling through the deep brush was exhausting by day, almost impossible by night. Parker made the risky decision to travel by day, using the woods as cover. During the trip, one man strayed from the group and was captured, and the group dodged several other patrols. Here is Parker's account:

> We made the river all right, but I was 24 hours ahead of my schedule, as Tom Collins had not figured I would travel by daylight. Consequently there was no boat awaiting our arrival. I had no other alternative than to push straight down the bank and take my chances. My chances proved very poor, because I ran into a patrol. Seeing the size of our party he turned and ran away. I knew that the whole countryside would soon be

> buzzing like a hornet's nest. Making my people throw away their bundles,
> I started along the bank as fast as I could go, with the fugitives following.
> I could see the lights of the town, but they might as well have been [on]
> the moon.[23]

At the ferry landing, Parker found a boat, and after some difficulty he located the oars. Then he realized that the boat was too small to carry them all. Two men were left on the riverbank. One of the women in the boat cried out that one of the men on the bank was her husband. Parker continues:

> Then I witnessed an example of heroism and self-sacrifice that made me
> proud of my race. For one of the single men safely in the boat, hearing
> the cry of the woman for her husband, arose without a word and walked
> quietly to the bank. The husband sprang into the boat as I pushed off.[24]

As he rowed the group to safety, Parker could hear the screams of the man who had been left behind, "[By] which I knew the poor fellow had been captured in sight of the promised land."

## John Rankin

Parker worked with every conductor in southern Ohio, but the one he admired the most was his neighbor in Ripley, John Rankin. Rankin was a Presbyterian minister and a frequent speaker on the abolitionist circuit. Rankin's house still exists, at the top of a high, steep hill. From his home, Rankin had a clear view the Ohio River, its changes and moods, each spring flood and winter ebb.

Today, the system of locks and dams regulates the river depth for navigation. But in Rankin's day, the river would sometimes be shallow enough to make it almost possible to wade across. And there was an occasional hard freeze, making it tempting for a fugitive slave to attempt a river crossing on the ice.

In *Beyond the River*, Ann Hagedorn describes an event that took place in January 1838. During a stretch of cold weather, a woman who was being held in bondage near Dover, Kentucky, fled, carrying her two-year-old child in her arms.

At a place called Stony Point, an old White man took her into his cabin and fed her. She explained that she planned to cross the river on the ice. The old man told her that she was too late. A thaw was well underway, and no one had been able to cross for several days. The ice was clearly unstable at the edges of the river, uncertain in the center. She would drown.

The sound of dogs barking in the distance jolted their conversation. They both knew what that sound meant. Sensing the woman's determination, the old man wrapped the baby up in a woolen shawl and rushed the woman outside. He tore a rail from the fence that she could use as a support if the ice broke, and he led the woman to the riverbank.

With her child in her arms, the woman began walking out onto the ice. Only a few feet from shore, the woman's feet broke through, plunging her feet and ankles into the frigid water. She kept going, breaking forward through the ice for a few feet until it became firmer and could hold her weight. Her pursuers reached the water's edge, where the dogs refused to go further. The men began yelling for her to come back. Then they fired shots over her head.

She kept going. The ice gave way again, plunging her into the water at a much deeper spot. She threw the child onto the ice ahead and used the rail to brace herself and climb back onto the ice. She walked further and again fell through the ice. With almost inhuman effort, she clambered once more back onto the surface. Reaching the Ohio shore, she collapsed.[25]

As she was trying to stand, a hand gripped her arm. It was a bounty hunter named Chancey Shaw. Shaw was part of the Ohio patrol. In addition to his work as a slave catcher, he was a heavy drinker, and he'd been arrested for assault at least twice. There's nothing in the record to suggest that Shaw was a compassionate man. Except this once. Shaw was stunned by what he'd just seen. He helped the woman to her feet and told her that any woman who crossed the river like that, with her young child, had earned her freedom. Shaw took the woman to the edge of Ripley, pointed the way up the hill to the Rankin Home, and let her go. Rankin's son John Rankin Jr. later recalled that night:

> I was aroused by father calling up the stairs for Calvin and myself. I had
> answered that night call too many times not to know what it meant. Fugi-
> tive slaves were downstairs. Ahead of us was a long walk across the hills
> in the dead of night under a cold winter's sky followed by the long cold
> walk back home which must be made before daybreak. So we were in no

pleasant mood when we came downstairs. Seated before the fire was a mulatto woman, with her baby in her arms and a pile of wet women's clothes on the hearth stones.[26]

Rankin told his sons, "She's crossed the river on the ice." One of them said, "But she couldn't!" And Rankin said, "But she did."[27]

Once the woman was fed and somewhat rested, Rankin, John Jr., and one of his brothers guided her six miles by foot to Red Oak, to the home of the Reverend James Gilliland. The next night the woman and her child were taken to Decatur. Eventually, they made it to northern Ohio, crossed Lake Erie on a steamer, and settled in Chatham, Ontario.

A year or so later, Rankin was visiting one of his sons at Lane Seminary. On a Sunday afternoon, Rankin called upon Professor Calvin Stowe, whose wife, Harriet Beecher Stowe, was also present. Rankin recounted the story of the woman who crossed over the ice. Harriet Beecher Stowe was struck by the idea. She used this episode when she wrote the story of Eliza in *Uncle Tom's Cabin*.[28]

*Uncle Tom's Cabin* was published in 1852. Today, it is understood that Stowe's descriptions of African Americans are patronizing. But at the time, the book was a sensation. For many Northerners, slavery had up to that time been an abstraction. *Uncle Tom's Cabin* made it vivid and real. Rankin's son Lowry later wrote:

> So far as we were concerned it was only another incident of many a similar character. Strange how this unknown fugitive mother figured into the history of this country. She had no name, no monument erected to her. We two boys had helped to make history and were deaf, dumb, and blind to its magnificence.[29]

## After the Civil War

After the Civil War ended, and slavery was finally abolished, Rankin left Ripley. He died in Ironton, Ohio, in 1886. John P. Parker stayed put. His house still exists. In the late 1880s he wrote:

> I am now living under my own roof, which still stands just as it did in the old strange days...Standing, facing the river, it has weathered the

storms of years, very much better than its owner and builder. But we have seen adventurous nights together, which, I am glad to say, will never come again.[30]

Slavery was abolished but rampant racism continued to exist. A few years later, his widow, Amanda Boulden Parker, decided to move to the Cincinnati area. Around 1907, she rented a home in the Norwood community, at 2944 Marsh Avenue.[31] She lived there with her grown daughters, Portia and Bianca, who were college-educated and made their living teaching music.

Today, however, there is no house at 2944 Marsh Avenue. And there's a story behind why there isn't.

Amanda Boulden Parker and her daughters lived there for a number of years. But then rumors began swirling that several nearby lots had been sold to African Americans, and the White people of Norwood feared that a "Negro colony" might be developing.[32]

White residents of Marsh Avenue repeatedly petitioned Norwood City Council to keep this from happening. The Norwood city solicitor, however, stated that there was no legal way "to remove several Negro tenants who

John P. Parker House in Ripley

already occupied one house on Marsh Avenue and that it was just as impossible to prevent other Negroes from purchasing property there."[33]

At the Parker residence, windows and shutters were broken. Amanda Boulden Parker had the windows replaced, but they were broken again. A health inspector arrived and told her that the broken windows were "health violations." On the basis of these violations, the Parkers received an eviction notice.[34] Bianca Parker went to the police, who were unhelpful, and then she appeared in court to fight the eviction, but the harassment continued.[35]

Amanda Boulden Parker was the widow of one of America's most brilliant and courageous heroes. But she couldn't beat the violent racism of Norwood. She and her daughters gave up and moved to Madisonville, a more integrated community, where Amanda Boulden Parker died in 1920.[36] No one seems sure what happened to Portia and Bianca after that.

Back in Norwood, the house at 2944 Marsh Avenue was still occupied by Black tenants, however, and the White Norwood community was still unhappy. Finally, the Norwood City Council hit on an idea: they would appropriate the land, tear down several houses, and create a park. On September 6, 1922, the *Cincinnati Enquirer* ran an article headlined "Park Is Solution of Puzzle." The article states:

> Action to appropriate property at Marsh and Beech Avenues, Norwood, for park purposes, was taken by Norwood City Council last night... The purchase...remedies a situation that puzzled councilmen for many months...The property includes the house in which the negroes live, and it is understood among the various property holders in the district that no more property will be sold to negroes.[37]

A number of African Americans protested to the Norwood City Council. Their protests are noted at the end of a follow-up article headlined "Norwood Mayor Praised."[38] The house at 2944 Marsh Avenue was demolished.

And that is why there is now a one-acre park in Norwood, called Marsh Avenue Park. There is no historic marker.

## CHAPTER 7

Scan to visit the
"Whitewater Canal"
route

# THE WHITEWATER CANAL ROUTE

## From Harrison, Ohio, to Cedar Grove, Brookville, and Metamora, Indiana

In a narrow slice of time, between the 1820s and the 1850s, America built, used, and then began to abandon a major transportation network of canals. A typical canal was around twenty-five feet wide at the base, with sloping sides, and the water was around four feet deep. A towpath ran alongside for the horses and oxen that pulled the ropes that towed the boats. A series of locks could raise and lower the boats to accommodate changing terrain.[1]

Most of these canals were located in Indiana, Ohio, Pennsylvania, Virginia, and New York.[2] The best known was the Erie Canal, which ran for nearly six hundred miles and connected Lake Erie to the Hudson River, giving access to the Atlantic Ocean. Another was the Miami and Erie Canal, which ran from the Ohio River at Cincinnati northward to Lake Erie, passing through

Restored Lock 25 and spillway

Hamilton, Dayton, and Toledo. The Whitewater Canal—which we follow in this chapter—ran north-south along the Whitewater River in eastern Indiana. The Whitewater Canal accessed Cincinnati via an east-west connector called the Cincinnati and Whitewater Canal. (This connector included a tunnel at Cleves, the remains of which can be seen on the *William Henry Harrison* tour.)

These canals and their associated locks, tunnels, and aqueducts were among the finest civil engineering accomplishments of the age, and their ruins still dot the landscape, if you know where to look.[3] But hardly anyone remembers anymore that these things ever existed.

## The Tour

Detailed information on this route is available on the *Bicycling through Paradise* community page. We invite you to leave additional information on route updates, detours, and businesses that will be helpful to future cyclists of this route. Here is the general idea.

We'll start in Harrison, Ohio/West Harrison, Indiana (the town is right on the state line). We'll ride north through small towns in Indiana, following, more or less, the route of the old Whitewater Canal, and we will often be within sight of the Whitewater River. The end point of the tour is Metamora, Indiana.

The tour is composed of three segments. Total one-way distance is thirty-four miles, but each segment can be ridden independently and has something historic to see. Each segment starts and stops in places where you can find parking, food, and bathrooms.

Mostly, we'll be on quiet roads on the west side of the river. But there are places where we will cross the river and use US-52. Traffic on this highway can be fierce, but for some stretches, there's no close-by alternative. Riders will want to consider what hours you will be on the road, and consider that riding in a small group may improve your visibility.

**Segment 1** goes from Harrison, Ohio, to Cedar Grove, Indiana (14.8 miles, flat to rolling). In Harrison you can see a couple of historic buildings associated with the canal. The R. E. Kaiser Hardware Store (201 N. State St.) was once the Kaiser Feed Mill. Originally, the mill was run by a waterwheel on the back side that was powered by the canal.[4] There is also a modest, Federal-style building from the 1830s or 1840s that fronted on the canal, at 107 Broadway Street. The canal ran where the railroad tracks are now.[5] From Harrison we will briefly head south on S. State Street, to see a historic marker showing where the Whitewater Canal (a north-south route) met the Cincinnati and Whitewater Canal (which ran east-west). Then we'll cross the Whitewater River and head north, taking quiet back roads on the west side of the river, including Pinhook Road and Barber Road. We'll cross back to the east side of the river, and take US-52 north, a busy highway, for 4.4 miles, until we reach Cedar Grove, Indiana. In Cedar Grove there's a convenience store (Beebe Marathon) for drinks and snacks, and you can wander over to the old church and cemetery across the street, Holy Guardian Angels.

**Segment 2** goes from Cedar Grove to Brookville, Indiana (9.2 miles, flat to rolling). This is the quietest, easiest segment on this tour. We'll head north on US-52 for just over a mile, then cross to the west side of the Whitewater River, which is the quieter side, and then head north on River Road and Blue Creek Road. We'll cross back to the east side of the river and briefly take US-52 north to the outskirts of Brookville. We'll use quieter roads to climb the hill into town. The Donald Jobe Overlook provides a great view of the Whitewater River, where you can see the swale where the canal used to be and the railroad tracks on the former towpath. Brookville has several lunch options.

**Segment 3** goes from Brookville to Metamora, Indiana (9.4 miles, rolling terrain). Starting in Brookville, we'll pass the home of James B. Ray, an early Indiana governor who was instrumental in canal planning. We'll also pass the 1820 "old brick church." Then we'll head northwest on the Metamora Road/ US-52, a busy highway. We'll pass the historic marker at Boundary Hill, an important boundary in the 1795 Treaty of Greenville. After another mile or so, we'll pass an unusual stone house on the right. This is the Mittendorf House, built over a forty-year period by the candy manufacturer John Mittendorf, incorporating boulders from (then) all forty-eight states.[6] Just past that house, on the left, is the trailhead for canal Lock 21. Tie up the bike, and just a few hundred yards down the trail is the ruined stone lock. Continuing north, we'll leave US-52 and take the Whitewater Canal Bike Trail for the last few miles, seeing another ruined lock in the process. Approaching Metamora, there's a restored lock on your right.

Metamora itself is a charming place with good options for food and lodging. Our tour ends at the Whitewater Canal State Historic Site. Here, there's a canal-powered gristmill. Even better, a short section of the canal has been restored, and you can ride on a genuine, horse-drawn canal boat and see a canal aqueduct over Duck Creek. (This is apparently the last covered wooden aqueduct in the United States.)[7] The easy, no-traffic alternative to this segment is to start and stop in Metamora and ride out and back on the Whitewater Canal Bike Trail, a round trip of about five miles.

## James B. Ray and the Canal Movement in Indiana

In Indiana a key figure in early transportation planning is James B. Ray, who served as governor from 1825 to 1831. He was a strong supporter of "internal improvements," or what we would now call infrastructure. In Ray's first address to the Indiana General Assembly, he talked about the importance of transportation and he cited Ohio's success with canal projects as evidence that canals had large economic value.

Ray was also a larger-than-life personality. He was tall and wore his hair long, tied in a ponytail. Some considered him egotistical. No matter where he went, he signed his name, "J. B. Ray, governor of Indiana and commander in chief of the army and navy."[8] An independent thinker, he never joined a political party. And he had a magnanimous nature, as shown by certain events from 1824 and 1825.

In November 1824 an old Revolutionary War soldier named Samuel Fields, who lived northeast of Brookville, was charged with assault. A young constable named Robert Murphy went to Fields's house with a warrant for Fields's arrest. Fields refused to go with Murphy but said he would appear the next morning.[9]

Constable Murphy, who was new at his job, went back to Brookville, but then he began to think that perhaps he had not been sufficiently assertive in the performance of his official duties. He returned to Fields's home, along with several other people. This time, however, Fields was prepared, having

James B. Ray House

whetted a large butcher knife and stuck it in a chink of the log wall just inside his front door.

Murphy approached the house and announced himself. Fields partially opened the door, and the two men had a conversation with Fields standing just inside. As Murphy placed a foot on Fields's doorstep, Fields pulled the knife out of the wall and stuck it into Murphy's left side. He immediately withdrew the knife and shut the door. Murphy died ten days later. A grand jury returned an indictment against Fields:

> We find that the said Samuel Fields, not having the fear of God before his eyes, but being moved and seduced by the instigations of the devil, did then and there, on the third day of November, eighteen hundred and twenty-four, with a butcher-knife, worth the sum of twenty-five cents, in his own right hand, thrust, stab, etc., the said Robert Murphy, causing the death of same.[10]

The trial was held in March 1825. Fields's own daughter, a Mrs. Thompson, testified against him with tears rolling down her cheeks. Fields was sentenced to be hanged.

Surprisingly, despite Fields's obvious guilt, public opinion on the case was divided. Fields's status as a Revolutionary War veteran made him a sympathetic figure.

The execution date was set as Friday, May 27, 1825. When that morning arrived, Sheriff Robert John came to the old log jail with a large group of deputies armed with flintlock muskets. They brought Fields out and placed him in a chair on the platform of a wagon, a coffin beside him.

They brought Fields to the town square, where there was "a large sycamore tree, that stood on the river bank at the foot of Main Street, and from which all obstructing branches had been lopped away, leaving one large horizontal limb for the rope."[11] A noose was tied around Field's neck, with Fields still sitting in the bed of the wagon.

An account of this ceremony was written in 1905 by James M. Miller, whose mother, as a thirteen-year-old girl, was present that day:

> A man named Walter Roff had charge of the horses that were hitched to the wagon. At the expiration of the time he arose, drew the lines and cracked his whip, and the horses surged forward, causing the wagon to move a little, which tightened the rope, drawing the prisoner up until he sat erect.[12]

At this moment a voice rang out, and all heads turned to see a man rushing up through the back of the crowd. It was Governor Ray, dressed in the uniform of a general in the Indiana Militia. He had ridden all the way from Indianapolis on horseback. He climbed onto the platform and placed a scroll of paper in Fields's hand saying, "Here, I give you your life."[13] Ray had granted Fields a pardon.

Reaction in the crowd was sharply mixed, with "shouts of approval from some" and "execrations from others."[14] But Ray stood by his decision, and so Fields kept breathing. Fields soon moved to Hamilton, Ohio, and then to Crawfordsville, Indiana, where he died quietly a few years later.[15]

Ray was a bold leader. Whatever the merits of his pardon in the Fields case, he knew that as governor, he had to make a decision. And he knew that whichever decision he made, some people weren't going to like it.

Two years later, in 1827, Ray faced a different decision. By this time, Governor Ray was starting to suspect that maybe canal-building wasn't really a great idea, and that maybe the state of Indiana should invest in railroads instead.

It wasn't obvious at the time that Ray was making the right decision. There were a few short stretches of steam railway in England, but railroads didn't really exist yet in the United States, except for some small and temporary experiments. Canals, by contrast, were a proven technology. The Erie Canal had started construction in 1817 and had been completed by 1825. This canal had opened up easy passage, for freight and passengers, all the way from the Great Lakes to the Atlantic Ocean. It was a clear victory.[16]

Still, Governor Ray became convinced that railroads would be cheaper and more efficient. He became an opponent of canal projects and a supporter of railroads. He wanted to see Indianapolis as a railroad hub, a vision that a committee of the legislature called "utopian" and "mad and impractical." Governor Ray persevered, and because of his leadership, the state's first railroad was planned and later constructed: a short line connecting Indianapolis to Shelbyville.[17]

## The Whitewater Canal

In 1836, several years after Governor Ray left office, the state of Indiana approved the Mammoth Internal Improvement Act. Reversing the course charted by Governor Ray, the act provided large funding for canals and turnpikes, but not much for railroads.[18]

For years, some state leaders had considered the desirability of a canal connecting the Whitewater Valley to the Ohio River, to help farmers bring produce to market. In 1834 Charles Hutchins had surveyed the area to determine the best route, and now, this project moved ahead. The project was an ambitious one. Plans called for seventy-six miles of canal, starting at Lawrenceburg on the Ohio River and progressing north through Harrison, Brookville, and Metamora, and eventually going on to Connersville, Cambridge City, and Hagerstown. The grades were steep, and this meant that the canal would require fifty-six locks and seven dams, plus an aqueduct at Metamora.[19]

Ground was broken on September 13, 1836. By June 1839, boats were running as far north as Brookville. When the first canal boat—the *Ben Franklin*—reached Brookville, "Joyful citizens went out to meet her, unhitched the mules, and towed her in by hand to the accompaniment of lusty cheers and thunderous cannonading."[20] But the Mammoth Internal Improvement Act was already straining Indiana's budget, and the state went into bankruptcy that summer. Further canal construction was suspended.

In 1842 the state of Indiana transferred its ownership in the canal to a private company, the White Water Valley Canal Company, with an agreement that the company would complete the route within five years. The company made good on its promise. The canal reached Connersville in 1845, Hagerstown in 1847.[21]

But then, in November 1847, heavy flooding in the Whitewater Valley washed out many portions of the canal, only a few months after the completion of the northernmost segment. The southern section, between Lawrenceburg and Harrison, was never rebuilt. The White Water Valley Canal Company incurred significant debt in making repairs, and this debt hamstrung the company for the rest of its history. Portions of the canal continued to be used until 1862.[22]

## What Happened to the Canals?

Not all of our country's canals have vanished. While the Erie Canal no longer carries passengers, it has been widened and is still used as an industrial barge canal.[23] Many of the others were equipped with water wheels providing power to gristmills, and sometimes those mills lasted for decades after the last canal boat had passed.[24] Some of the canals were simply abandoned. The most common fate, however, after a canal company went bust, was that a railroad company would purchase the land to use the towpath as a rail bed. That's what happened to the Whitewater Canal; it was purchased by the Indianapolis and Cincinnati Railroad.[25]

Occasionally the canals have continued to have a ghostly existence in other ways. A common joke in nineteenth-century Cincinnati was that since many of the German immigrants lived on the north side of the Ohio and Erie Canal, they lived "over the Rhine." The name stuck, and today the neighborhood is called Over-the-Rhine. The road that replaced this stretch of canal is today called Central Parkway. There's an abandoned, never-completed subway tunnel under this road. There have occasionally been proposals to put the canal back, using the shell of the tunnel, to make Central Parkway into something like the San Antonio River Walk.[26] It seems unlikely that this idea will come to fruition.

Interestingly, the railroads that replaced the canals have had a similarly mixed fate. Many rail lines are still in use, though often they are now freight-only, with no passengers. Other rail lines have been converted to roads or bike paths, and some of the old rail lines have simply been abandoned, like some of the canals.

This pattern must cause us to wonder: what might happen, in another hundred years, to the Interstate Highway System? Time will tell.

In 1827 Governor Ray decided to throw his support behind railroad companies rather than canals. He acted on incomplete information, knowing that there were competing interests, and knowing that whatever decision he made, some people would object. His leadership was fiscally smart and put his state technologically ahead.

Our own political leaders and private developers, now and in the future, will face the same kinds of choices. Is it better to have a bus line or a streetcar? A road or a light rail line? A parking lane or a bike path? Highway or hyperloop?

Decisions must be made, knowing all the while that if you bet on the wrong horse, you can waste a lot of money—either taxpayer money, or private investment, or both. When the White Water Valley Canal Company sold out to the railroad, they received only a small fraction of the cost of construction.[27]

So Ray did all right, and we can only hope that our vision is as clear as his. We are sorry to report that after he left the governorship, Ray had a lackluster career. He held lower office a few times (state senator, state representative), but he lost more elections than he won. He practiced law in Indianapolis, but he wasn't very successful, and he gave it up. He then moved to Cincinnati and died there, of cholera, in 1848. He is buried in Spring Grove Cemetery.[28]

# PART II

## PARADISE

Scan to visit the
"Bicycling
through Paradise"
route

# BICYCLING THROUGH PARADISE

## Mariemont, Perintown, Harmony Hill, Felicity, and Utopia

Town planners and founders tend to have high aspirations. Within fifty miles of Cincinnati there are towns named Edenton, East Enterprise, Felicity, Friendship, Loveland, Independence, New Harmony, Union, and Utopia. There are towns named after great cities of the old world: Carthage, Florence, Sparta. There are biblical names: Bethel, Mount Carmel, Goshen, Hebron, Lebanon, Palestine, Pisgah, Zion Station. There are towns named after saints and their churches: St. Bernard, St. Martin, St. Peter. And sometimes the founders name the towns after themselves: Cozaddale was founded by John Jackson Cozad. Kings Mills, by Ahimaaz King.

Main square at Mariemont

Some of these communities have thrived. Some haven't. One of the success stories is the village of Mariemont, founded by the philanthropist Mary Emery. Emery was intrigued by the question of what makes an ideal place. In 1910 Emery directed her business manager, Charles Livingood, to start visiting planned communities in England and Germany.[1] Livingood was especially impressed by the Garden Cities movement in England. This movement promoted the idea of self-contained small towns, each with a central commercial area, with boulevards radiating outward, and with lots of green space, especially at the perimeter. Livingood worked with Emery and an architect named John Nolen to realize this vision at Mariemont.[2]

Other planners have had other visions, including the surveyor William Lytle, who laid out the town of Williamsburg (originally called Lytlestown), and who created a farmstead for himself, called Harmony Hill. Or the socialist Josiah Warren, who in the 1840s created a commune on the Ohio River at a place he called Utopia. All of which raises the question: What makes an ideal place? How will we know when we have reached Paradise?

## The Tour

More detailed information on this route is available on the *Bicycling through Paradise* community page. We invite you to leave additional information on route updates, detours, and establishments that will be helpful to future cyclists of this route. Here is the general idea.

This is a long tour, starting in Mariemont, east of Cincinnati. We'll ride through historic small towns further east, then turn south and descend into the Ohio River Valley. We'll cross the river on the Augusta Ferry and end in Augusta, Kentucky. The terrain is rolling to hilly, and there are some stretches that carry significant traffic, so on the whole this is a very challenging tour. For the busy stretches, riders will want to consider what hours you will be on the road, and consider that riding in a small group may improve your visibility.

The tour is composed of eight segments. Total one-way distance is a little over eighty-three miles, but each segment is fun to ride independently and has something historic to see. Each segment starts and stops in places where you can find parking, water, and bathrooms. There are bed-and-breakfasts at the halfway point (Batavia), at the three-quarters point (Bethel), and at the end point (Augusta).

**Segment 1** goes from Mariemont to Perintown (10.7 miles, flat to rolling). We'll start on Wooster Pike, and for much of the time, we'll be on the Little Miami Scenic Trail. We'll get off the trail at Milford and take S. Milford Road. For the last 3.6 miles, we'll be on Round Bottom Road, which can be very busy. Perintown is an unincorporated community where there is a convenience store for snacks and ice cream, and where we can see the old Perintown Methodist Cemetery, with the grave of the steamboat captain Isaac Perin.

**Segment 2** goes from Perintown to Owensville (9.2 miles, hilly). This is a very beautiful segment, mostly along low-traffic roads, including Binning Road, Olive Branch-Stonelick Road, and Benton Road. We'll see the beautiful St. Philomena Church and cross over the Stonelick Covered Bridge. The last 1.5 miles are on US-52, a busy highway. Owensville has a convenience store and a pizzeria. Make sure to read the historical marker in front of the 1859 Methodist church (now the town hall).

**Segment 3** goes from Owensville to Williamsburg (10.1 miles, rolling). We'll head east on Jackson Pike and then south on McKeever Pike. In Williamsburg, on Gay Street, we'll ride past the historic homes of two prominent abolitionists—Charles "Boss" Huber and Leavitt Thaxter Pease. In the next block, we'll see the Williams House. It's on the National Register of Historic Places because when Morgan's Confederate raiders came through Williamsburg, this house was used to hide a Confederate soldier who was deserting from Morgan's cavalry. We'll also see the 1805 Samuel Davies Home, which is where the local militia met during the War of 1812. On the outskirts of Williamsburg, we will visit William Lytle's farm, Harmony Hill, which includes his tiny dairy house, built in 1802 and thought to be the oldest standing structure in Clermont County.

**Segment 4** goes from Williamsburg to Batavia (12.7 miles, flat and then a steep descent). We'll take the Williamsburg-Batavia Bike Trail, which goes through East Fork State Park. Then we'll take Greenbriar Road and Elklick Road, descending steeply to reach OH-222. From here the next segment will head south, but going briefly north will take us to Batavia, home to Grammas Pizza, plus a good bed-and-breakfast, the 1861 Inn.

**Segment 5** goes from Batavia to East Fork State Park (10.8 miles, hilly). We'll head south on OH-222 on a segment with significant traffic and challenging terrain. Then we'll take Berry Road east (from this point, a brief spur west would take you to the Lindale Grocery for a snack, which is important because the end point of this segment only has a water fountain). We'll reenter East Fork Park at the south entrance. We'll see the Old Bethel Church, built in 1818 (and largely rebuilt in 1867). The segment ends when we reach the beach at William H. Harsha Lake. Here there's a bathhouse with public bathrooms and drinking fountains.

**Segment 6** goes from East Fork State Park to Bethel (9.8 miles, rolling). This is the quietest, easiest segment on this tour. Leaving East Fork State Park, we'll take Williamsburg Bantam Road and ride past the Bantam one-room schoolhouse. We'll take Sugar Tree Road and other back roads heading south and then east, then take OH-232 into Bethel. We'll take a short loop around the town, visiting the Old Settler's Burial Ground (with its Tomb of the Unknown Hunter). The segment ends when we reach the center of Bethel. Note that the Poplar Creek Bed-and-Breakfast is less than two miles northeast of Bethel.

**Segment 7** goes from Bethel to Felicity (10.4 miles, mostly flat). We'll head south on back roads, including Bethel-Maple Road, Donald Road, and Hoover Road, and then join Highway 133. This highway follows the old Bullskin Trace, which was a buffalo trail, a Native American path, a pioneer road used by Simon Kenton and Daniel Boone, and a supply route during the War of 1812. At Felicity we'll pass by the store building once owned by Oliver Perry Spencer Fee (1823–73), a conductor on the Underground Railroad who used this store to provision escaping slaves with clothing and supplies.[3] In Felicity there are a couple of food options, and the Henderson House Bed-and-Breakfast is only a mile outside town.

**Segment 8** goes from Felicity, Ohio, to Augusta, Kentucky (9.6 miles and rolling, with a long descent heading south). We'll descend into the river valley, using Felicity Cedron Rural Road until joining US-52, which will take us to Utopia, founded in 1844 by a group of socialists. The commune later dissolved, but they did learn a few things in the process, as we shall see. Two miles west of Utopia, taking OH-52, our bike tour ends when we cross the Ohio River on a ferryboat into Augusta, Kentucky, which is also a stop on the *Ohio River and the Search for Freedom* tour. In Augusta there are a number of good options for lunch, dinner, and overnight lodging. You can also visit the Baker Bird Winery, the oldest commercial winery in the United States, and an excellent place to stop for a glass.

So there's a lot to see on the tour. This chapter focuses on just four of the places we will visit: Mariemont, the old cemetery at Perintown, the Lytle farm at Harmony Hill, and Utopia.

## Mariemont

By 1915, Mary Emery and Charles Livingood had selected a town site about ten miles east of Cincinnati, in an area of sparsely populated farm fields, on a bluff overlooking the Little Miami River. Livingood began acquiring property, working through agents in other cities to conceal the scope of the project. Over time, Emery acquired some 253 acres, much of which had belonged to the Stites and Ferris families.[4]

When most of the property had been acquired, Emery and Livingood hired their architect: John Nolen, a distinguished urban planner who lived in Cambridge, Massachusetts. Livingood explained to Nolen that the new village should be "a small community to house people employed in nearby factories." Livingood said, "The village or town was to be for all classes of people, and would have some special features, one being a development on a cooperative basis for pensioned employees."[5] It's important to note, however, that the vision for "all classes of people" did not extend to African Americans. As the village developed, the sale of lots would be restricted to White people only, a practice that would continue in Mariemont for many years.[6] Nolen laid out a graceful plan of streets, houses, apartments, and parks, with a shopping district in easy walking distance of the residential areas. The buildings around the main square were designed in a British half-timbered style. The plan also called for an industrial district at the foot of the bluff.[7]

The ceremonial groundbreaking was held in 1923. Emery stuck a silver spade into the soil. The backdrop for the ceremony was the oldest house in the area: the Eliphalet Ferris House, built in 1802–3 near the center of the new development.[8] (The house still exists, at 3915 Plainville Road. A tiny granite monument marks the spot where Emery turned the first spade of soil.)

Shortly after the ceremony, Nolen sent a book to Emery. It was a collection of stories by Edgar Allen Poe. Nolen underlined some passages in "The Domain of Arnheim," which is about a castle and landscape of supreme loveliness. Emery wrote back to Nolen: "A marked book is more intimate than a conversation and I have taken to heart one of Poe's conditions of bliss, viz, 'to have an object of unceasing pursuit'—of course that is what Mariemont represents."[9]

Mariemont is now one of the most beautiful neighborhoods in the Cincinnati region. It's an economic success story, too. The main square is busy. The buildings around the perimeter contain a movie theatre, an ice cream parlor, a charming hotel, a wine shop, Starbucks, and several very good restaurants.

So Emery conceived Mariemont as an ideal community, and her experiment has been wildly successful, but perhaps not in exactly the way she intended. Emery saw Mariemont as a place for factory workers of modest means. Mariemont has succeeded instead by becoming a bastion of wealth. There's no sign of that "industrial district," or of any other significant source of employment within the village. Which raises the question again: what makes an ideal place?

## The Perintown Cemetery

In 1946 the American poet Archibald Rutledge published an essay about a short trip he had once taken, crossing a southern river on a tugboat. Rutledge found that there was a new engineer, a man who was "fat and squat but immaculate," sitting in the doorway of the engine room reading a Bible. Rutledge was astonished to find that the engine room had been cleaned up so that it no longer stank. The bilge water was gone, and the engine "gleamed and shone." Rutledge asked the engineer how he had managed this feat. "Cap'n," the engineer said, nodding toward the engine, "It's just this way: I got a glory."[10]

This is a good story, because it speaks to the individual and personal nature of glory. And it's natural to be reminded of this story when we visit the old cemetery at Perintown, because there we can see the tombstone of a man named Isaac Perin, who was a young steamboat captain in the 1830s, long before Rutledge was born. Isaac Perin was a proud man because he was captain of the *Moselle*, the fastest steamboat on the Ohio River.[11]

Captain Isaac Perin was the nephew of Samuel Perin, the principal founder of Perintown. Samuel Perin was from Massachusetts and moved to southern Ohio around 1805. Working as a millwright, Samuel Perin earned enough money to purchase fifty acres in Stonelick Township. In 1814 he put into operation the first sawmill in the area. He built a small gristmill, and then a larger one, and acquired additional property. He built a tannery, then a distillery.[12]

By this time, several of Samuel Perin's relatives had moved here, including his nephew Isaac, born in 1814.[13] Isaac grew up to be "a young gentleman of great ambition and enterprise," and by 1838, when Isaac was only twenty-four, he was captain of the *Moselle*.

The *Moselle* was brand-new. She was regarded as "the very paragon of western steamboats; she was perfect in form and construction, elegant and superb in all her equipments, and enjoyed a reputation for speed which admitted of no rivalship."[14] The *Moselle*'s first voyage, from Portsmouth to Cincinnati, a distance of 110 miles, was made in seven hours and fifty-five minutes, a record.[15] On another early voyage, Captain Perin and the *Moselle* delivered passengers to a farm owned by William Henry Harrison, to witness the groundbreaking ceremonies for the Cincinnati and Whitewater Canal.[16]

Captain Perin's exploits had gained him a certain level of celebrity. It all ended on April 25, 1838. The *Moselle* pulled into the river port at Fulton, Kentucky, to take on passengers. That accomplished, the bow of the boat was pushed from shore, and the *Moselle* began steaming away. At this moment, her boilers exploded. The whole of the vessel forward of the wheels was blown to splinters. Eyewitnesses stated that "fragments of the boiler and of human bodies were thrown both to the Kentucky and Ohio shores, although the distance to the former was a quarter of a mile."[17]

Hundreds of volunteers rushed to the riverbank. On the shore lay "twenty or thirty mangled and still bleeding corpses."[18] Other bodies were still being dragged from the wreck. The survivors were as pitiable as the dead: "Fathers were distractedly inquiring for children, children for parents, husbands and wives for each other. One man had saved a son, but lost a wife and five children."[19]

At least eighty-nine people were killed, including the captain himself, whose body "was thrown to a considerable height on the steep embankment of the river."[20] Captain Perin's body was returned to Perintown.

The Perintown Methodist Cemetery contains the grave of Samuel Perin, the founder of Perintown, plus Samuel's wife, Mary Simpkins Perin, and many other relatives. Among the graves, it's easy to spot Isaac's tombstone. It's a large, fancy stone with a long inscription:

> SACRED To the memory of CAPT. ISAAC PERIN who met an early death by the fatal explosion of the steamboat MOSELLE on the 25th day of April 1838 aged 24 years 8 months and 16 days. Amidst the gay and cheerful multitude... the vigor of youth...soul broken from these cold remains... youthful friends...

Perintown Church and Cemetery

What the stone doesn't tell you is that the disaster was Captain Perin's own fault. He was hotdogging. When the *Moselle* pulled in to port at Fulton, Perin should have let off steam. But he kept the pressure in the boilers high, because he wanted to show everyone that his steamboat could take off like a shot after a full stop. The excess pressure caused the explosion.[21]

And because the truth came out quickly, it's likely that whoever wrote Captain Perin's epitaph knew all this. The stone doesn't call him a hero. It doesn't say that he was skillful or smart. The stone doesn't praise Captain Perin for anything except "the vigor of youth," which he had. It was his tragic flaw and his last glory.

## Harmony Hill

William Lytle (1770–1831) was from Pennsylvania. He first came down the Ohio River when he was only nine and a half years old but he was already a skilled sharpshooter, traveling with his father (also named William). The father and son were part of a large expedition, with sixty-eight flatboats carrying nearly a thousand men and women who were intent on settling in Kentucky.

Many years later, William Lytle the younger recalled his first trip down the Ohio River. On April 11, 1780, the company "arrived without molestation at Limestone, now Maysville" in Kentucky. A hunting party also went out and killed several buffalo, and William "now for the first time tasted their flesh."[22]

William Lytle and his father settled near Lexington, Kentucky, and this is where the boy grew up. By the early 1790s, William Lytle the younger was a surveyor whose work often brought him to Clermont County, Ohio. By 1794, Lytle had a semipermanent surveyors' camp in the area.[23] Many Revolutionary War veterans had been given land in Ohio in exchange for their military service, and Lytle made a lot of money surveying these land grants. Lytle also inherited land from his father, and he eventually owned a large part of what is now Clermont County.

By the time he was twenty-six, William Lytle was planning a town, which he called Lytlestown, and which we now call Williamsburg, on the east fork of the Little Miami River. Lytle's plan included a mill site and a public square. Lytle promised a free lot to each of the first ten families who would promise to build a house there. There were plenty of takers.[24]

For his own homestead, Lytle reserved six hundred acres immediately outside the town, on a high rise of ground. Lytle called his tract Harmony Hill.[25]

In 1798 Lytle made a trip to Philadelphia, where he met Eliza Stahl. Lytle wrote to his friends that he had finally found "the one to keep him at home."[26] He and Eliza were soon married, and he brought her back to the frontier.

In 1800 Lytle had a land office built at Harmony Hill, where settlers came to register their claims. That same year, Lytle began construction of his own home. In 1802 Lytle hired a stonemason to improve the house and add a second story. Also in 1802 Lytle added a tiny stone dairy house next to his well.[27]

By 1803, William and Eliza Stahl Lytle had the finest home between Chillicothe and the Little Miami River. William and Eliza's first four children were born at Harmony Hill between 1800 and 1806. But then the Lytle family decided to leave Clermont County. Business opportunities would be better in Cincinnati, and so would educational opportunities for the children. So the Lytles sold Harmony Hill.[28]

Harmony Hill stayed a working farm for a long time, but by the mid-twentieth century, the house and the land office had deteriorated, and both were torn down. Today, the only trace of William Lytle's farmstead is the dairy house, which has been restored. In Cincinnati the Lytles purchased a large town lot and built a mansion. The mansion is gone, but the location is easy to find—it is now Lytle Park.[29]

Among William and Eliza Lytle's children, the most prominent was their son Robert Todd Lytle, born at Harmony Hill in 1804. In the early 1830s, Robert Lytle represented Ohio in the US House of Representatives. The scion of the family was Robert's son William Haines Lytle, born in 1826. When the boy was five years old, his grandfather William Lytle wrote of him, "Thank God I now have a boy who will keep up the name of Lytle when the rest of us are laid in the dust."[30]

William Haines Lytle grew up to be a brilliant young man who man studied law and wrote poetry. He served in the Mexican-American War, and he came safely home again. He spent two terms in the Ohio House of Representatives. He got engaged to a woman named Lily, but the engagement collapsed. He wrote a poem titled "Tis Only Once We Love" about "The heart that throbbed at Glory's voice," and about how the light of love can fade at evening-time, even though at morning it was "fair as dawn on Eden."[31]

When the Civil War broke out, William Haines Lytle returned to service. This time he was killed in battle, at Chickamauga, by a musket ball to the head. He was thirty-seven. He had never married.[32] Here is his poem "The Haunted River":

> *Through a desolate dim region,*
> *Rolls a haunted river,*
> *Shapes and shades whose name is legion,*
> *Vex its tide forever.*
>
> *Round it loom steep promontories*
> *Fringed with morning's ruddy glories,*
> *In the olden day,*
> *Now, wan and gray;*
> *And still this sad, mysterious river*
> *Goes sweeping, moaning on forever.*
>
> *Once amid enchanted islands,*
> *Where the May reposes,*
> *Starred with flower-crowned highlands,*
> *Drunk with breath of roses,*
>
> *Flashed its current in the sunlight,*
> *Sung its waters in the moonlight,*
> *Sung to Dian,*
> *And Orion;*
> *Now, this sad, mysterious river,*
> *Sweeps and moans along, forever.*[33]

## Reaching Utopia

Some miles south of Harmony Hill is Utopia, Ohio, which still has a road sign with the town name, plus a gas station, and a historical marker, but not much else. The village of Utopia was originally a socialist commune. It existed first under the name the Clermont Phalanx, and was located about a mile west of where it is now.[34]

The Clermont Phalanx issued its constitution and prospectus in 1844. The prospectus explained that all land would be owned collectively. For a fee of $25 per year, a family would be able to live in a small, communally owned dwelling. Work would be done cooperatively, and the results of labor would be shared.[35]

The people who issued this prospectus were followers of the French socialist philosopher Charles Fourier (1772–1837). Fourier believed that cooperative societies would be able to eliminate poverty by paying sufficiently high wages, with a "decent minimum" paid to those who were not able to work.[36] Fourier also believed in greater rights for women. (He coined the word feminism—*feminisme*—in 1837).[37]

In Fourier's writings, a community based on these principles would be called a *phalange*, but in English this was usually rendered as *phalanx*, like the military formation in which soldiers work together.[38]

Not everyone believed that Fourier's business model could succeed. In particular, a social economist from Cincinnati named Josiah Warren visited the nascent community on the Ohio River and said it wasn't going to work.[39] Warren told them that many of Fourier's ideas were good, but that some of his rules were too absolute.[40] Full communal ownership of land, Warren said, would never succeed. People needed to own their own property.[41]

Warren, now in his mid-forties, had already seen several experimental communities in action, including the New Harmony community founded by Robert Owen in Indiana. Josiah Warren still believed in cooperative economics, but he thought that there needed to be more room for individualism than was allowed for in a fully socialist system.[42]

The Fourier disciples were not swayed by Warren's critique, and the Clermont Phalanx proceeded as planned. According to a later newspaper account:

> All sat down to meals together in the great dining room—first the grown people, then the children. There was a separate building where meetings of the council were held. The whole made a charming white village among the trees...The people were drawn from all classes. They were mostly dreamers who had made a failure of life, but all were virtuous and intelligent, and many highly cultured.[43]

It wasn't long before they ran into trouble. There was "a hand-to-hand scramble for some of the 'common property,'" and less than three years after its founding, the Clermont Phalanx broke up.[44]

In June 1847 Warren visited by steamboat, and he was met at the landing by a man named Daniel Prescott, who told Warren, "Well, we have failed just as you foretold; it worked exactly as you said it would, and if you had been a prophet you could not have told more accurately what would happen. Now I am ready for your method."[45]

And so Warren finally had a chance to put his ideas into practice. He called his system Equitable Commerce. The prices of goods, he said, should be set not to maximize profit. Instead, the prices of goods should be closely pegged to the amount of labor required to produce those goods. Warren encouraged the use of "time notes"—worth so many hours of labor—as scrip, instead of currency.[46]

There was some available land about a mile upstream that was owned by Henry Jernegan, "a believer in Equitable Commerce."[47] An agreement was made that Jernegan would lay out a town in quarter-acre lots.[48] The town was skinny and long, two blocks wide along the Ohio River and extending several blocks to the north. The road that is now called U.S. Ohio Highway 52 bisected the town. (Most of the original street grid still exists.) The new location was "most beautiful, and healthy; forty miles above the city, and the soil rich and productive beyond comparison."[49]

The new town was named Utopia. This experiment was considered important enough that another prominent social reformer arrived at just around the same time that Warren did: John Otis Wattles.

John O. Wattles and his brother Augustus Wattles had both attended Lane Seminary in Cincinnati, the school founded by Lyman Beecher. The Wattles brothers had become ardent abolitionists,[50] and they also had a strong interest in spiritualism: trances, spirit rappings, and so on.[51] John O. Wattles was described as a "spontaneous clairvoyant, that is, he enters the clairvoyant state by power of his own will."[52]

Wattles attracted a crowd of followers in Utopia, and they built a large, brick building right on the shore of the Ohio River, to use for religious ceremonies

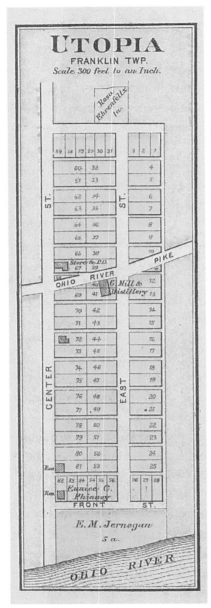

Map of Utopia in 1891

and, presumably, séances. The building was completed in late 1847.

The mortar between the bricks was not yet dry when there was a sudden flood, on November 15. Rising waters covered the first floor of the building, but Wattles and some of his followers believed that they would be safe on the upper level. Just as the water reached the second floor, the brick walls began to collapse. Some of Wattles's followers jumped into the river and were drowned, others were crushed in the ruins.[53] Seventeen people died.[54]

John O. Wattles and his wife, Esther, were among the survivors, but they did not stay in Utopia long after that. John's brother Augustus Wattles, another social reformer, stayed for a few more years,[55] but then Augustus moved away.[56] Josiah Warren left, too, in 1850.[57]

So the community of Utopia reached a point where they had already failed once, as the Clermont Phalanx. Their largest building had collapsed, killing seventeen people. And all of their leaders were gone. That might have been the end of the experiment. But it wasn't. The people of Utopia stuck to their principles of cooperation and fair distribution of labor. Utopia got a sawmill, then a gristmill. The people exchanged time notes for work.

Years later, one of the residents, a shoe-and boot-maker named Enoch Cubberly, recalled that "the labor notes put us into a reciprocating society—the result was, in two years twelve families found themselves with homes who never owned them before." Cubberly built himself a brick cottage, one and a half stories high, and the total cost in cash was only $9.81, since "all the rest was effected by exchanging labor for labor." Cubberly's verdict was: "Mr. Warren is right, and the way to get back as much labor as we give is by the labor-cost prices."[58]

Josiah Warren came back to visit Utopia, Ohio, once, in the winter of 1855–56. Warren had to admit, even then, that Utopia was not much to look at. (This hasn't changed.) Still, he was encouraged by what he found:

> My visit to that little germ of Equitable society...has given me higher hopes and expectations than I had before dared to entertain. It is not the display that the little group of buildings makes to the eye...but knowing the means by which these...have been acquired.[59]

The principle of equitable commerce, Warren wrote, "Had lost nothing with those who first took hold of it...but had gained...from year to year in their highest judgment and affectionate regard."[60]

Utopia didn't last forever, but it lasted longer than almost anyone expected. The town was still a healthy, semi-socialist community into the late 1850s, and some work was still being done in exchange for time notes into the mid-1870s.

Warren, for the rest of his life, continued preaching his brand of cooperative economics plus individualism. This was his unceasing pursuit. He wrote:

> I do not mean to be understood that all are of one mind. On the contrary, in a progressive state there is no demand for conformity...Peace, harmony, ease, security, happiness, will be found only in Individuality.[61]

Josiah Warren was a restless soul. After leaving Ohio, he moved to another utopian community, in New York City, and then another one, in rural

Massachusetts. He died in Boston in 1874.[62] Did Warren find paradise? We think he did. But he also learned that every glorious paradise here on earth is individual, personal, and temporary.

The story of the disastrous flood and building collapse at Utopia, and the story of ill-fated steamboat captain Samuel Perrin, and the mournful poetry and too-soon death of William Haines Lytle—these stories all remind us that the only thing that endures is the old and haunted river.

Scan to visit the "Party Tour" route

CHAPTER 9

# THE PARTY TOUR: BREWERIES AND INCLINES

## Amusements Past and Present in Over-the-Rhine

Geography is destiny, unless you can build an incline and climb out of the city basin, via a coal-powered streetcar to reach a dazzling height above the smog and industry below. In the late 1800s, much of what is now downtown Cincinnati was a riot of tenement housing, saloons, congested filthy streets, and factory smoke, finished off with a canal that smelled like a cesspool. Before the inclines, population density in downtown Cincinnati was approximately thirty-two thousand people per square mile, making it one of the densest cities in the United States.[1] Today it is about four thousand people per square mile.[2]

In the late 1800s and early 1900s, thousands of Cincinnati residents, night after night, escaped uphill for a few hours. The most popular incline and the longest-lasting one was the Mount Adams Incline, in operation for seventy years until 1947. Once on the mount, dancing, pyrotechnics, locally and globally brewed beer, and food all awaited, most of it at the Highland House; sometimes as many as eight thousand people were at the house on a weekend night. The Highland House was a two-story brightly lit colorful building. The scene was so romantic and high-spirited that it bolstered the claim that Cincinnati was the "Paris of the U.S." Whether due to the brews or the views, Highland House was a hip place to be.[3] And it was one of three restaurants and dancing venues at the top of an incline in the late 1800s and early 1900s. But there is more—national origin (geography in another sense) also deeply influenced Cincinnati's vibrant beer producing economy. Germans, particularly in Over-the-Rhine, owned and operated dozens of breweries from the early

1800s through the mid-1900s, though Prohibition took its toll. This tour will take us past the ghosts of this late nineteenth- and early twentieth-century scene in Cincinnati as well as two contemporary breweries: Christian Moerlein and Rhinegeist.

## The Tour

More detailed information on the route is available on the *Bicycling through Paradise* community page. We invite you to leave additional information on route updates, detours, and establishments that will be helpful to future cyclists of this route. Here's a general idea of the route.

This is a short tour, 8.5 miles round-trip and flat. We begin and end at Findlay Market, where the choices for eating are practically endless, and parking is available either in the market lot or on the street. From there, riders travel from east to west to visit the base of each of the inclines. None of them exist anymore but steps in two cases give a sense of the topography conquered by the trains and, in one case, Fairview, the staircase is complete enough to climb most of the way up the hillside (totally recommended, after locking your bike). Start at the bottom of Mount Auburn Incline and then travel along McMicken Avenue to the base of the Bellevue Incline. In between, are several old brewery buildings and the present-day Christian Moerlein Brewing Company. From Bellevue, visit Rhinegeist Brewery on Elm Street before reaching the next incline, Fairview. The final incline to be visited is Price Hill, located on the west side of town, via 8th Street. The current Incline Public House is located where the top of the incline used to be. The Mount Adams Incline, unfortunately, cannot be visited as its base lies in the tangle of I–71 east of Eggleston Avenue.

## Brewing

By the 1880s, Cincinnati was known as the "beer capital of the world."[4] Starting with an English brewery in 1812 and then a German one in 1829, by 1870 Cincinnati was home to about 22 breweries, most of them making popular lagers that made use of a yeast that was active on the bottom of the barrel (rather than top-of-the-barrel yeast, which characterizes ales).[5] But between

Findlay Market

1812 and today, 250 breweries opened and closed. Unlike inclines, for most of the last two centuries, beer has been a constant presence in the Cincinnati economy, both in terms of production and consumption. Beer brewing received a significant boost with German immigration to the city starting in the 1840s. German immigrants shared a cultural appreciation for beer and a good time that was not as common among English-speaking immigrants.[6]

A related industry developed in Cincinnati at this same time: yeast making. Originally developed from yeast in the brewing process, the Fleischmann brothers commercialized a stable, consistent brand of yeast that made for lighter, less dense bread than had been the standard in the United States up to that point.[7]

In 1891 the export value of beer and whiskey was twice as much as that of livestock.[8] The most visible remnants of the nineteenth-century beer-making industry are on McMicken Avenue in Over-the-Rhine, very close to several of the bases of inclines. Most of the breweries were built near the Miami and Erie Canal (where Central Parkway is now) because it provided access to the Ohio River and points south as well as the Great Lakes to the north. One can see at 133 E. McMicken Avenue the brewery building that was first Bauer (1865), then Schmidt (1875), and finally Crown (1905). And at 24 W. McMicken Avenue stands the city's oldest brewery building, Lafayette. By 1900, twenty-two breweries employed two thousand workers and supported ten thousand more in related industries.[9]

The men who made Cincinnati the beer capital of the world were self-made, hardworking Germans who loved their beer and their city. They were active citizens, supporting public institutions and the congregations of which they were a part. The Christian Moerlein Brewery on Elm Street grew from a casual enterprise at Moerlein's blacksmithing shop to Ohio's largest brewery and the nation's fifth largest in the early 1900s. Moerlein walked three hundred miles to board a ship to the United States. Once here, he first took a job digging ditches, but eventually turned to brewing where he became an innovator. He was one of the first brewers to pasteurize his beer so that it could be safely transported across the country and world. He also shipped it in barrels and had it bottled closer to its point of sale to keep it fresher.[10]

Louis Hudepohl's beer became strongly associated with quality Cincinnati beer. It started as Buckeye Brewery on what is now McMicken Avenue; you will ride by the building on your right after Vine Street. Hudepohl, the first American-born beer baron, and his partner bought Buckeye in 1885. They survived Prohibition by abandoning brewing for a few years until it was repealed, and then returning to their buildings and equipment and picking up again.[11] The company was creative and nimble, producing light beers, specialty beers, and marketing special cans for Reds and Bengals games.[12]

The John Hauck Brewing Company was second only in production to Christian Moerlein for decades. You will pass by his Italianate home on Dayton Street as part of the tour. In the late 1800s, the street was known as "millionaire's row" and "beer barons" row. Hauck's brewery was a block away from his house on Central Avenue. When the founder of the Zoological Garden, Mr. Erkenbrecker, died, Hauck paid the debts of the garden and bought the land on which it had been established for $135,000 and leased it to the Zoological Garden for ninety-nine years. Hauck immigrated to the United States in 1852 at the age of twenty-two and moved to Cincinnati where his uncle, a brewery owner, lived. Hauck married in 1858 and became brewmaster in his father-in-law's Lafayette Brewery. After his father-in-law's death, his mother-in-law sold the brewery and Hauck joined Johann Windisch to open a brewery in

1863. Windisch died in 1879, and Hauck bought the interest of his deceased partner for $550,000. This was the largest transaction that had ever taken place in the Hamilton County Recorder's Office. Hauck closely monitored the quality of his company's beer. He was reluctant to switch to bottling in the 1870s, convinced that beer should be kept in wood. Similarly, he demanded that his workers handle the kegs gently in getting them on and off the wagon and taking them in and out of the cellar, where they were stored in the cool air. When Hauck died in 1896, his son Louis continued to operate the brewery until Prohibition.[13]

The moniker "beer capital of the world" also refers to rates of consumption. As in many places, beer was safer than local water. In 1889 there were 1,841 saloons in the Cincinnati area. In 1902 there were 136 saloons up and down Vine Street alone. Saloons were community centers where business and political relationships were forged and severed. In pre-Prohibition days, Cincinnati residents drank two to four times the amount of beer annually than the average US citizen, forty gallons for every person in the city. Three-fifths of the beer brewed in Cincinnati stayed in Cincinnati in the nineteenth and early twentieth centuries.[14]

Employees were allowed to drink beer all day and were paid well. At John Kaufmann's brewery (founded in 1844), one worker named Vantzy drank two hundred glasses of beer each shift. The glasses were apparently smaller than our pint glasses, but still. The brewery's employees usually drank an average of thirty-five glasses apiece on a shift. Other breweries did limit consumption: Moerlein employees averaged twenty-five glasses per day, and at the Jackson

John Hauck House

Brewery, they were allowed six to fourteen glasses a day depending on age, build, and quality of work.[15]

Breweries, like many nineteenth- and early twentieth-century industries, were dangerous places to work. Accidents, sometimes fatal, were frequent. Beer vats and casks exploded, refrigeration pipes created ammonia fountains, scaffolds collapsed, men fell into huge hot mash tubs, into cellars through shafts, and there were fires. One story will suffice to convey the horror. This ran in the *Cincinnati Commercial* on November 26, 1876. Green Township farmer Peter Hensler traveled to downtown Cincinnati with his wagon to purchase a load of malt barley sprouts from Schaller and Gerke Brewery, located on the corner of Plum Street and Canal Street. As Hensler climbed down into the cellar, his long coat accidentally wrapped around a spinning axle. "First his coat was wound up in a few revolutions of the shaft, and then the man was wound up and whipped against the stairs and the floor above." The injuries were fatal: broken ribs, punctured lungs, and back and head injuries.[16]

From the early years of the United States, there was concern about alcohol consumption. In 1831 Cincinnati passed a law prohibiting liquor sales on Sundays, but the law was not enforced until 1889. In 1880 the Cincinnati Red Stockings (now the Reds) had been kicked out of the National League for selling beer and playing on Sundays. In 1889 they stopped playing on Sundays for the remainder of that season.[17]

The path toward Prohibition reflected Cincinnati's rural and urban interface and ethnic makeup. There was a conflict between those in rural areas and those in Cincinnati about the value of Prohibition. Rural counties, like Warren and Clermont, became dry by 1909. In 1913 the Ohio Legislature limited the number of saloons a city or town could have, forcing hundreds in Cincinnati to close. Cincinnatians voted overwhelmingly against Prohibition, but with World War I, Prohibition became associated with anti-German sentiment, and it was approved and became law in 1920. Consumption and production continued in significant quantities, despite federal legislation to the contrary. Cincinnati was deemed in one publication the third "wettest" city in the country, behind New York and Chicago.[18] But the impact on the brewing industry was profound. Three large pre-Prohibition breweries closed:

Christian Moerlein, Windisch-Mulhauser, and John Hauck. Prohibition devastated Over-the-Rhine—they lost breweries, brewery-related businesses, and the jobs associated with both. Prohibition extinguished the Over-the-Rhine community.[19]

Some, of course, made their fortune as bootleggers. In fact, George Remus, the inspiration for *The Great Gatsby*, moved to Cincinnati to take advantage of the illegal beer-brewing economy. Remus had been a lawyer in Chicago; in Cincinnati he built a distribution network that covered nine states and employed three thousand people. He lived in a Price Hill mansion (atop the incline), complete with a $100,000 Grecian swimming pool, tennis court, stable, and baseball diamond. His friends protected his illegal operation for some time, but he was caught in 1924. He served in federal prison for two years. During this time, his wife had an affair with the federal agent who had arrested him. When Remus was released, he murdered his wife in Eden Park. He was only given six months in Lima State Hospital for the murder because he convinced the jury that he went insane due to jealousy and rage.[20]

When the Eighteenth Amendment was repealed in 1933, only six breweries came back, including Hudepohl, Wiedemann, and Bavarian. One at least had brewed near-beer throughout so was immediately ready for beer production.[21]

Starting in the 1960s, Cincinnati's breweries faced stiff competition from Anheuser-Busch and Miller, among others. These companies focused on marketing, national distribution, and also responded to demand for lite beers and other changes in consumer interest. Brewers elsewhere had been more dependent on exports than Cincinnati because they lacked the density of population and consumption. Busch, for example, was the first to use refrigerated rail cars to get their beer to distant markets.

By the late 1970s, signs of Cincinnati's beer-making demise were everywhere. The Reds, Oktoberfest, and the Labor Day fireworks were sponsored by breweries from outside the city, and local watering holes were serving more and more national and European beers. None of the local breweries survived into the twenty-first century.[22]

Now, with the resurgence of micro-and craft brewing, Cincinnati has once again gained national attention. In 2017 the area was home to twenty-one microbreweries, making the city, per capita, one of the leading cities in beer brewing. The tour highlights Rhinegeist Brewery, which is located in the old Christian Moerlein bottling plant, and the new Christian Moerlein Brewery, with an original 1860s malt house and historic underground lagering cellars.

## Inclining

Climbing the steps of the Fairview Incline provides a strong sense of the impediment that Cincinnati's geography was to mobility and settlement. Before vehicles, people or animals would be the only means to climb out of the basin to the hilltops around Cincinnati. Those with enough money could afford private carriages to climb the hills and build homes in Mount Auburn and Clifton. Others could take a horse-drawn bus. In 1850 the trip from the city center to Mount Auburn took two hours, in part because the horses had to rest multiple times on the steep grade.[23] When the Main Street Incline opened in May 1872, the *Cincinnati Enquirer* wrote that the hilltops were now accessible to all:

> The barbarians of the lower plan have at length scaled the rugged ascent
> to their fastnesses, and will soon be besieging their castle gates, clamor-
> ing for admission to the broad fields, the sunny slopes and the pure air of
> the upper plateau. And here will they build their homes, leaving the city
> with its crowded streets, its smoky, begrimed houses, its odors and its
> filth to commerce and manufactures.[24]

There were five different inclines in Cincinnati in the late 1800s through the early 1900s: Mount Auburn, Bellevue, Fairview, Price Hill, and Mount Adams. Much of the information below is drawn from Melissa Kramer's *The Inclines of Cincinnati*. They took their inspiration from Pittsburgh, where the Monongahela Incline was built in 1870. Inclines were also called funiculars and had parallel railroad tracks. Connected by a cable that moved through a pulley, passenger cars traveled up and down simultaneously, controlled by two steam engines at the top. Stilts raised the rear of the cars to keep them horizontal as they moved. The inclines were relatively safe. However, there were fires from time to time and an accident in 1899 on the Main Street Incline killed six passengers.

The Mount Auburn Incline (sometimes called the Main Street Incline) opened in 1871 and closed in 1898. This was the shortest operating of all the inclines. The Lookout House was the entertainment venue at the top of the Mount Auburn Incline. It was the first of the hilltop venues to be built in 1872 and became the model for the other incline houses. According to the transportation curator John H. White Jr., initially it was a simple two-story structure. A kitchen, bar, and wine room were on the first floor and a dance hall and smaller refreshment room were on the top floor. Entertainment at the Lookout House would ensure both incline traffic and more guests at the house, so much like the Highland House, there were fireworks and other attractions. In 1876 the German Military Band played to a crowd of ten thousand. A year later a white whale was on display until it perished in its makeshift home. Bowling alleys and a theater were added as well.[25]

The Bellevue Incline (also known as the Elm Street Incline) opened in 1876 and closed in 1926 and also had a restaurant and bar at the top, the Bellevue House, a beautiful three-story building with a four-hundred-foot rotunda and a veranda on all sides of the building. A park is located where the Bellevue House used to be and it has a beautiful gazebo structure and view, both of which are worth checking out. The Bellevue Incline is known for a few other pieces of interesting history. The Jackson Brewery was located just to the west of the incline, and just to the east of it was a school of mortuary science that became the University of Cincinnati. The lore is that sometimes students would wave body parts out the windows to the surprise, if not horror, of incline passengers.

The Fairview Incline opened in 1892. It covered the shortest distance, about 650 feet. In 1921 the Fairview Incline was temporarily closed for repairs. It was never to reopen, for the company opted to spend $85,000 to build a road that extended from McMillan Avenue from Fairview Avenue down the hill to Central Parkway. The cost to rehabilitate the Fairview Incline would have been $55,000. The ease of traveling by car up to the suburbs made the maintenance of the inclines no longer cost effective. So it closed in 1923.

The Price Hill Incline had two tracks—one for freight and one for passengers. The former opened in 1877 and closed in 1929. The latter opened in 1874

Fairview Incline Steps

and closed in 1943. This was the steepest incline, with a grade of 47 percent for seven hundred feet. It was also the only one with a hilltop resort that did not serve alcohol, as a result it was called Buttermilk Mountain. Like the other entertainment venues, visitors could eat, walk, picnic, take in the views of the city below, and continue their journey by horse-drawn carriage. The current Incline Public House sits in the same location as the former Price Hill House.[26]

The larger infrastructure of the inclines included streetcars that connected passengers from the bottom stations of the inclines to Fountain Square and Governor's Square and other destinations downtown. Once at the head gates, or the top of the inclines, streetcars ferried people to other popular destinations, such as the Cincinnati Zoo, which was once home to the orchestra, or Burnet Woods. From the Mount Adams Incline, Eden Park and the Art Museum were popular destinations.

There were some who wanted to maintain those that were most beloved (Price Hill and Mount Adams) for the sake of tourism and history as the cities of Pittsburgh and San Francisco have done. But Cincinnati's inclines had no strong champions and none of them were saved.

CHAPTER 10

# TOWN AND COUNTRY

## Mt. Airy Forest, Winton Woods, Greenhills, Glendale, and Sharon Woods

In some ways, this tour picks up thematically where the *Path Dependency* tour leaves off, above the Mill Creek Valley, where people sought to escape the dangers and challenges presented by the creek and its development. Here we are north of the city in green rather than industrial spaces, and communities with green spaces. The suburbs on the tour all sought to rectify much of what was perceived as wrong about human occupation of the landscape, particularly urban development.

Jediah Hill covered bridge

## The Tour

More detailed information on the route is available on the *Bicycling through Paradise* community page. We invite you to leave additional information on route updates, detours, and establishments that will be helpful to future cyclists of this route. Here's a general idea of the route.

In two segments, this tour travels from Everybody's Treehouse in Mt. Airy Forest to Sharon Woods Park near Sharonville. Cycling from Mt. Airy to Sharon Woods can be a bit gritty as we pass through industrial and suburban areas that were not designed for anything other than automobile and truck traffic. So be careful and choose days (weekends) and times (midday) when traffic will be lighter. There are also some wonderfully tranquil sections through Winton Woods and Glendale.

**Segment 1** goes from Mt. Airy Forest to Greenhills (9.4 miles total, a bit hilly at the end). The first segment starts in one of Cincinnati's city parks and then travels through suburban Cincinnati (Mt. Airy, College Hill, and Mt. Healthy). After several miles, the tour descends into the valley of the West Fork of the Mill Creek, passing close to Jediah Hill Covered Bridge. The route here peacefully winds along a river and then into Winton Woods, where we suggest a spin around the lake/reservoir. A brief uphill climb on Winton Road ends the first segment as we enter the commercial district of Greenhills. Public parking and a café, the Village Troubadour, are available here.

**Segment 2** goes from Greenhills to Sharon Woods (8.5 miles, mostly downhill). This segment starts in Greenhills on some of the curvilinear streets of this planned community until we end up on Sharon Road. We will pass through Forest Park and Springdale (where we join a bike path briefly) and then reach historic Glendale. Riding through Glendale, we experience the garden design of this community through its parks and curvilinear streets. Food, refreshment, and parking are available here. The tour continues on Sharon Road through industrial areas, passing over the Mill Creek, and then through downtown Sharonville on Reading Road briefly. The tour ends in Sharon Woods Park, where the Visitor Center has bathrooms and parking. We recommend walking through the historic village and the Gorge Trail. Both are inspiring in their own way.

## Town and Country

In the late 1800s, people and planners sought living environments that were free of the noise and pollution of industrial cities. But rural areas were not idyllic either. They were largely deforested as a result of farming and increasingly could not provide a decent living for humans or the plants and animals that had first attracted settlers to this region. Several solutions surfaced and were sometimes combined. One was to leave the city and create communities, what would come to be called suburbs, away from the crowds and pollution and with access to trees and lawns. In this chapter, that search takes the form of Garden Cities, which would combine the best of urban and rural living (For another suburb inspired by Garden Cities, see the *Bicycling Through Paradise* tour). Designed and developed before the era of the automobile, they were meant to be small, relatively dense, mixed-use cities ideal for pedestrian (and bicycle) travel. Glendale represents this kind of vision. With the increasing use of the automobile, these designs, like that of Greenhills, became associated with lower density, expensive, and racially segregated land use. In 1931 Calvin Wilson published a book of poems about Glendale. The first is titled "Glendale the Beautiful" and captures this sentiment:

> *Village of the winding streets,*
> *Where we dwellers taste the sweets*
> *Of city and of country too*
> *Urban charm and Nature's dew,*
> *Looking over wide-spread lawns,*
> *Under sunsets, under dawns,*
> *With our tall and noble trees*
> *Answering unto every breeze,*
> *Where in chorus they are heard*
> *Harmonious notes of many a bird,—*
> *We salute you, lovely town,*
> *Whose beauties all our senses drown.*[1]

The other solution was to ensure that city residents had access to parks and green spaces so that they could readily escape the city and be restored. This solution also called for reforesting or preserving some forested areas in perpetuity, ensuring that the entire landscape would not be stripped of trees in the pursuit of rural or urban development. In Cincinnati, by the early 1900s, the landscape architect George E. Kessler was concerned that rapid growth and land acquisition would close off an opportunity for parks and green space that he felt were so essential for all resident's health and well-being. His 1907 plan called for purchasing land as quickly as possible and then developing it slowly as funding would allow.[2]

This approach was one of Kessler's signature ways of proceeding, and the plan did become the foundation for the city and county park systems Cincinnatians benefit from today. German-born and educated, George Kessler was the most prominent architect in the Midwest in the early 1900s, working briefly in Ohio, and much more extensively in Missouri, Indianapolis, Tennessee, and Texas. But his projects can be found in twenty-three states, Mexico, and China. His other ideas, still visible in Cincinnati, were to create citywide park systems so all residents, no matter their means, had access to park space. His plans often included boulevards and parkways to provide green corridors of travel within the city.[3]

## Glendale the Beautiful

Long before the twentieth century, the first planned railroad commuter town in the United States, Glendale, was built.[4] Since the early 1800s, it had been the site of an inn, a stopping point on the Cincinnati–Hamilton Road. And it was also the site of a Presbyterian church, led by the Reverend Robert Warwick in the early 1800s, whose sermons could run four hours. If he needed refreshment, he drank buttermilk from the pulpit.[5] The luxury of being able to live miles from work in the city in a nice suburban home surrounded by green space and in a garden-like setting was only available to those who could afford to commute such a distance on a regular basis. Closer neighborhoods like Mt. Adams, Walnut Hills, and Clifton were accessible by walking, horse, or incline.[6]

Glendale was established in 1852 after the Cincinnati, Hamilton and Dayton Railroad was constructed. The commute to Cincinnati was about an hour and a quarter, so at the outer limits of a practicable daily distance. By the 1880s there was an express train that took only thirty minutes. The Amtrak to

Main square in Glendale

Chicago still goes through this small town (in the middle of the night). The train was a prominent feature of Glendale life; not only did people travel to Cincinnati and back on it, but it carried mail and goods to Glendale. One could order food or other items from stores in Cincinnati and have them delivered to Glendale by train for free if one had a commuter pass. Cubicles on the train station wall had the families' names on them for delivery of such goods. Mothers and children in family carriages often met working men at the station at the end of the day, providing a social time for members of the community.

The location was desirable for other reasons as well. It was beyond the flooding of the Mill Creek Valley, two streams ran through town, and the rolling country was covered in forest and fertile farms. It was the first in Ohio and one of the nation's first planned communities. The design included forested greenbelts and parks, curved streets, and large lots.[7] The community, like many planned communities, was designed for wealthier families and often became racially segregated, if not by design then by default.[8]

Several educational efforts are worth noting. The first is that Glendale was home to the Glendale Female College, first opened in 1854 (under the name the American Female College) as a Presbyterian girls' school. It occupied the building that had been the Hotel Ritter House, on the corner of Sharon Road and Laurel Avenue, where families stayed while their houses were being built.

Contrary to its name, the American Female College was not a college or even a college preparatory school. College education for women was rare in the United States in the mid-1800s. In 1865 Vassar College became the first institution in the United States to offer a bachelor's degree to women. Glendale Female College was a "finishing school." Students came from all over the country to attend.[9]

The Reverend Potter, president of the Glendale Female College from 1865 to 1901, fifty years later was remembered for educating women for rich lives full of varied interests. Students learned English, history, philosophy, science, French, German, Latin, rhetoric, mathematics, music, and Bible study. Students were required to attend church every Sunday and to attend any other religious services held by the school. Competition from tax-supported public high schools, a fire in 1918, and a series of poor principals all led to the closure of the school in 1929.[10]

The Glendale Lyceum, inspired by the Greek Lyceum, and still standing on Congress Avenue, started as an effort to provide literary, musical, and social entertainment for the residents. Originally home to a library and natural history collection, it now serves as a recreation and meeting space. The town also has a strong historical connection to the protection and aid of runaway slaves and education of African American children. The Eckstein School, located on Washington Avenue, educated African American children from kindergarten through eighth grade from 1915 to 1958.[11] After eighth grade the students joined their White counterparts in the high school.

At the intersection of Oak Road and Chester Road, stood the home of John Van Zandt (1791–1847), known as one of the most active stations on the Underground Railroad. Harriet Beecher Stowe used Van Zandt as the abolitionist character John Van Trompe in *Uncle Tom's Cabin*. The following incident demonstrates the risks he was willing to take. In April 1842 Van Zandt had taken a load of farm produce to Cincinnati, where he spent the night with a friend near Lane Seminary in Walnut Hills. In the morning, eight Black men and women asked him for help getting to Canada. He obliged. But as he took them north, some of his neighbors heard his wagon and pursued him. Mr. Van Zandt was arrested, imprisoned and fined $1200 and found guilty of breaking the law. Seven of the eight runaways were returned to their owners in Kentucky.[12]

Glendale is also home to black squirrels, a variation of the gray squirrel, introduced to the town in the 1940s. The black squirrels have been in North America prior to European arrival in the 1500s when the eastern United States was thickly forested. Their dark color likely protected them in this habitat. Black squirrels also have a higher tolerance for cold. As settlers cleared land for farming, perhaps the advantage was not as great and gray population probably took over. To celebrate the town's 150th anniversary hand-painted four-foot fiberglass squirrels were placed around town.[13]

## Mt. Airy Forest the Beautiful

Currently, Mt. Airy is the largest Cincinnati city park. Its size is in part a direct response to Kessler's vision, for he wanted city parks to be large enough to accommodate a large proportion of the population at any one time and to bring the country within easy reach of city dwellers. And it is beautiful. The description from a 1914 editorial is still apt: "It is no exaggeration to say that the Mount Airy Forest comprises the most picturesque assortment of hills, valleys, streams, woods, lawns and wild scenery that we have within the city limits. It has been described with justice as a magnificent bit of romantic scenery."[14]

Agriculture was a destructive enterprise. The hilly terrain around Cincinnati, much like that of ancient Rome, unless properly cultivated and protected against erosion, soon became unsuitable for any kind of food production, as did Rome's. Mt. Airy Forest was first envisioned in 1911 as a solution to the abused hillsides that had supported both vegetable and dairy farms and were no longer suitable for either. It became one of the nation's first city reforestation projects. Several decades later, it was home to a Civilian Conservation Corps (CCC) camp of African American laborers who are responsible for the rustic buildings, such as shelters and bathrooms, noted by the federal government in designating it on the National Register of Historic Places. The first African American workers from Fort Hill, Ohio, built their own camp to live in over the course of three months in 1935. Over the next two years, 200 CCC men planted more than one million trees to stop the erosion and restore the soil, and built stone steps, stone walls, guard rails, trails, and footbridges. Mt. Airy's camp is interesting for two reasons. African American CCC camps were unusual, making up about 150 out of about 2,600 camps, and urban camps were also uncommon.[15]

A more recent addition to the park is Everybody's Treehouse, a fully accessible treehouse off of Trail Ridge Road. The treehouse was funded by local organizations and businesses and built by volunteer laborers, including youth, in 2006 to provide access to a play and gathering space for all. Meyer Lake and the Arboretum are also lovely spots to visit while in Mt. Airy.

## Greenhills: A Twentieth-Century Garden City

Greenhills was one of three New Deal greenbelt towns built by the Division of Suburban Resettlement in the 1930s. The other two were Greendale, Wisconsin, and Greenbelt, Maryland. In many ways, implementation of the vision fell far short. The original vision was fifty experimental greenbelt communities across the nation. Further, Greenhills was planned to be much larger than it was constructed. Like many New Deal programs, the development of Greenhills was a solution to multiple problems at once: provide jobs for skilled and unskilled laborers, make use of garden design principals to give residents access to green space both communally and individually, create a walkable community, and relieve an acute housing shortage. Planned communities, like Mariemont or Glendale, catered to the wealthy, whereas those involved in designing and planning the greenbelt communities hoped to meet the needs of the average laborer. In 1924 one estimate was that three-quarters of the suburban houses built that year were within reach of only one-tenth of the nation's families.[16]

Greenhills and the other garden cities were inspired by Ebenezer Howard's *Garden Cities of Tomorrow* (1902). His premise then was that people should not continue to pour into crowded cities and deplete the countryside. He sought to restore people to the land and sky. Both romantic and pragmatic, Howard understood that people were attracted to the cities for legitimate reasons that must be addressed by any possible solution. "Each city may be regarded as a magnet, each person as a needle; and, so viewed, it is at once seen that nothing short of the discovery of a method for constructing magnets of yet greater power than our cities possess can be effective for redistributing the population in a spontaneous and healthy manner."[17]

Howard saw that both town and country had benefits and drawbacks. The town lacked nature; the country amusement. The town offered employment and social opportunity; the country an abundance of water and fresh air. A blend of town and country could achieve the best of both worlds with few of the drawbacks of the other. The Garden City that he conceived would be one-sixth urban area and five-sixths rural with a size of thirty-two thousand inhabitants.[18]

With this in mind, the planners of the greenbelt communities in the United States in the 1930s, as the historian Joseph Arnold put it, "Thought they were planning a new world." Partly this was because they were given tremendous latitude, more than in any other public housing project up to that time. Like Glendale, however, it was designed for White residents. Officials sought poor White families but not African American families, who were not allowed to live in the communities at all.[19]

Farmers owned the land that eventually became Greenhills, and at least one of them was reluctant to sell. Labeled a "stubborn German" by one historian; one imagines Muehlenhard had an honest material and spiritual attachment to his land and home. A government official was flown in from Milwaukee to strong-arm him into selling his land. Instead, Muehlenhard ran him off his property, threatening him with a three-foot corn knife. Eventually, Muehlenhard came to the company offices where planners shared the full scope and vision of the project and pleaded with him to sell his land for the sake of the slum children whose parents would move to the community. After five hours in the office, the farmer signed papers to sell his land.[20]

In Greenhills, as in other greenbelt towns, enthusiasm for the social mission often outran the practicalities of the project. For example, men were hired to construct the community in December 1935, but construction began in March 1936. Between one to two hundred laborers were employed each day, even though there was little work. The first homeowners moved in in 1938.[21]

Residents built a community and cooperative economic institutions including a farm, store, credit union, and library. But all were difficult to maintain as residents moved in and out of the community, particularly with the destabilization of World War II. Arnold, though, praises the cooperative efforts of greenbelt towns for education, medical services, and transportation, noting that they were "without parallel in twentieth-century American cities." The commercial district still exists. It is one of the oldest strip malls in Ohio.[22]

These nationally planned communities were attacked for being socialist and poorly managed. After World War II, the federal government sold off its portion of the communities, leaving them in the hands of residents who bought their own homes. Critics also were concerned with the space-consuming nature of the projects. Rather than build decent, denser housing and leave rural areas for pristine enjoyment, garden cities took up what had been rural areas and turned them into private, sprawling residential areas.[23]

Cycling away from Greenhills through Forest Park, there is a magnificent vista of the Cincinnati basin, much like the one that Greenhills' residents had when the community was first established above the "grimy but busy" Mill Creek Valley.

## Flood Control on the Mill Creek

Ohio has very few natural lakes. Almost all of them have been constructed as part of flood control measures. East Fork Lake, Miami Whitewater Lake, Sharon Lake, and Winton Lake all are examples. The recreation that the lake and surrounding woods provide today was originally secondary to their development.

Flooding of the lower industrial Mill Creek led to the damming of Sharon Creek and the West Fork of the Mill Creek upstream. Two lakes were created that are now at the heart of Winton Woods Park and Sharon Woods Park. The barrier dam at the mouth of the Mill Creek on the Ohio River had been the first step in preventing flooding; the next was to control the amount of water that came down the creek during heavy rains. The Sharon Creek Dam was built in 1937 and the reservoir incorporated into a Hamilton County Park. You will cycle over Sharon Creek on your way to Sharon Woods. As you travel east, you

Boathouse in Winton Woods

will ride over a large railroad yard, and just to the east of the yard is a narrow corridor of trees that marks the creek. Further south it joins the main branch of the Mill Creek. The West Fork Reservoir project was completed in 1952. The dam is located on the eastern end of the lake just to the east of Greenhills. These lakes help to preserve the livelihoods of tens of thousands of people near Cincinnati and provide the greenspace and recreation that Ebenezer Howard and George Kessler both thought was essential to human thriving.[24]

Sharon Woods has much to explore. The historic village has a nice array of homes and buildings along a tree-lined lane. The gorge is a favorite for hiking. The trail is 0.7 miles one-way and well worth walking up and back. The Sharon Woods Gorge is ninety-feet high and has exposed fossils that are more than 450 million years old (from the Ordovician Period) when this part of Ohio was covered by an inland sea. In addition, the rocks on the floor of the creek bed bear ripples that formed from waves.

# A Holy City: Churches, Synagogues, Seminaries, and Shrines

## Northern Kentucky, Downtown Cincinnati, Walnut Hills, and Evanston

A holy city represents a place with special significance to the adherents of one or more religions. While, like most titles in this book, this one is meant both reverently and a bit provocatively, the reality is that for many people of faith, nineteenth-century Cincinnati offered opportunities for fuller human expression than could be found elsewhere. But the title also refers to the ways in which humans as individuals and communities give rise and shape to such cities through their visions, houses of worship, and sacred sites.

Cincinnati has been home to prominent Jewish settlers and leaders, German Catholics, pioneering Black ministers, and outspoken abolitionists. This is a city that has been a center of religious life, and of religious diversity, since its founding. Cincinnati is home to the oldest Jewish congregation west of the Allegheny Mountains, K. K. Bene Israel, which was established in 1824 and still has a thriving congregation (now in the Amberley Village neighborhood, and also known as Rockdale Temple). The oldest standing Christian church in Cincinnati is Old St. Mary's Parish Church in Over-the-Rhine, built in 1842. Other important Catholic sites of worship range from the St. Peter in Chains Cathedral in downtown Cincinnati to the Cathedral Basilica of the Assumption in Covington, Kentucky. Protestants have also left their stamp. Historically Black congregations include Union Baptist Church, right downtown, and Allen Temple AME, located in Bond Hill.

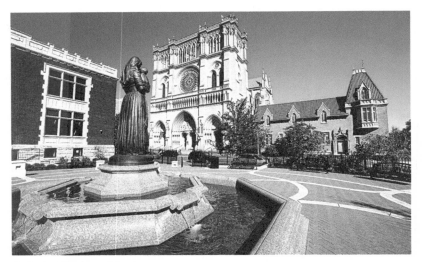

Cathedral Basilica of the Assumption

## The Tour

More detailed information on the route is available on the *Bicycling through Paradise* community page. We invite you to leave additional information on route updates, detours, and establishments that will be helpful to future cyclists of this route. Here's a general idea of the route.

This tour, in two segments, will take us past a variety of religious sites that reflect the diversity of the city's population, past and present, as well as the strong human impulse to connect to the transcendent. Temples, churches, cathedrals, and meeting houses act as a central gathering point for co-believers, as a point of communication between heaven and earth, a little piece of heaven on earth, and a place for the indwelling of God, according to Harold Turner in *From Temple to Meeting House*.[1] This tour starts in Covington, Kentucky, and makes its way north to Evanston, Ohio, visiting a wide variety sites along the way. The first segment is short but with a brief, steep climb to a hill overlooking downtown Cincinnati where the Garden of Hope is located. Segment 2 involves a winding route through downtown Cincinnati before heading out of the basin to Walnut Hills and Evanston to see the Harriet Beecher Stowe House and United Jewish Cemetery.

**Segment 1** is the Garden of Hope Spur (2 miles each way, hilly). This segment begins and ends in Covington, Kentucky, on or near the corner of 6th Street and Madison Avenue. Parking and a variety of places to eat are available in downtown Covington. The first stop is Seminary Square. At the highest elevation in Covington, the neighborhood boasts stately nineteenth-century homes, some of which were used by the faculty of the Western Baptist Theological Institute, established in 1840. From here we will eventually climb a steep hill up on Edgecliff Street to Garden of Hope for a great view of the city and a chance to wander the grounds. On our return, the tour passes the Cathedral Basilica of the Assumption. The cathedral is one of only thirty-five minor cathedral basilica (a designation for a Catholic church of particular importance or significance) in the United States.

**Segment 2** goes from Covington to Evanston (7.6 miles, hilly). This segment begins at the same place as the first segment and includes a wide variety of historical and religious sites including, in this order: Union Baptist Church (and George Washington Williams historical marker), St. Peter in Chains Cathedral, Plum Street Temple (or Isaac M. Wise Temple), Sherith Israel Temple (now condominiums but marked by an historical plaque), Old St. Mary's Church, Lane Seminary historical marker, Harriet Beecher Stowe House, and United Jewish Cemetery in Walnut Hills. The first few miles are relatively level, zigzagging through downtown streets to (mostly) view these structures from the outside. Both Plum Street Temple and St. Peter in Chains Cathedral are worth seeing from the inside. Tours are given of the temple on a regular basis. Find out more on their website, https://www.wisetemple .org/. After passing Old St. Mary's, the tour climbs out of the city basin along Gilbert Avenue, riding by the historical marker for Lane Seminary and then the Harriet Beecher Stowe House, which is open on the weekends (Friday–Sunday). The final stop is United Jewish Cemetery where we can, again, get off our bikes and explore. A bit further up Montgomery Road, the tour ends in Evanston at the corner of Dana Avenue and Montgomery Road, where food and parking are available.

## Judaism: Plum Street Temple/Isaac M. Wise Temple

The authors of *The Jews of Cincinnati* wrote:

> Perhaps the central surviving symbol of Cincinnati Jewry's nineteenth-century grandeur is historic Plum Street Temple. Looking at it, one is struck anew by the vision that it represents of boundlessness, triumphalism, and daring...The ornate structure...[is] a monument to days gone by when Reform was young, Cincinnati was booming, and hopeful dreams abounded.[2]

Plum Street Temple is Moorish and Byzantine in its design (like a number of synagogues and temples in Germany and Eastern Europe in the mid-1800s) and the interior has been recently restored so a visit today permits one to fully appreciate the above statement. Bold colors, ornate woodcutting, detailed and varied stenciling, Hebrew inscriptions from the Bible, vaulted ceilings with beautiful blue domes, and stained-glass windows all bedazzle and humble the observer. The temple uses sixty-five different colors and more than one hundred stencil designs on its high walls and ceiling, the effect of which is to make one feel enclosed in luxurious warmth and beauty.[3]

In 1840 a group of Jewish German immigrants left an English-speaking congregation in Cincinnati to form a new congregation that would follow their national rites and customs—K. K. Bene Yeshurun. A similar German-language movement was afoot in the Catholic Church as well. A synagogue was dedicated in 1848, and a religious school followed in 1849. Plum Street Temple, a testament to the dream of its new rabbi, Isaac Mayer Wise, was dedicated in 1866. It was designed as a temple rather than a synagogue so as to be a place of celebration. Temples are not used for mourning. It was opposite the city's leading Catholic and Unitarian churches: "Symbolic of the co-equal role that Wise...believed Judaism should play in the city," as recorded in *The Jews of Cincinnati*.[4] On the fourth corner sat the city building, hence giving a remarkable confluence of large buildings representing two important sectors of daily life. As a daily paper wrote at the time, "Cincinnati never before had seen so much grandeur pressed into so small a space."[5] For a while, Plum Street was known as the street of spires for all the religious buildings along it.

Jewish settlers in Cincinnati had made a significant mark by the end of the 1800s. A Chicago Jewish newspaper claimed that no other Jewish community anywhere on earth had "accomplished so much good in the interest of Judaism and its people."[6] These efforts included a hospital and several aid societies before 1850. But their impact was felt far beyond the Jewish community, as Jews were important businessmen (particularly in the garment industry), philanthropists, and neighbors. Coming from a Europe often hostile to Jews and their culture and faith, the mutual goodwill that existed between Jews and Christians in nineteenth-century Cincinnati was welcome and encouraged big dreams about the growth and significance Judaism might achieve in the West.

Cincinnati Jews had several powerful leaders in the mid- to late eighteenth century, one of whom was Rabbi Isaac Mayer Wise (1819–1900). Jewish reformers asked Rabbi Wise to come to Cincinnati and he agreed on two conditions: (1) that he be appointed rabbi for life, and (2) that he be unanimously chosen by the leadership. In 1854 Rabbi Wise became the spiritual leader of the congregation. As a reformer, he introduced a number of changes, including a choir, an organ, and permission to pray without a head covering.[7]

Rabbi Wise was a towering figure in American Jewish history and an eloquent proponent of the grandiose visions many had for Cincinnati in the mid-nineteenth century. More about his work and vision is in the *Crosstown Missions* tour. As the authors of *The Jews of Cincinnati* wrote, "In a city filled with bold planners and grand schemers, one that envisaged itself becoming the greatest city in America if not the world, he found himself right at home."[8] The grand Plum Street Temple is a fitting legacy for Rabbi Wise. In fact, it was his dream to preside over a congregation that worshipped in such a beautiful and large space. Many today refer to it either as the Plum Street or Isaac M. Wise Temple because the vision for the building was part of Rabbi Wise's religious dream and vision. When Rabbi Wise died in 1900, his chair on the pulpit was draped in black and kept vacant for a year. By the year 2000, Wise Temple had more than 1,400 families as members.

Wise founded two newspapers, one in German (*Die Deborah*), and one in English (the *Israelite*). The latter became the oldest Anglo-Jewish newspaper in the world. They had overlapping content, the same editor, and both were voices for Reform Judaism.[9] A series of pieces that Rabbi Wise wrote for *Die Deborah* were compiled into a short book, "The World of My Books." These personal reminiscences captured both the intensity and versatility of Rabbi Wise's thinking and work. They chronicle a very long list of books that he published, all despite not liking to write. When arriving in the United States, Rabbi Wise found no substantial writings on Jewish history or culture in English. Thus, "The desire to write awoke in me, weakly at first, then ever more strongly, until I had overcome my dislike of writing and had forgotten my lack of knowledge. I wrote."[10] Later, lamenting the neglect of both reform and literary criticism within the Jewish world, he took up writing about both. Thus, Rabbi Wise led his synagogue, the American Jewish community, and the city of Cincinnati to a stronger future.[11]

## Catholicism: Old St. Mary's and St. Peter in Chains

Bishop Fenwick, originally serving in northern Kentucky, created the Diocese of Cincinnati in 1821. The first Catholic church was built in the 1810s on the corner of Liberty and Vine Streets where the Church of St. Francis of Assisi is now located.

The oldest standing place of worship in Cincinnati is Old St. Mary's Catholic Church. In the 1840s, two hundred German Catholics a day were moving to Cincinnati. In response to the large size of the German Catholic population, land was purchased for a new German Catholic church. At its opening in 1842, a procession marched through the city from Holy Trinity Church to the new St. Mary's. It was the first such processional in the city. The sermon that Sunday, delivered by Father Henni, lasted almost two hours. Record has it that his message held the believers spellbound despite the heat and humidity. Initially, a predominantly German congregation, priests at St. Mary's have at various times delivered masses in French, Spanish, and Hungarian. Today, masses are held in English, Latin, and German. It is the only church in the United States with a weekly German mass. Like Plum Street Temple, the interior is a beautiful, light-filled space of wood and color. The church bell was installed in the clock tower in 1843. Levi Coffin, who helped more than three thousand slaves escape bondage, cast the bell. For some years, it was the fire alarm for the northeastern part of the city.[12]

St. Peter in Chains Cathedral is the most important Catholic church in the diocese and a symbol of the bishop's authority. It was built in 1845 with a shorter steeple than it now has. The current steeple was built to sit higher than that of the Plum Street Temple across the street. With time, Catholicism became the dominant faith in the city. In 1910, 70 percent of city residents were Roman Catholic.[13]

## Garden of Hope

The Garden of Hope provides access to important religious structures and artifacts for Christian believers. This space is further evidence that architecture matters and that the structures in which we live, pray, work, and recreate shape us spiritually and materially. It is a reminder of the strength of individual visions.

The Garden of Hope creates an imagined universe for the believer based on replicas of religious sites. The Garden of Hope brings some of the Holy City of Jerusalem to Cincinnati. The Reverend Morris H. Coers of Immanuel Baptist Church in Covington had a vision while visiting the Holy Land in 1938

View from the Garden of Hope

and built this respite in response.[14] The centerpiece is a replica of the tomb of Jesus.

The Reverend Coers was ordained at the age of eighteen and was pastor of an Indianapolis church by nineteen. There, over the course of five years, membership in the church increased by 50 percent.[15] A pioneering spirit, he became a Red Cross field director during World War II.[16] Then, seeing the ways in which radio and television could be used to spread the Word of God, he launched a radio program, *The Temple of the Air*, which lasted for ten years. He also had his own daily television show, *The Chapel of Dreams*. Coers held Easter services in 1950 in a drive-in theater so that people could worship in their cars.[17]

In 1946 the Reverend Coers became pastor of Immanuel Baptist Church in Covington, Kentucky. Ten years later, he found a place to build his vision—a two-acre parcel high on a hill with a stunning view of downtown Cincinnati. Unfortunately, the property owner wanted $1,000 for it. The Reverend Coers did not have that kind of money, but he kept returning and asking if the owner could lower the price. One day the landowner asked how much money he had and he said, "Five dollars." That was the amount the Reverend Coers paid for the land. Over the next two years, a carpenter's shop (filled with tools that would have been in use during the time of Christ) was built and a mural painted inside. The chapel was built with a stained glass windows donated from Christ Church Cathedral in Cincinnati and the large tomb was constructed out of cement. The Chapel of Dreams (named after his television show) is modeled after a sixteenth-century Mexican mission. The flowers and shrubs were native to Israel and former Israeli prime minister David Ben-Gurion donated the carpenter's tools on display in the carpenter's shop.[18]

In these first years, it was a popular destination, and the Chapel of Dreams was used as a wedding venue while various churches used the tomb for services. The eclectic replication of Christian holy sites on this high hill in Cincinnati is a strong reminder of the strength of an individual's vision, the power of buildings to shape the human experience, and the transitory nature of both. Today volunteers from the Immanuel Baptist Church support the garden. It is not visited as much today as in years past, but picnic tables and a wonderful view of the city invite a cyclist to at least stop and rest for a while, if not pray.

## Protestantism: Lane Seminary and the 1834 Slavery Debates

Some slaves from the South found refuge in Cincinnati. Slaves' attempts at freedom were supported by some free Black people and Americans of European descent, many of them also of Christian belief, particularly the Quakers. Quakers and other Christians supported slaves' quest for dignity and freedom by providing support on the Underground Railroad and by participating in the fight for abolition.

Lane Seminary, a Presbyterian theological college from 1832 to the late 1800s, is known for the role it played in the abolition movement and its location is highlighted on this tour. The seminary itself, while sadly no longer part of our landscape, was an important element in the discussions. It was not an accident that the event that came to be known as the debates was held at a seminary in a space built to educate men for a life in service to God. Questions about human dignity and equality are deeply informed by our values and ethical systems, and these in turn are shaped, for many, by religious expression and community.

In the early 1800s, in the United States, there were multiple views, in the White community, on the future of slavery and role of free Black people in society. One view was to grant slaves abolition immediately; the other was to send free Black people to other parts of the United States, to the Caribbean, or back to Africa to eliminate the problems that some White people, including Thomas Jefferson, perceived would follow from free Black people coexisting with White people. In the United States and other slaveholding societies, fear on the part of White people—fear of rebellion (one of the debate speakers noted that Kentucky slaveholders slept with muskets), fear of eventual economic and political power on the part of those who had been brutally enslaved, fear of mixed relationships and offspring, and fear of free Black people and White people living side by side—fueled this idea of colonization. To be fair, some supporters (both White and Black) believed Black people would be better off elsewhere, far from racist America. The Society for

Harriet Beecher Stowe House

the Colonization of Free People of Color of America, more commonly known as the American Colonization Society, was founded in 1816 to return free Black people to Liberia.

Lyman Beecher was the first president of Lane Seminary in 1832.[19] His family lived in the historic home at the corner of Gilbert Avenue and Martin Luther King Drive, also on this tour. His daughter Harriet Beecher Stowe is well known for her novel, *Uncle Tom's Cabin*, and another daughter, Catherine Beecher, opened multiple schools for women across the United States.

Against the wishes of the school trustees and Lyman Beecher (and in his absence), in February 1834, for two and a half hours for nine nights, a group of abolitionist students held a series of discussions.[20] Speakers addressed two questions: (1) ought the people of slaveholding states to abolish slavery immediately, and (2) are the doctrines, tendencies, and measures of the American Colonization Society, and the influence of its principal supporters, such as render it worthy of patronage of the Christian public? Of the influence of the debates and speeches, one attendee said that the result "presents one of the noblest exhibitions of the power of truth upon the hearts and consciences of man, that the world has ever witnessed." In an account written up afterward, tremendous detail is given of both the content and emotions of the evenings. A brief excerpt will give a sense of the depth and richness of the conversations:

> James Bradley, the emancipated slave above alluded to, addressed us
> nearly two hours; and I wish his speech could have been heard by every
> opponent of immediate emancipation, to wit: first, that "it would be
> unsafe to the community;" second, that "the condition of the emanci-
> pated negroes would be worse than it now is; that they are incompetent
> to provide for themselves; that they would become paupers and vagrants,
> and would rather steal than work for wages." This shrewd and intelli-
> gent black, cut up these *white objections* by the roots, and withered and
> scorched them under the sun of sarcastic argumentation, for nearly an
> hour, to which the assembly responded in repeated and spontaneous
> roars of laughter, which were heartily joined in by both Colonizationists
> and Abolitionists. Do not understand me as saying that his speech was
> devoid of argument. No. It contained sound logic, enforced by apt illus-
> trations. I wish the slanderers of Negro intellect could have witnessed
> this unpremeditated effort.[21]

Bradley pointed out that slaves take care of themselves, their families, and
their masters, so they would more than be able to take care of just their families were they emancipated.

The votes at the end of the two weeks of lively speeches were strongly in
favor of immediate abolition and the cessation of colonization activities.[22] The
ideas discussed in Cincinnati those evenings circulated broadly and became
part of the movement toward the abolition of slavery in the United States.
Religious leaders and believers, here and elsewhere, were instrumental in
building and shaping the movement. But the school's trustees, many of them
with business ties in the South, ordered the students to abolish their anti-
slavery society. As a result, most students quit the school, many taking their
abolitionist fervor with them to Oberlin.[23]

## Protestantism: Union Baptist Church

Union Baptist Church is the oldest Black Church in Cincinnati and the second
oldest in the state. Like German Catholics and Jews, free Black Baptists sought
to form their own church where they would be free to "worship in dignity
and true freedom" as the church website puts it, rather than be segregated. In
1830, at the same time as a new round of Black laws was passed to try to drive

free Black people out of the state, Enon Baptist Church banished its minority Black membership to the balcony. In 1831 ten men and four women boldly requested dismissal from Enon Baptist Congregation. By 1835 they had their own church building and a church school. Union Baptist Church was originally called African Union Baptist Church but the first part was dropped shortly to be inclusive of all people. The Union Baptist Ladies Church Association provided food and clothing for runaway slaves. By the 1950s, the church was in its fifth building and had more than one thousand families in membership. Its current location, on 7th Street, is its sixth location.[24]

One of the more well-known ministers in Union Baptist Church history is George Washington Williams. You can see the historical marker in his honor at the church on the tour. Williams was called to the pastorate in February 1876.[25] At the time, Cincinnati had a population of about two hundred thousand and a little less than six thousand were Black (2.7%).[26] The Black community had created a variety of clubs and societies but churches were the most important, and by 1876, there were seven Black Baptist churches in the city.

Williams was an enormous figure, "as enigmatic as he was brilliant, as hedonistic as he was energetic," his biographer John Hope Franklin describes.[27] As a Black man in the latter half of the nineteenth century, he sought as many opportunities as he possibly could, regularly pushing up against norms and boundaries that kept most African Americans in "their places." He was "the first serious historian of race, the first Black columnist for a major American newspaper, the first Black member of the Ohio legislature, the very first critic of King Leopold's policies in the Congo."[28] And all of this before he died at the age of forty-one. Franklin stumbled upon Williams first in a library where he saw his two-volume, thousand-page work—*A History of the Negro Race in America from 1619 to 1880; Negroes as Slaves, as Soldiers, and as Citizens*—published in 1882.

Nine hundred people attended Williams's installation in March 1876. The White pastor of the Ninth Street Baptist Church preached at the installation sermon. Such cooperation, reminiscent of that enjoyed between Jews and Christians in nineteenth-century Cincinnati, was characteristic of the cosmopolitan nature of the city. Williams gave a brief address that lived up to his reputation as an excellent speaker. A few months later, a paper remarked of Williams's oratory that few clergy in the city could match "the young colored divine as a speaker, or preach a sermon marked by such natural eloquence and originality of interest as characterize his address."[29] In December 1876 Williams became a regular contributor to the local paper, the *Commercial*, where he wrote a weekly column under the pseudonym Aristides.[30] He mostly wrote on religious, cultural, and military topics. Within a year, he was one of Cincinnati's best-known citizens. He eventually left Cincinnati and went on to the accomplishments listed earlier. While he might have only found a holy city in his own mind, he contributed to creating more awareness and opportunity for those who followed him.

CHAPTER 12

Scan to visit the
"Immortality and its
Consequences"
route

# IMMORTALITY AND ITS CONSEQUENCES

## Miamitown to Fernald Preserve
## and Whitewater Shaker Village

Our landscape holds the stories of people who have struggled against the limitations of human mortality. Some of these people had ambitious plans for the future, which can leave their traces on the earth for a long, long time. But the ideas behind those plans can be shorter-lived and have ambiguous or unintended consequences.

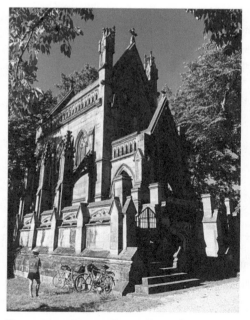

Dexter Mausoleum at Spring Grove Cemetery

## The Tour

More detailed information on this route is available on the *Bicycling through Paradise* community page. We invite you to leave additional information on route updates, detours, and establishments that will be helpful to future cyclists of this route. Here is the general idea.

Our chapter starts with a discussion of Spring Grove Cemetery. Spring Grove does not currently allow bicyclists inside the gates, but it's an essential destination for trying to understand how Cincinnatians have tried to achieve earthly immortality. Go here for a day hike. Spring Grove is full of hundreds of curving paths, so be aware that the dashed white line indicates the main road from the front gate to the rear gate. Walking up this road from the main gate, after a third of a mile, you can look to your left and you will see the Dexter Mausoleum. Also, it's worth checking the Spring Grove tour schedule, because they offer many special-interest tours.

Most of this chapter (and the next) will focus on historic sites in the watershed of the Great Miami River. Bicycling from Spring Grove to the Great Miami Valley can be fun, but very it's very hilly, and there's a good bit of traffic. So the directions for the cycling portion of our tour will start at a much more modest cemetery, the Miami Cemetery in Miamitown, Ohio. From there, we'll head generally north to Hamilton. Mostly, we'll be on rural roads. We'll use a few miles of the Miami Whitewater-Shaker Trace Trail, plus the southernmost section of the Great Miami River Recreational Trail. There will be one long climb, between Shandon and the Venice Pavilion.

The cycling portion of the tour is composed of three segments. Total one-way distance is over 37 miles, but each segment is good to ride independently and has something historic to see. Each segment starts and stops in places where you can find parking, food, and bathrooms. Overnight accommodations are available at Hamilton for anyone planning a weekend trip.

**Segment 1** goes from Miamitown to New Baltimore (6.7 miles, mostly flat). We will start at the Miami Cemetery, a modest, small-town graveyard, and ride north through the historic village of Miamitown. (Be sure to patronize Ari and Mia's Small Town Café, and be aware that you are not far from Kreimer's

Bier Haus.) We'll take Harrison Avenue west and then E. Miami River Road north. This road is quiet and flat. On the outskirts of New Baltimore. we'll cross the Great Miami River and proceed to Sam's Corner store, where you can get drinks, snacks, and sandwiches.

**Segment 2** goes from New Baltimore to Venice Pavilion (19 miles, mostly flat-to-rolling but with one serious climb. You can reduce the total distance by 2.4 miles if you pass by the entrance to Fernald Preserve and do not bike in to the visitors' center.). Starting at New Baltimore we'll go north and west on River Road and then Willey Road, soon reaching Fernald Preserve. Fernald was once a nuclear materials processing center. Now, it's a nature preserve with eight miles of hiking trails. From there, we'll continue west on Willey Road and north on the Shaker Trace Bike Trail to Oxford Road and Whitewater Shaker Village, where you can see the exterior of more than a dozen Shaker buildings. We'll continue north on Oxford Road, then east on Highway 126, until reaching the village of Shandon: site of the earliest Welsh settlement in Ohio, where we'll see an 1824 Welsh Meeting House with its traditional Welsh "death door." We'll continue east on Hamilton-New London Road and Layhigh Road to the Venice Pavilion Antiques Mall at Ross, Ohio. There's a convenience store nearby for snacks and drinks.

**Segment 3** goes from Venice Pavilion to Hamilton (11.2 miles, mostly flat). We'll head briefly south on Cincinnati-Brookville Road, then take East Miami River Road until we reach the Great Miami River Bike Path at Waterworks Park in Fairfield. From there, we'll be on a dedicated bike trail all the way into Hamilton, which has numerous options for food and overnight accommodations. Special praise goes to the Almond Sisters Bakery. An easy, no-traffic alternative to this segment is to start at Waterworks Park on Groh Lane in Fairfield and ride to Hamilton via the Great Miami River Bike Path, a little over five miles one-way.

## The Dexter Mausoleum

Early one morning in April 1870,[1] dozens of carriages were lined up in Spring Grove Cemetery. They were not there for a funeral. The occupants of those carriages wanted to get a glimpse inside a brand-new, still empty, high-gothic mausoleum built for the Dexter family. It looked like a small cathedral, complete with flying buttresses. And it would be open for public viewing exactly once, that day, and never again.[2]

The Dexter family opened the doors to the chapel and the catacombs, as Cincinnatians swarmed the building and the grounds. Today, those doors are padlocked.

The Dexter Mausoleum was built to house the remains of a whiskey baron named Edmund Dexter Sr. He was not a distiller but a rectifier—someone who buys raw whiskey in bulk, blends it, ages it, bottles it, and sells it. This business had made him very, very rich.[3] Edmund Dexter Sr. died in 1862 and was buried initially in a typical grave in Spring Grove. His five sons were the ones who then commissioned the mausoleum, and three of them—Charles, Julius, and Edmund Jr.—are interred there as well.[4]

This small architectural wonder was not just an honor to their father. The sons were also staking a claim for themselves. In nineteenth-century Cincinnati, if you were someone like one of the Dexter boys—not famous, but very rich—a big mausoleum at Spring Grove was your best shot at earthly immortality. Today, walking or cycling through Spring Grove, we can see, again and again, expressions of the deep human desire to make something last forever.

Making something last forever is a tall order, however. In 1878 the spire of Dexter Mausoleum was struck by lightning, breaking all the windows. The shock "splintered the strongly riveted door in the front of the chapel into atoms."[5]

By the early twentieth century, all the fancy Gothic stonework at Dexter Mausoleum was in poor condition, and the Dexter heirs were not as rich as they had been. Charles Dexter had two daughters, Annie and Alice. When Annie Dexter died in 1916, her will included a bequest of $5,000 to the Spring Grove Cemetery Association, to keep the Dexter Mausoleum perpetually in "good repair." But the money was so far short of the stated purpose that Spring Grove refused the bequest. The money was delivered instead to Annie's sister, Alice.[6]

In 1924 Alice Dexter appeared at a meeting of the cemetery's board of directors. The meeting minutes, from October 9, state that Mrs. Alice Dexter Walker has requested that "the question of razing" the Dexter Mausoleum should "be re-opened." The minutes ask for a report to be presented at the next meeting by Burton Hollister, an attorney who had been Annie Dexter's executor.[7]

There's no further mention of the name Dexter in the cemetery's records. So it's not clear exactly what happened next, except that the mausoleum is still standing. But the building still needs restoration, now more than ever. So there's an open question here about what happens to these monuments after the families are gone or no longer have money to burn. Who pays for all this pricey immortality?

## The God of the Sky

In Fernald, Ohio, there is another expression of the desire to control the future. A large chemical plant was built there in the 1950s, when the village was just a dot on the map. Later on, "Fernald" just meant the plant. The sign outside said, "Fernald Feed Materials Production Center." The plant had large smokestacks, and it had a water tower that was painted in a friendly red-and-white checkerboard pattern, like the Purina logo.[8] By the late 1970s, many people who lived in the area assumed that the Feed Materials Production Center was just making dog food, or something.

The plant workers knew differently, of course, but they couldn't even tell their spouses or closest friends exactly what they did for a living, not without breaking laws that could get a person sent to prison.[9]

And only a few people understood that radioactive dust was falling out of the sky.[10]

You could start the story of Fernald in 1951, when ground was broken for the plant. Or the story could start in, say, 1789, when a chemist named Martin Heinrich Klaproth, working in his laboratory in Berlin, isolated a new chemical element.

Klaproth wasn't sure what he should call his new element. Klaproth wanted to be careful, because names can be powerful, and because scientific naming had political implications.

A separate scientific naming controversy was already underway. Nine years earlier, in 1780, the astronomer William Herschel had discovered a new planet. Because Herschel was a British subject with a streak of political pragmatism, he proposed that his new planet should be named for the reigning British monarch, King George III. The planet, Herschel said, should be named *Georgium Sidus*—the Star of George.

Outside Great Britain, this proposal was less popular. Several other suggestions were made (including *Herschel*). In 1782 the German astronomer Johann Bode suggested that the convention of mythological names should be maintained. The new planet was closest to Jupiter and Saturn. In classical mythology, the god Jupiter was the son of Saturn, and Saturn was the son of Ouranos. So Bode proposed that the new planet should be called Ouranos—or, as he spelled it, Uranus.[11] There was another reason, too, why Uranus was a good name for a planet—Uranus was the god of the sky.[12]

So when Martin Klaproth discovered his new chemical element, he decided to throw support behind the planetary name proposed by his fellow countryman Johann Bode. Klaproth named his new element Uranium.

Gradually, the chemical properties of uranium were uncovered through the process of scientific method, a process that in the long run is self-correcting, because it is designed to contain and counteract the inevitable rivalries, grudges, secrets, crackpot ideas, and other misbehavior to which individual scientists are sometimes prone.

In 1896 the French scientist Henri Becquerel noticed that uranium could emit a sort of energy, but he did not grasp the importance of this. Becquerel's student Marie Curie correctly interpreted the experimental results and coined the term *radioactivity* for the new phenomenon. In 1938 the physicists Lise Meitner and Otto Frisch, working in Germany, discovered that the nucleus of a uranium atom could be split in two, a process they called nuclear fission. Other scientists quickly recognized that if a fission reaction emitted enough neutrons, a chain reaction could potentially occur, releasing enormous amounts of energy. Nuclear weapons were developed. These weapons ended World War II and became a central fact of the Cold War.[13]

The Fernald Feed Materials Production Center was fabricating uranium fuel cores to be fed into nuclear missiles. Missiles that would someday, if it seemed necessary, rain down upon the Soviet Union. Fernald represented an attempt to project national dominance across the globe and into the future.

Safety measures at Fernald were lax, but the emphasis on national security kept anyone from saying much. Then, toward the end of 1984, there was a release of three hundred pounds of uranium dust from the smokestack. This wasn't the first release, or the biggest, but this time, word got out.

One of the local residents was Lisa Crawford, who rented a house across from the plant. She lived there with her husband, Ken, and her young son, Kenny. The house had a vegetable garden, and they got they water from the well in the yard. Years later, in 1999, Lisa Crawford was interviewed:

> And I can remember Christmas Eve, we were making cookies and a TV reporter knocked on our back door and said, you know, "Would you like to comment to us about what's happening with the dust releases across the street at this facility." And I was like, "Can't really comment because I don't really know anything."

> Mr. Knollman [the landlord] had called and told Ken, you know, that there was a problem with this well, it was gonna be made public in the next few days, and he thought we should hear it from him...And, uh, Ken called me at work right away and said, "Something's wrong here," you know, "When you come home tonight and you pick up Kenney, don't drink any of this water."

And after that, Crawford said, "All hell broke loose."[14]

It gradually became clear that there was significant environmental contamination both at the plant and in the surrounding area. The Department of Energy (DOE) finally admitted that there had been several large-scale releases of uranium through the smokestacks as well as groundwater contamination. Some people living near the plant had been diagnosed with cancer, and they strongly suspected that these uranium releases were to blame. Lisa Crawford, along with several of her neighbors, filed suit against the DOE.[15]

In 1989 the DOE finally closed the plant and began environmental cleanup efforts. The problems at Fernald were vast. There were 2.5 billion pounds of waste, including 31 million pounds of uranium products (mostly low-level radiation materials) stored in various buildings. There were silos and waste pits full of sludge, and thousands of waste drums were scattered across the site.[16]

The federal government set up a compensation fund for workers and residents, to pay for medical treatment and for the loss of property value. The government agreed to provide free annual checkups and preventative care, over a long period of time, to anyone who had lived near Fernald during the period of contamination.[17] They also paid to have a new municipal water line brought in from Hamilton, so that people didn't have to drink well water anymore.

In 1993 the DOE finally created a citizens' advisory board, allowing public input into the question of what should happen to the Fernald site.[18] Lisa Crawford was a prominent member. High-level waste was removed and taken by train to storage facilities in Nevada. Low-level waste was buried in specially constructed trenches, with monitoring devices to make sure that no contamination leaches out.

Today the landscape is dotted with small, blue sheds. On group hikes, docents get asked what the sheds are for. The answer is, "They're for groundwater remediation. We pump water out of the aquifer, treat it to standards that are better than the standards for drinking water, and pipe it into the river." On a recent hike, someone asked, how long will this need to go on? The answer was, "Forever."[19]

It really is safe to go for a hike at Fernald. It's safe to go for a lot of hikes there. Fernald has become a favorite place for birdwatchers, and wildlife has come back. But the preserve still does not allow swimming in the pond, or sleeping on the ground, or gathering mushrooms.

It turns out that small particles of uranium, so long as they're outside your body, are actually pretty harmless.[20] (The stuff buried in underground trenches at Fernald cannot hurt you.) The previous problems at Fernald occurred because if uranium dust gets stuck in a person's lungs or other tissues, it will keep emitting radiation over the long term. How long depends on which isotope of uranium is involved. But the primary type which was used at Fernald—the primary type in fissile weapons—is uranium 235. Which has a half-life of seven hundred million years.[21]

We should enjoy Fernald Preserve. But it won't ever be safe to ignore Fernald, or to quit monitoring the groundwater, or to forget how it all happened.

## Clothed with the Sun

Not far from Fernald, on the west side of Oxford Road, just north of New Haven, Ohio, there's a cemetery. In the middle of that cemetery there's a large monument, which reads:

> *Erected by the Society of Shakers*
> *Whitewater Village*
> *An Order*
> *Of Celibate Christian Communists*
> *To Honor the Memory of the*
> *Members Whose mortal Remains*
> *Are Interred in This Lot*
> *1827–1916*
> *They That Have Done Good*
> *Until the Resurrection of Life*
> *Whose Abiding Place is Immortality*

The Shakers were an ecstatic, communal, religious sect founded in eighteenth-century England by a woman named Ann Lee. Because of the frenzied dancing during their worship services, they were called "Shaking Quakers," first as an insult, though they later embraced the name.

Ann Lee was an intense and magnetic woman. She was born in 1736, the daughter of a blacksmith named John Lee or Lees. She was raised in the slums of Manchester, England. During her twenties, Ann Lee found her calling as a religious leader and preacher. Because of her disruptive teachings, she was repeatedly jailed. She always emerged from jail with a stronger sense of vocation.

She married a blacksmith named Abraham Stanley and bore four children, all of whom died young. She separated from her husband and took back her maiden name. And somewhere along the way, Ann Lee developed a strong antipathy toward sex. She believed that sexual relations were the primary cause of separation between humans and God. Within the Shaker movement, marriage was forbidden. [22]

In 1770 Ann Lee had a vision in which it was revealed to her that she was the female incarnation of divinity. Jesus was the father of the church, and she was the mother. From this point forward, Mother Ann's followers identified her with the woman in the Book of Revelation, chapter 12: "A woman clothed with the sun, and the moon under her feet, and upon her head a crown of twelve stars"—the woman who contends with the great dragon.[23]

Mother Ann Lee sailed to America in 1774 and soon established the first Shaker commune in Niskayuna, New York.[24] Mother Ann taught the values of simplicity, neatness, productivity, hospitality, and thrift. She taught that work itself was an act of prayer, so that there was spiritual significance to any task performed well.[25] Children and adults were encouraged to learn to read and write and to gain practical skills.[26]

These values would define the Shaker movement to outsiders, as anyone could perceive the quality of Shaker furniture and buildings. The Shakers were master gardeners and they made and sold brooms, baskets, and garden seeds.[27]

Mother Ann Lee died in Niskayuna in 1784, at age forty-eight. The great expansion of Shakerism took place later, during the first half of the nineteenth century. By the mid-1820s there were four Shaker villages in Ohio: one near Cleveland, one near Kettering, one in Lebanon, and the Whitewater settlement.[28] The only one of the four that still has extant buildings is Whitewater, which was the smallest of the four, with a peak population of around two hundred.[29]

Whitewater Village got a slight membership boost in 1844. At the time, there was a rival religious movement of Millerites, who followed the teachings of William Miller (1792–1849). The Millerite movement was primarily concerned with the return of Jesus—literally, visually, in the clouds of heaven. William Miller calculated, based on his reading of the Book of Daniel, that Jesus would reappear and the world would end on October 22, 1844.[30]

In the weeks leading up to this date, twenty Millerites established themselves at Whitewater Village, mooching off the Shakers and generally making a nuisance of themselves. The Millerites expected that the Shakers could be

converted to Millerism. It turned out to be the other way around. The jour-
nalist Frank Grayson, writing in 1932, tell us that the Millerites at Whitewater
were ready:

> The men, women and children of the group donned white robes and
> waited for the appointed hour when their delusion of being translated
> into another sphere would become a reality. They had sought the country
> for departure from this mundane sphere, but as the hours passed and
> the grasshoppers kept on chattering and the birds kept on singing, and
> their feet were still planted on good old Ohio turf, instead of the pearly
> streets, the Millerites bitterly reflected upon the hardships they would
> have to undergo to walk back to Cincinnati. As the easiest way out of their
> dilemma they up and joined the Shakers.[31]

The Shakers at Whitewater Village were governed by four elders: two male and
two female.[32] There were separate dormitories for men and women. The community raised cattle, wheat, corn, and garden vegetables. They had a schoolhouse, a mill, beehives, and workshops. In 1903 a man named J. P. MacLean
visited the Whitewater community and wrote:

> Although I had never seen the Shaker lands, the moment I struck them
> I knew I was on their possessions. The fences were in good condition
> and the lands cared for, and there was the general aspect of thriftiness.
> When I caught sight of the first house, my opinion was confirmed that I
> was on the lands of the Shakers, for the same style of architecture, solid
> appearance, and want of decorative art were before me.[33]

Today at Whitewater, more than a dozen buildings survive. The main cluster
is north of the cemetery, and these are owned by the Hamilton County park
system. The meetinghouse survives, as does the main residence, one of the
barns, a milk house, an icehouse, workshops, and outbuildings. The buildings
have been stabilized but are somewhat rundown. Still, it is possible to sense
some of the harmony that MacLean saw. For people in the nineteenth century,
visiting from squalid cities, a Shaker village must have looked a little like
heaven. Perhaps enough to make the observer wonder whether the Shakers
might know more about heaven than other religious groups did. The village

A portion of Whitewater Shaker Village

itself was—consciously or unconsciously—a Shaker recruitment tool, and perhaps the best one they had.

Recruitment was not enough, however. The Shakers' adamant opposition to marriage meant that no children were born into Shaker communities. The Shakers at Whitewater adopted orphans from the orphan asylum in Cincinnati and raised them. When the orphans reached adulthood, they were given the choice of joining the Shaker community or going out into the world.[34] Few of them stayed.

Increasingly, cheap manufactured goods from outside put pressure on the sale of Shaker-produced baskets and brooms. Industrialization in the outside world also opened up new opportunities for persons who otherwise might have joined the Shakers. The Whitewater community ceased to be economically self-sustaining and began to decline.[35] There were occasional slipups in the celibacy department. Sometimes, members left the order.[36]

By the early twentieth century, membership at Whitewater was perilously low. Then in 1907, a disastrous fire destroyed many buildings and killed several elderly Shaker women.[37] In 1916 the remaining community members made the decision to disband.[38] It was a sad end, but the last members were comforted by having lived well.

One of the Shakers buried in the cemetery at Whitewater is Ezra Sherman (1805–82), whose last words were:

> Don't be too hard on [Shakers], for they mean well...Don't judge us by the bad ones among us...Although there are some among us who are not true believers, be good to our people. Don't pay any attention to creeds, but live right. Do right and when you are called to enter the great hereafter, you will have nothing to regret.[39]

## The Death Door

In the village of Shandon, there's a historical marker, noting that this was the first Welsh community in Ohio, founded in 1801 when William Gwilym purchased land here on the stream now called Paddy's Run.[40] The marker also notes that a Congregational church was formed here in 1803, meeting initially in members' homes. The marker reads: "A brick Meetinghouse, complete with a Welsh Death Door leading to the cemetery, was constructed in 1824."

That meetinghouse still exists, less than two blocks from the marker, on Millville-Shandon Road. The "Death Door," sadly, is not very photogenic, since it has been bricked up, and there is now an air conditioning condenser in front of it. But it's there.

During a funeral, the coffin would be placed up by the altar. The Death Door was positioned so that as soon as the funeral was over, the pallbearers could make a beeline straight into the cemetery.

This custom may be related to the traditional belief that a corpse should be carried out feet-first, to keep the spirit looking ahead, with less temptation to attach to a familiar setting, or familiar people.[41]

Having a Death Door was yet another attempt to control the distant, intangible and perhaps frightening future. The deceased person's spirit should be immortal, yes, but not here.

Scan to visit the "Immortality, Continued" route

CHAPTER 13

# IMMORTALITY, CONTINUED

## Hamilton, the Hollow Earth Monument, Chrisholm Farmstead, and Miamisburg Mound

Here we continue the previous chapter with more stories of people who struggled against the limitations of human mortality, and whose ambitious plans for the future have left marks upon the earth, while their ideas have mostly disappeared.

### The Tour

More detailed information on this route is available on the *Bicycling through Paradise* community page. We invite you to leave additional information on route updates, detours, and establishments that will be helpful to future cyclists of this route. Here is the general idea.

This tour starts at Hamilton, Ohio, and runs north and east to Miamisburg. Much of the time, we'll be following a dedicated bike path: the Great Miami River Trail. The trail is

Hollow Earth Monument

mostly flat. But not all sections of the trail are contiguous yet, so we'll be using regular roads and highways to connect them, taking some hills in the process.

The tour is composed of three segments. Total one-way distance is just over thirty-seven miles, but each segment is fun to ride independently and has something historic to see. Each segment begins and ends in places where you can find parking, food, and bathrooms. Overnight accommodations are available in Hamilton and at Miamisburg for anyone planning a weekend trip.

**Segment 1** goes from Hamilton to Trenton (15.3 miles, flat to rolling). We'll take a quick loop around Hamilton to see the Hollow Earth Monument—a small tribute to the peculiar ideas of John Cleves Symmes the younger (1779–1829), who lectured widely on his theory that the earth was "hollow and habitable within." We will pass through the German Village Historic District and then pick up the bike lane on Ford Road heading east. We'll ride out Canal Road and then join the Great Miami River Trail, riding east along the towpath of the old Miami Canal. The trail ends at Rentschler Forest Metropark. From there we'll take a stretch with significant traffic, using Indian Meadows Drive, Millikin Road, and Liberty Fairfield Road until we can head northeast on Woodsdale Road, where we'll visit the Chrisholm Farmstead, once home to the leader of the Amish congregation in Butler County (and now owned by Butler County Metroparks). We'll continue on Woodsdale Road and Radabaugh Road until we brush by the edge of Trenton, Ohio. The segment ends when we cross the Great Miami River and rejoin the Great Miami River Trail. (A quiet, easy version of this segment would be to start in Hamilton and ride to Rentschler Forest Metropark and back, a round trip of around 8 miles.)

**Segment 2** goes from Trenton to Franklin (12.4 miles, mostly flat). We'll take the Great Miami River Trail north from the Trenton trailhead to the south edge of Middletown. We'll turn right on the trail spur that leads to Ninth Avenue. Then we'll ride north on S. Main Street, which heads into Middletown along a row of fine mansions including the Sorg Mansion, once the home of the industrialist Paul Sorg, who owned the Miami Bicycle Company and much else. We'll rejoin the Great Miami River Trail, heading north. Depending on trail construction, you may have to jog over to Verity Pkwy/OH 73-E from Access Road to Baxter Drive. We'll rejoin the tail and continue into Franklin, where we'll see a two-story log post office built in 1802, and we'll have a chance to visit the Museum of Spiritual Art.

Segment 3 goes from Franklin to Miamisburg (10 miles, flat for a while and then a good climb). We'll take the Great Miami River Trail north. Just past Crain's Run Nature Park, we'll turn east on the Medlar Bikeway and climb to the top of the hill. We'll head north on Miamisburg-Springboro Pike and then take Benner Road and Mound Road to Miamisburg Mound—one of the largest Native earthworks in the eastern United States, built between two thousand and three thousand years ago. From there, we'll descend and continue on to downtown Miamisburg. (Alternatively, you could skip the climb up to Miamisburg Mound and take the nice, flat, Great Miami River Trail straight to downtown Miamisburg.) There are several good restaurants here, and for those staying overnight, the English Manor Bed and Breakfast is an especially good option.

## The World Within

John Cleves Symmes was born in 1779 in New Jersey. (He was the nephew of an older man, also named John Cleves Symmes, who was a famous pioneer and landholder sometimes known as "Judge" Symmes.) The younger man distinguished himself first by bravery in the War of 1812. He then moved to St. Louis, where in 1818 he published a pamphlet, beginning:

> TO ALL THE WORLD! I declare the earth is hollow, and habitable within; containing a number of solid concentrick [sic] spheres, one within the other, and that it is open at the poles 12 or 16 degrees; I pledge my life in support of this truth, and am ready to explore the hollow, if the world will support and aid me in the undertaking.[1]

The possibility of exploration was especially alluring because Symmes believed that the interior of the Earth was probably already inhabited, "by animals if not by men."

A year after writing this pamphlet, Symmes moved to Newport, Kentucky. Five years after that, in 1824, Symmes moved to Hamilton, Ohio. Symmes lectured widely but never wrote a full treatise of his ideas. One of Symmes's most ardent supporters, however, was a man named John McBride, and McBride did write a book, published in 1826 under the title *Symmes' Theory of Concentric Spheres: Demonstrating that the Earth is Hollow, Habitable Within, and Widely Open about The Poles.*

For Symmes, the natural world provided ample evidence that the earth was something more complex than a simple, solid sphere. Take volcanoes, for example. The hot gasses escaping from them—where exactly were those gasses coming from? The same could be asked about hot springs and geysers. Earthquakes, too, were puzzling. If the Earth were indeed solid and compact, then wouldn't a major earthquake be felt all across the globe? The vibrations from major earthquakes might not actually be felt more than a few hundred miles away. Didn't this suggest that the planet wasn't as solid as it seemed?[2]

As Symmes pointed out, the great seventeenth-century astronomer Edmund Halley—for whom the comet is named—had also believed that the Earth was hollow. Halley believed that the outer shell of the Earth contained another sphere, and another one inside that. Halley believed that these concentric spheres could rotate independently, and that this movement explained the fluctuations in the readings of magnetic compasses.

Halley had presented his ideas before the British Royal Society in 1691. In a paper published the following year, he addressed several possible objections to this theory. For example, it might be argued that these internal spheres would not stay in position, but would bump against each other. Halley said no, the concentric spheres would stay in place, in much the same way that Saturn's rings stay put.[3]

By the time Symmes started giving lectures, these ideas were no longer regarded as credible, and Symmes's work gained him a wide reputation as an oddball and a crank. But Symmes persevered. He was confident that openings into the interior sphere must exist at the poles and could be found. He was likewise confident that the entire interior could be explored because—and this is crucial—Symmes felt sure that the interior globe would be illuminated with adequate sunlight falling "on every part of the inner sphere."[4]

On the face of it, this seems unlikely. The sun spends its time more or less above the equator and is never directly above the poles. So the polar openings would never receive light except at an oblique angle, providing hardly enough light to illuminate the entire interior, concentric globe. Symmes responded that even a large room can be lit by a north-facing window, where direct sunlight never enters.[5]

Symmes's convictions about this illumination were more theological than scientific. Why, he reasoned, would an all-wise Providence create an interior world, or any world at all, without allowing it the conditions to support life?[6] Symmes's disciple John McBride continued the argument in his book. If the interior of our planet is assumed to be dark, then one might as well conclude "that the immense planet Jupiter, situated so far from the sun as he is, can be nothing but a dark, cold, and barren waste." To Symmes (and McBride), this vision of a cold, dark universe was distasteful. McBride continues with comments about Saturn and Uranus (which he calls by its old name, *Georgium Sidus*):

> The light and heat which Saturn receives from the sun is estimated at only the one hundredth part of that of the earth; and the planet Georgium Sidus, revolving such an immense distance further from the sun, must enjoy still less light and heat; according to which we would conclude... that those vast planets are not fitted by the God of nature for the residence of intelligent beings; however I am inclined to believe that both light and heat are communicated to them, in some way not well known to us, sufficient for the purpose.[7]

Since Symmes was convinced that Earth's interior must be habitable, he and his supporters petitioned both Congress and the Ohio legislature for funding to mount an expedition to find one of the polar openings and then proceed into the center of the planet. The funding did not materialize.[8]

John Cleves Symmes died in 1829. He was buried in a small cemetery on Third Street in Hamilton with an unusual tombstone—an obelisk, surmounted by a stone orb which is open at both ends and through the center—a fine representation of the hollow earth itself. With this small memorial, John Cleves Symmes has gained a tiny measure of immortality as a colossal dope.

But while John Cleves Symmes was wrong about a lot of things, he was right about one big thing: he was right, in the main, about scientific method.

Symmes did not ask that his ideas be accepted uncritically. He only asked for the chance to test his hypothesis. He wanted to go have a look. McBride writes:

> Many of the theories which have been advanced respecting the earth, are vague and uncertain, and will remain so forever...Not so with the theory of concentric spheres. Its correctness admits of ocular demonstration. The interior of the sphere is declared accessible, and the whole extent capable of being accurately explored; thereby establishing the theory, or disproving and putting it at rest forever.[9]

More than a hundred years after Symmes died, Hamilton city leaders decided to make a public park out of the land that contained Symmes's grave. Some nearby graves were moved. But John Cleves Symmes was different. He was a favorite son of the town, and his unusual tombstone was a local landmark. An iron railing was erected around the tomb, and bronze plaques were added, explaining Symmes's ideas. The city leaders had a good idea, too, about what to call the new park—they named it Symmes Park.[10]

## Chrisholm Farmstead

The early nineteenth century, when John Cleves Symmes was giving his lectures, was also a period of religious creativity and ferment. America had become home to groups of Shakers and Quakers, Millerites, Mormons, Mennonites, and Amish. Many of these groups had distinctive lifestyles, communities that were largely separate from outsiders, and implicitly utopian beliefs. Each group had to strike a balance between uniqueness and assimilation, as each attempted to preserve their religious identity over the long term.

In 1819 a group of German-speaking Amish farmers arrived in the Great Miami Valley from Alsace-Lorraine, on the French-German border. They were led by Christian Augspurger, who would eventually purchase nearly two thousand acres here. In 1830 Christian Augspurger built a fine house, which he called Chrisholm. The current Chrisholm House is an 1873 replacement, built by his son after a fire, but much of the farmstead is intact.[11]

Back in northern Europe, the Amish had suffered from generations of religious persecution because they opposed the Catholic practice of infant baptism. Also unlike Catholics, the Amish did not pray for the souls of the deceased, believing that the final state of the dead was already decided. America provided the Amish the freedom of worship that they craved.

The Amish in America were nearly always farmers. The Amish were generally suspicious toward education, which was believed to make boys lazy and girls morally lax. The Amish disapproved of the use of musical instruments, especially in worship. And they had strict dress codes: women wore bonnets, while men sported beards and broad-brimmed hats. Clothing was fastened with hooks-and-eyes; buttons were forbidden as being too modern.[12]

In 1832 another group arrived in the Great Miami Valley and settled close by the Amish. This was a group of around one hundred Mennonite farmers. The Mennonites were an offshoot of the Amish with nearly identical religious beliefs and with only slightly more relaxed rules of dress and decorum. The new settlers had come mostly from Hesse-Darmstadt, Germany. Partnership between the two groups seemed natural.

Prominent among the Mennonites was Christian Iutzi (1788–1857). Iutzi kept a diary, in which he tells how he and his family, along with several related families, sailed from Bremen to Baltimore in 1832. They spent two weeks in Baltimore, resting and gathering supplies. They traveled overland to Wheeling, West Virginia, and then by flatboat to Cincinnati. In Cincinnati Iutzi and

Chrisholm Farmstead

his family loaded their belongings (including a piano) on a canal boat and traveled up the Miami and Erie Canal to Hamilton. From there, Iutzi scouted land in several locations. On Christmas Day 1832, he writes:

> It was decided that we buy land in Butler County, and I have made the start. I bought 195 acres in Madison Township. Chr[istian]Augspurger is my neighbor, and right beside his land my brother-in-law John Holly bought 145 acres. My brothers Peter and Jacob bought 188 acres of the so-called Red Buck [farm].[13]

The Amish and Mennonite neighbors attended the same church and shared German as a common language. English was spoken only to conduct business with outsiders. The two groups cooperated in other ways as well: Christian Iutzi's diary from September 1834 tells how he and his family "were at Jacob Augspurger's and helped set up a new dwelling for him."[14]

Christian Iutzi's diary contains only brief notes of everyday events. Iutzi kept a farmer's eye on the weather. He speaks of the river, its freezes and thaws. He noted the solar eclipse that took place on November 30, 1834. He describes going to Hamilton to hear a speech by William Henry Harrison. He mentions birthdays, and illnesses, and the market prices of farm goods.

Beneath the apparent harmony of farm life, however, tensions were brewing. Iutzi and the other Mennonites had a favorable view of education that did not sit well with the Amish. Iutzi's piano was a minor scandal. And the relaxed dress code of the Mennonites was a problem, because they allowed buttons on their clothing. This last issue turned out to be an intractable problem, because there isn't much middle ground between buttons and no-buttons. On May 8, 1835, Iutzi wrote:

> Today the meeting was at Joseph Augspurger's, and it was decided that from now on, two congregations should exist, one on this side of the Miami River, and one on the other side.[15]

The congregation had split. From this point forward, the Amish congregation was also called the "Hook-and-Eye" church, and the Mennonites were the "Button" church. Both survived for the next sixty years. During that time, both suffered setbacks. Christian Augspurger died in 1848. His son Samuel took over Chrisholm and built a paper mill on the riverbank, across the road from the house. But in 1880 a disastrous fire destroyed the mill, and a flood that same year hurt many local farmers and left Samuel Augspurger bankrupt.[16]

By this time, strict Amish practices were declining in Butler County, as people gravitated to the more relaxed views of the Mennonites. In 1897, the "Hook-and-Eye" church and the "Button" church merged,[17] in what was billed as an act of cooperation but was clearly a victory for the Buttons. The combined congregation still exists at Trenton.[18]

Nationally, both groups still soldier on, using different strategies for survival. The old-order Amish, with a lifestyle nearly unchanged from Christian Augspurger's day, now have over two hundred thousand members in the United States.[19] The Mennonites, through a process of accommodation and assimilation, have created a denomination ten times as large, though many of their practices are scarcely distinguishable from the practices of mainline Christian churches.[20] The Amish and the Mennonites, like many mainstream religious groups, still await a future cataclysm that will usher in a changed world.

## The Sky at Night

Around 1797, a man named Zachariah Hole built a blockhouse and stockade on a high point beside the Great Miami River, near what is now Miamisburg. It's long been rumored that local Native Americans told Zachariah Hole to name the place Star City.[21] That story is surely apocryphal, but Miamisburg has indeed been nicknamed "Star City" at least since 1885,[22] and the nickname does sound nicer than what the stockade was actually called—Hole's Station.

Zachariah Hole cannot have failed to notice the seventy-foot tall mound, now known as the Miamisburg Mound, on a ridge not far from his stockade. The mound has been a source of wonder ever since. The town of Miamisburg was platted in 1818 (just a year before Christian Augspurger arrived in the Miami Valley), and the first formal excavations of the mound took place in 1869.[23]

Many of the Native American earthworks in Ohio were built by people now referred to as the Adena. The Adena culture arose in the Ohio River Valley around 800 BCE and lasted until around CE 100 or so. The Adena were among the first people in Ohio to make pottery, and they were the first to build mounds here. Most of their mounds have been destroyed, but not this one.

The mound at Miamisburg is the largest conical mound in Ohio and the second largest in eastern North America. It's sixty-five feet tall (a few feet shorter than it once was), and it contains fifty-four thousand cubic yards of earth. Layers of ash inside the mound, and a layer of stone around twenty-four feet below the surface, indicate that the mound was built in stages.[24]

The Adena people are believed to have spent around nine hundred years constructing Miamisburg Mound, and today, no one is sure exactly what the mound was for. Was it a lookout post? A royal residence? A tomb? An observatory, a fortification, a boundary-marker, a place of sacrifice? Or was it simply a manifestation of the deep human desire to create something that will last forever, to leave a mark upon the earth?

No one knows the complete answer, and probably, no one ever will. But we do know part of the answer. The mound has never been fully excavated, but the partial excavations in 1869 revealed that eight feet below the peak there was a skeleton, "Entombed in a sitting posture and facing due east."[25] Nothing more is known about that great Native leader, who is now and forever nameless. But at least we know that the mound was, at least in part, a tomb. We also know that the Adena people, like people in many cultures, often left

Miamisburg Mound

grave goods, especially food, in their burial pits. All of this implies some sort of belief in an afterlife.

It's also likely that Miamisburg Mound, and others like it, functioned as observatories. Certainly, the great Serpent Mound in Adams County, Ohio, had astronomical significance. Serpent Mound was built in the shape of a giant snake, and the snake's head points to the sunset at summer solstice. Several archaeologists (especially Robert Fletcher and Terry Cameron) have argued that there are additional solar and lunar alignments in the coils and the tail.[26] Other researchers have suggested that Serpent Mound is constructed in the shape of the constellation we call Draco, the Dragon.[27]

Further archaeological studies may confirm or refute these ideas. Archaeology, like the hard sciences, moves slowly, in a long arc of incremental improvement. Today, perhaps the best we can do is just to stand on top of Miamisburg Mound and look up at the sky.

The night sky was always a primary fact of ancient life. We don't know what stories the Adena told about the sky. But we know what stars they saw. Adena culture lasted long enough for Halley's Comet to come and go a dozen times. The Adena watched the stars in their rotation, and they watched the planets wander among the stars. They watched Mercury, Venus, Mars, Jupiter, and Saturn. But the planet we call Uranus can't be seen with the unaided eye, even when there's no light pollution. So the Mound Builders never saw the planet that we named after Ouranos, the god of the sky. That one was too dark and too far away.

# Part III

# Big Ideas

CHAPTER 14

# HOMELAND INSECURITY

## Military Installations from Fort Washington to Newport Barracks to Fort Thomas, Kentucky

The army came to Cincinnati in 1789 with the construction of Fort Washington: a large stockade enclosure with blockhouses at the corners, located near what is now Broadway Street, just north of the street now called Fort Washington Way. This was the major military outpost of the Northwest Territory, used for both defense and aggression against Native Americans. It remained an active base throughout the 1790s as General Arthur St. Clair and other leaders attempted to consolidate control over the territory.[1]

Newport Barracks Monument

Since that time, greater Cincinnati has been home to a number of subsequent military installations, and this area has come under some form of military threat more often than we tend to realize.

## The Tour

More detailed information on this route is available on the *Bicycling through Paradise* community page. We invite you to leave additional information on route updates, detours, and establishments that will be helpful to future cyclists of this route. Here is the general idea.

This tour is composed of two loops, each of which starts and stops at the south end of the Purple People Bridge in Newport, Kentucky. Each loop has one long climb and one steep descent. The first round-trip loop is 8.9 miles, and the second is 15 miles.

In the process, we will visit the sites of four historic military installations. First is a monument to Fort Washington. Second is the monument to the old Newport Barracks in Kentucky, an active base from 1803 until 1895. Third is the overlook at Devou Park, Kentucky, not very far from the site of a Civil War artillery installation called Battery Bates. Fourth is Fort Thomas, Kentucky, home to an active army base from 1887 to 1964.

**Segment 1** is the Devou Loop (8.9 miles, with one long climb and one steep descent). We will start by crossing the pedestrian bridge, heading north into downtown. We'll see the monument to Fort Washington on Fourth Street (just across Ludlow Street from the Lincoln Statue at Lytle Park). We'll recross the river on the John A. Roebling Suspension Bridge and head down to the Covington riverfront, passing by a park dedicated to General George Rogers Clark, a Revolutionary War hero. We'll see a historic marker describing the significance of the river during the Civil War, and then we'll see the Roebling murals at the foot of the bridge. We'll continue along the riverfront using KY-8, until it's time to take a steep climb up Parkway Avenue into Devou Park. Along the way we'll pass Prisoners' Lake, originally a stone quarry worked by prisoners from the Covington jail. At the top of the hill, we'll reach the Behringer-Crawford Museum, which houses Civil War artifacts, along with a lot of other cool stuff. We'll descend out of the park via Montague Road and come back into Covington on Pike Street. We'll cross the Licking River on the bridge at East Fourth Street, and then we'll ride along the top of the floodwall until we reach General James Taylor Park, the home of the Newport Barracks Monument. From there we'll return to our starting place.

**Segment 2** is the Fort Thomas Loop (15 miles, with one long climb and one steep descent). We will start at again at the pedestrian bridge and take a long, gradual climb up Covert Run Pike to the town of Fort Thomas. Many buildings from the 1880s still exist, including the stone water tower, and there's a small museum of Fort Thomas history. Then we'll descend via River Road and return along the river on the Mary Ingles Highway/KY-8 (sometimes called "Old" Kentucky 8), coming through Dayton and Bellevue, Kentucky. In Bellevue, there are several good places to eat. Save room for Schneider's Homemade Candies.

This tour will give us a chance to think about the military history of our country, and how we got to where we are today.

## The Development of a Standing Army

Back in the 1770s and 1780s, many colonists feared the idea of a standing American army. After the Revolutionary War, the Continental Army was completely and intentionally disbanded. No modern regiment can trace its lineage directly to any Continental unit.[2] In 1787 James Madison gave a speech before the Constitutional Convention in which he said:

> In time of actual war, great discretionary powers are constantly given to the Executive Magistrate. Constant apprehension of War, has the same tendency to render the head too large for the body. A standing military force, with an overgrown Executive will not long be safe companions to liberty. The means of defence agst. foreign danger, have been always the instruments of tyranny at home.[3]

Patrick Henry, George Mason, and Eldridge Gerry also felt that a large, standing army could become a danger to democracy, though Madison also admitted that it might be a necessary danger.[4] So when the Constitution was written, Article 1 gave Congress the power "to raise and support Armies, but no Appropriation of Money to that Use shall be for a longer Term than two Years." The next sentence allows Congress "to provide and maintain a Navy," without the two-year limitation.

At first glance, the meaning seems clear. Ships need to be maintained, so a navy has to be permanent. Armies, however, should be raised only as needed, and for a limited time. A second glance says otherwise. No limit is placed on congressional authority to "raise and support" an army. The only limit is on the timing of appropriations, and nothing forbids continual reappropriations. So from the beginning of the republic, a standing army has been allowable and perhaps inevitable.

By the late 1780s, there was a detachment of soldiers at Fort Washington in Cincinnati, and the United States has maintained a standing army ever since.

In 1803 a new barracks was built in Newport, Kentucky, just across the Ohio River from Cincinnati. During the War of 1812, soldiers were deployed from here to northern Ohio. Some of them fought in the Battle of Lake Erie in 1813, and they brought British prisoners back to Newport Barracks.[5] The War of 1812 dragged on into 1814, when the British burned the U.S. Capitol building in Washington, DC. A peace treaty was signed in December 1814, but word did not reach the armies until after the Battle of New Orleans in January 1815.

During the War of 1812 and throughout the early nineteenth century, the US Army was small, its size usually hovering between four thousand and twelve thousand soldiers. State militias filled out the force as needed.[6] In this way, the United States fought the small wars of the early nineteenth century—including the Seminole War of 1817–18 (Florida), the Black Hawk War of 1832 (Illinois and Wisconsin), the Creek War of 1836 (Alabama), the Second Seminole War of 1835–42 (Florida), and the Mexican-American War of 1846–48—among others.[7]

These conflicts were far away from Cincinnati. Still, Cincinnati was not a completely safe place, because of domestic unrest. The first major race riot in Cincinnati took place over several weeks in August 1829, when hundreds of White men, mostly Irish, attacked a Black neighborhood in the First Ward, in an attempt to drive out Black residents. By the end of August, between 1,100 and 1,500 African Americans had left Cincinnati for good, some heading to Canada.[8]

Cincinnati's worst race riot was probably the one in 1841, when a mob of White men met in the Fifth Street Market and marched on Bucktown, a Black neighborhood along the riverfront. Hundreds of Black men were armed and waiting. The White men rolled a cannon down Sixth Street, faced it toward Bucktown, and fired. There were an unknown number of fatalities. Three hundred African Americans were arrested.

At other times, the perceived enemies shifted. The Cincinnati riots of 1855 were fought between German Americans and anti-immigrant nativists. The nativists supported a mayoral candidate from the American Party, James D. Taylor, whose speeches included inflammatory attacks on immigrants. On Election Day, fights broke out, and the nativists managed to destroy the ballots in two German wards. Riots erupted in which several people were killed. The German Americans organized militia units and built a barricade across Vine Street where it enters Over-the-Rhine. The nativists attacked the barricade, and the German Americans fired a cannon over their heads.

There would be later riots, too, including the 1884 courthouse riots, in which more than fifty people died and the courthouse was destroyed.[9]

## The Civil War and the John Hunt Morgan Raid

When the Civil War broke out, both sides raised huge armies. In Ohio the war was broadly popular. Between 1861 and 1865, Ohio alone provided nearly 320,000 volunteer soldiers. By the end of the war, among Ohio men between eighteen and thirty-five years of age, 60 percent had served in the military.[10]

During the early phases of the Civil War, the Union Army constructed a long line of artillery fortifications across northern Kentucky, to try to keep Confederate forces from crossing the Ohio River. These included Fort Mitchell and Fort Wright, plus other, smaller, artillery installations, including one called Battery Bates, in what is now Devou Park. But then, in July 1863, a large Confederate raiding party under General John Hunt Morgan slipped through the lines west of Louisville, crossed the Ohio River from Kentucky into Indiana, rode eastward into Ohio, and then rode across Cincinnati's northern suburbs.

General Morgan commanded a force of nearly 2,500 men. They entered Ohio on July 13, 1863, in the town of Harrison. On this particular bike tour, we won't intersect the route taken by Morgan's raiders, but on many of our other tours, you'll see markers of the John Hunt Morgan Heritage Trail. General Morgan and his men passed east from Harrison through New Baltimore, Whitewater Shaker Village, Glendale, Camp Dennison, Perintown, Owensville, and Williamsburg—all places that are on the tours in this book. (For Morgan's full route, see Cahill and Mowery's *Morgan's Raid across Ohio: The Civil War Guidebook of the John Hunt Morgan Heritage Trail.*[11])

General Morgan's raid was purely diversionary. He did not intend to attack any particular military target. He only wanted to distract Union forces, to take pressure off a larger Confederate force commanded by General Braxton Bragg. General Bragg had liked the idea of a raid, but he wanted General Morgan to stay on the south side of the Ohio River. Morgan disobeyed those orders.[12]

The raid was brilliant, foolhardy, and chaotic. General Morgan's men would routinely sweep out miles from the main column across surrounding farms to steal fresh horses, so that they could move fast and deprive their pursuers of fresh mounts. The only way the 2,500 raiders could eat was to enter farmhouses uninvited and demand food. When they ran out of ammunition, they stole it. They also had to scavenge forage for the horses. Yet they managed to move quickly enough to evade capture.

General Morgan's men would break into telegraph offices, send out false reports of sightings that concealed their true location and direction, and then cut the telegraph lines. Newspapers in Cincinnati hastily set type to send out special editions several times a day, warning of the approach of the raiders. Panicked farmers tried to hide their horses, food, and valuables, but they were often outsmarted by the Confederates.

After leaving the Cincinnati area, General Morgan's raiders continued east until they reached Pomeroy, Ohio, near the West Virginia border. Then they headed north and made it all the way up past Wellsville, Ohio. This was the northernmost point ever reached by the Confederate Army, further north even than Gettysburg, Pennsylvania. Here, Morgan and his men were finally captured and imprisoned, after a month-long raid that had taken them over a thousand miles from their starting place in Tennessee.[13]

General Morgan escaped from his Ohio prison in November 1863. He returned to the South, rejoined the Confederate Army, and was killed in battle on September 4, 1864.[14]

## The Post–Civil War Period and the Founding of Fort Thomas

At the close of the Civil War, the army contracted sharply in size, as enlisted men were discharged. But it never went back to being as small as it had been before. Out of the Civil War emerged a new generation of military leaders, some of whom had expansive ideas about military staffing and infrastructure.

The old Newport Barracks remained an active military post throughout the Civil War and for some time thereafter. But it was prone to flooding, so eventually, the army began to consider other locations. They ended up selecting a site at what is now called Fort Thomas, Kentucky, on a high, windy ridge four miles west of Newport. According to local historian A. Vinton Stegman:

> It may appear strange to some, that the U.S. War Department would have located an Army Post in such a non-strategic location as the Highlands of Campbell County, Kentucky, but in 1887...the army was still looked upon as a protector of local communities in many parts of the country. There were posts spread over the United States during the early part of [the twentieth] century, and it was not until World War II that the army was stationed in huge bases (i.e., Fort Campbell, Fort, Bragg, etc).[15]

The selection of the site of Fort Thomas was largely the work of a single man—a Kentucky businessman named Samuel Bigstaff. Bigstaff was a sweet talker and a natural salesman. He was born in Kentucky in 1845. He enlisted in the Confederate Army, was captured, and was sent to Newport Barracks as a prisoner. He charmed his captors and soon had full run of the barracks, plus permission to eat in the officers' club. While he was nominally a prisoner at Newport Barracks, he met Alice Webster, the daughter of a prominent Newport lawyer. Samuel and Alice were married soon after the war ended. Samuel became a lawyer and developed significant business interests. In the postwar period, he was often known as "Major" Bigstaff.[16]

Bigstaff knew that it might be possible to purchase land on the highlands at a bargain price because one of the area's largest landholders, Eli Kinney, was in financial distress, having made several bad business decisions in Cincinnati. Kinney was forced to sell his holdings in 1883, and by 1887, Bigstaff had put together a consortium of just four property owners (himself and three others), who collectively owned a contiguous parcel of 111 acres—tiny by the standards of today's military bases, but roughly ten times the size of the old Newport Barracks.[17]

In May 1887 Bigstaff gave a horseback tour of the highlands to several uniformed men, including Colonel Melville Cochran, who was commandant of Newport Barracks, and General Philip Sheridan, a Civil War hero who had become chief of staff of the US Army. They rode from Newport, through woods and orchards, until reaching a panoramic view overlooking the Ohio River. Here, General Sheridan said, "Gentlemen, this new fort will be the West Point of the West!"[18]

The new post was named after General George H. Thomas, another Civil War hero. The new Fort Thomas would house the 6th Infantry Division. Forty buildings were planned. The first to be constructed was the base commander's house, completed in 1888. The city of Covington provided a water line to fill a water tower—a huge metal pipe encased in a stone tower—that was completed in 1892, and still exists. And by 1893, the Green Line streetcars were operating, making it easy for soldiers to travel to Cincinnati and back. The primary owner of the streetcar company was Bigstaff.[19]

The first base commander was Colonel Cochran, who moved up from Newport Barracks. Colonel Cochran was a great lover of plants and flowers, and he often detailed soldiers to work on the landscaping around his house. But his ideas extended beyond his own residence. He decided that the soldiers should raise their own vegetables, and in 1891 he leased additional land for this purpose.[20]

And so things went on quietly at Fort Thomas until May 1898, when word reached the fort that there had been an incident in Havana Harbor, Cuba. Both Spanish and American ships were present at Havana. There had been an explosion, possibly caused by a Spanish torpedo, and the USS *Maine* had sunk to the bottom of the harbor.

## Remembering the *Maine*

The USS *Maine* had been commissioned in 1895. She was 324 feet long and armor plated, with gun turrets on either side. She was steam powered, using coal-fired boilers. But there was a potential flaw: the coal used in the *Maine* was bituminous coal, which can release a gas called firedamp. And firedamp is pyrophoric, which means that it can burst into flame on contact with air. If the *Maine* were to have a spontaneous fire in the coalbunker, and if that fire could not be contained before it reached the powder magazine, it was possible that the *Maine* could suffer a deadly explosion.

At the time the *Maine* was commissioned, Cuba was fighting a war of independence against Spain. In January 1898 fighting broke out in Havana between Cuban separatists and Cubans who were loyal to Spain. There were Americans living in Havana, and the fighting endangered both the lives of the Americans and their control of sugar plantations. The *Maine* was sent to Havana Harbor to protect American interests. Three weeks later, on February 15, the *Maine* exploded, killing 266 sailors.

To this day, no one knows for sure why the *Maine* exploded. There were Spanish ships nearby, and it's possible that one of them fired a torpedo. But a much likelier explanation is that the *Maine* explosion was caused by a spontaneous fire in the coal bunker.[21]

In the United States, two major newspaper publishers—William Randolph Hearst and Joseph Pulitzer—used the disaster to boost circulation, and both urged the United States to declare war on Spain. Privately, Pulitzer said that "nobody outside a lunatic asylum" could believe that Spain was responsible for the explosion. But the relentless drumbeat for war was good for newspaper sales.[22]

US Naval forces began a blockade of Cuba, to keep Spanish ships out. US Army forces, including the 6th Infantry Division, landed on the island and, fighting alongside Cuban separatists, forced the surrender of Spanish nationalists after only ten weeks of war.[23]

These were glory days for the soldiers of Fort Thomas. As trophies, they brought back two Spanish cannons that had been cast in the 1760s. These cannons are supreme examples of the art of casting and engraving, with elaborate decoration and inscriptions. These canons now sit at the base of the stone water tower in Fort Thomas, at the entrance to the old fort.[24]

After the Spanish-American War was over, Fort Thomas went back to being a sleepy place, and there was talk that the fort might be abandoned. But when the United States entered World War I, these calculations changed. Fort Thomas became a recruitment and induction center. And in 1917 some soldiers from Fort Thomas became bit players in an interesting drama: they were sent to arrest Ernst Kunwald, the conductor of the Cincinnati Symphony Orchestra (CSO).[25]

## World War I and the Ernst Kunwald Case

The United States had entered World War I in 1917, two years after a German submarine had torpedoed the *Lusitania*. (Three of those who died onboard were from Cincinnati.) Cincinnati's many German-born citizens were suddenly suspected of being disloyal at best, spies at worst. German-language classes were dropped from schools. German teachers were dismissed. German-language newspapers were shut down.[26]

Dr. Ernst Kunwald was a first-rate conductor. He'd been conductor of the Berlin Philharmonic Orchestra before coming to Cincinnati in 1912, where he replaced Leopold Stokowski as conductor of the Cincinnati Symphony Orchestra. But he wasn't immune from anti-German sentiment. Kunwald's political troubles began in November 1917, when the CSO was scheduled to perform in Pittsburgh. The Pittsburgh Police Department became convinced that Kunwald was a German agent because his program was scheduled to include German music.

Kunwald was actually Austrian, rather than German. But Austria was a German ally, and it isn't clear that this distinction mattered much to the Pittsburgh Police anyway. Kunwald was not arrested, but he was forbidden to appear at the concert. The CSO delayed the performance until a replacement conductor could be found, and then the performance went ahead with no German music and no Kunwald.

Kunwald was sufficiently pro-Austrian to raise a few eyebrows, at least during a time of war. He made it clear that he was a loyal subject of the

Austro-Hungarian Empire, and he thought Woodrow Wilson was a fool. It was rumored, rightly or (probably) wrongly, that Kunwald had said at a dinner party that he would assassinate President Wilson if the Austro-Hungarian emperor told him to.

Kunwald submitted a letter of resignation to Anna Sinton Taft, president of the orchestra association, saying that he did not want to be a distraction. But Taft supported Kunwald, and the board unanimously rejected the resignation. A few days later, the CSO played at Camp Sheridan in Chillicothe, Ohio, again under Dr. Kunwald's baton. He began the program with "The Star-Spangled Banner."

On December 5, 1917, however, the United States declared war on Austria-Hungary. The federal government issued an order requiring all male Austro-Hungarian citizens over the age of fourteen to report to a US Marshall for registration. Kunwald didn't even get the chance to register: he was immediately arrested under the Alien Enemies Act for allegedly speaking out against the US government. He was released and was allowed to return to his home in Avondale. But then just a few days later, soldiers from Fort Thomas came to his home and arrested him again. This time he was taken to Fort Oglethorpe in Georgia, where he was held until the end of the war.

At Fort Oglethorpe, Kunwald helped organize an orchestra, but he frequently quarreled with Karl Muck, director of the Boston Symphony Orchestra, who was there for the same reason. Soldiers pretending to be prisoners took notes of their conversations, and they gathered enough evidence to deport Kunwald back to Austria at the end of the war.

As Hitler began rising to power, an aging Ernst Kunwald tried to get back into the United States, but he died before receiving permission. Ernst Kunwald died in Vienna on December 12, 1939, at the age of seventy-five.[27]

## World War II and the Cold War

In 1941, after the attack on Pearl Harbor destroyed the US Pacific fleet, a Japanese invasion of California suddenly seemed possible. More than 110,000 Japanese Americans were rounded up and sent to internment camps, including some who passed through a temporary detainment station in Cincinnati.[28]

As World War II continued, Cincinnatians began to worry about air raids. (Neither Germany nor Japan had planes with the range required to reach Ohio, but that didn't seem to make people feel better.) In November 1941 the Hamilton County National Defense Council (HCNDC) issued a call for civilian volunteers. Five months later, Xavier University hosted a "commencement" ceremony for more than six thousand newly trained air raid wardens who'd been instructed in blackout techniques, fire defense, and first aid. HCNDC also called for civilian volunteers to guard bridges, railroads, and public utilities against the threat of sabotage. By June 1942 more than sixty-two thousand people from greater Cincinnati had volunteered.[29]

The Soviet Union tested its first nuclear device in 1949, and by 1952 it was clear that the USSR did indeed have long-range bombers capable of reaching targets in mid-America. In 1953 local officials issued the *Cincinnati-Hamilton County Civil Defense Handbook*, and in 1956 the Ohio Valley Civil Defense Authority came up with an even better title—*Civil Defense: Will to Survive*. These handbooks recommended that local citizens should consider constructing family bomb shelters in their basements or backyards.

To counter the threat of long-range bombers, the US military began developing new surface-to-air missiles. Around 1960, four new Nike missile bases were constructed to defend the area around Cincinnati and Dayton. The bases were at Wilmington, Felicity, and Oxford, plus one in Dillsboro, Indiana.[30] But then, the Soviets began testing intercontinental ballistic missiles, which would be impervious to Nike missiles. It was widely rumored that Wright-Patterson Air Force Base, outside Dayton, was third on the Soviet target list, suggesting that Cincinnati would be incinerated in the process. (It's worth noting that dozens of other places in the United States also claimed to be number three or number four on the Soviet target list.[31])

## The Cincinnati Subway Shelter

In response to these escalating threats, local civil defense authorities stepped up efforts to provide large, public nuclear fallout shelters, many in the basements of large buildings in downtown Cincinnati.

Most Cincinnatians know that underneath downtown there are unfinished, abandoned subway tunnels from the 1920s. And many people know that in the early 1960s, one tunnel area was converted into a fallout shelter. This was the east underground platform of the Liberty Street Station, at the intersection of Liberty Street and Central Parkway. (This location is on the Canal Bikeway but is not included in the directions for this tour, because today, there's not much to see.)

The east underground platform and bathrooms of the Liberty Street Station were cleaned up, and a portion of the platform was divided into smaller rooms with new concrete block walls. Bunk beds, water storage drums, medical equipment, and communications equipment were brought in. An entrance was modified.[32]

The subway tunnel was only one shelter among many. But the subway shelter piqued public curiosity. And officials of the General Services Administration (GSA) were coy about the project. In April 1963 the *Cincinnati Enquirer* finally got an interview with a GSA official. The official, who wouldn't allow his name to be used, made reference to the "alleged" shelter. The *Enquirer* reports:

> He admitted it may look like a fallout shelter. If one raps upon its metal doors, it may even sound like a fallout shelter. The contractor, who finished work on it last December, may have thought he was building a fallout shelter, but..."It's not a fallout shelter now," the official said. "It's an experiment. It won't be a fallout shelter until the government puts up a sign and says it's a fallout shelter."

The *Cincinnati Enquirer* continues:

> To ease the confusion, the government official ordered workmen to dismantle the large metal frame, which had rested upon the surface doors of the fallout shelter, which wasn't a fallout shelter, in the subway, which wasn't a subway.[33]

## Where We Are Now

All of that was before the terrorist attacks of September 11, 2001, and before the time when the George W. Bush administration advised everyone across the country to purchase duct tape and plastic sheeting, so they could seal up rooms in their houses in case of a biological weapons attack by Saddam Hussein.

So despite an apparently protected location in the heartland, the good people of Cincinnati have had quite a bit to worry about, over the years.

Back in the 1780s, the question was whether we needed a standing army. Now that we have grown accustomed to what James Madison called the "constant apprehension of war," the question has changed. The question is now whether we must accept a condition of permanent warfare.

In October 2002 President Bush gave a speech in Phoenix in which he said, "It used to be that oceans could protect us. We used to be able to sit back here in America and feel safe and confident, because there's two vast oceans to protect us from potential enemies."[34]

President Bush made versions of this remark dozens of times in public statements over the next few years. And he was right about how people felt at that moment. But he was wrong about history. Over the wide sweep of years, the citizens of Cincinnati have felt unsafe again and again. The 9/11 attacks admitted us to a club to which every previous generation already belonged— the society of people who know that our heartland and our hearts are still and always vulnerable. So it is up to us to learn how to react wisely to the next real or perceived threat, and the one after that.

# People, Animals, Water, and Salt

## Anderson Ferry, Burlington, Rabbit Hash, Big Bone Lick, and Walton, Kentucky

One of the features of the Ohio River in the Cincinnati area is the deep northward route that it takes after leaving Maysville, Kentucky, until reaching Madison, Indiana. South of the river is an area that has been connected to Cincinnati and its history in a variety of ways despite the broad river dividing the two landmasses. In fact, this is one of the themes of this tour, Ohio River as connector rather than divider. Paralleling the Ohio River for some time and connecting a number of historic sites, this tour reminds the rider of the many forces that have shaped this region's history. One highlight will be our visit to Rabbit Hash, Kentucky, a small river town. It is believed that the town name was chosen after the flood of 1847, when high water drove the rabbits to higher ground, and they became a food staple. But no one knows for sure, because subsequent floods—in 1884, 1913, and 1937—destroyed many of the town's records. The town itself is an object lesson in both the benefits and challenges of riverside living and the difficulty of reconstructing history.

It is also an area that illuminates a couple of broader themes in the region's and nation's history. The first is that the livelihood of humans and animals overlapped in interesting and profound ways. Also, humans have hunted animals for thousands of years relying on their hides, milk, meat for their welfare and sustenance. Second, needs of animals and people are similar in many ways, since humans are an animal. And all animals need water and salt to survive. On this tour, there will be a number of opportunities to consider the Ohio River as conduit and danger for people and animals.

Rabbit Hash General Store

## The Tour

More detailed information on the route is available on the *Bicycling through Paradise* community page. We invite you to leave additional information on route updates, detours, and establishments that will be helpful to future cyclists of this route. Here's a general idea of the route.

There are four segments in this tour, with a total one-way distance of forty-three miles. We will start in Embshoff Woods Park in Delhi, Ohio, and end in Walton, Kentucky. Along the way we will descend, climb up out of the Ohio River Valley, descend into it again and gain a ridge in Walton. None of the climbs are very steep. And the scenery both up on top of the ridge and down in the valley is fairly pastoral. The two significant towns are Burlington and Walton Kentucky, where one can find a good meal and plenty of history. Spending the night on one end or the other is a bit more challenging on this route. One can camp at Big Bone Lick or stay at the Old Hashienda, a furnished apartment, in Rabbit Hash. A new ferry between Rising Sun, Indiana, and Rabbit Hash, Kentucky, makes eating and staying in Rising Sun an option on this tour as well. And for the adventurous, from Rising Sun, one could ride along Route 56 to Aurora, Indiana, where the William Henry Harrison and the Shawnee tour ends.

**Segment 1** goes from Delhi, Ohio, to Burlington, Kentucky (12.5 miles, mostly flat terrain, one big downhill and one big uphill). Embshoff Woods is a Hamilton County Park and requires a day or yearly pass to enter. There are restrooms available at the park and ample parking. This segment includes riding on the Anderson Ferry (bicyclists pay $1 to cross one-way), traveling the perimeter of the Greater Cincinnati Regional Airport (CVG) on KY 20, skirting downtown Hebron, and arriving in quaint downtown Burlington, which contains several restaurants, including the recommended Tousey House Tavern.

**Segment 2** goes from Burlington to Rabbit Hash, Kentucky (11.4 miles, hilly and rolling, mostly downhill). This segment takes us by the Dinsmore Homestead and Middle Creek Park on KY 18, both places for a nice stroll through the woods, and ends at the Rabbit Hash General Store, where one can sit by the river and enjoy not-so-easy-to-find soft drinks and snacks. On the weekend, they sell barbecue as well. There are portable bathrooms at Dinsmore Homestead and Middle Creek and more sophisticated ones in Rabbit Hash next to the General Store.

**Segment 3** goes from Rabbit Hash to Big Bone Lick State Park (9 miles, mostly flat along the river bottom). The museum and outdoor exhibits at Big Bone Lick are definitely worthwhile. There are bathrooms at the museum but no food is available here. The route follows Lower River Rd and then KY 388 to the park.

**Segment 4** goes from Big Bone Lick to Walton (9.8 miles, mostly uphill). We will travel mostly uphill on Beaver Rd/Walton Rd/KY 1292 to Walton Community Park (35 Old Stephenson Mill Road) with restrooms and parking. A short ride from the CCC historical marker via Alta Vista Road takes us to Family's Main Street Café (on Rt. 25, 104 N. Main Street) for breakfast, lunch, or dinner. An optional extension to the Gaines House and Museum, an old tavern and waypoint and the oldest building in Walton, is 1.2 miles north of town and well worth a visit.

Big Bone Lick State Park

## Anderson Ferry

Most of this tour is spent in Kentucky. It was granted statehood in 1792 (eleven years before Ohio) but we start in Delhi at the top of the ridge overlooking the Ohio River Valley on the Ohio side. A steep descent (do not spend too much time thinking about the ride back; you can always walk up) brings the rider to the Anderson Ferry. The Anderson Ferry opened in 1817 but there was likely a ferry in operation prior to this, as it had been a popular crossing point on the Ohio River for millennia.[1]

Geologically and geographically, the location of the Anderson Ferry is significant. The Ohio River is 981 miles long, running from Pittsburgh, Pennsylvania, to Cairo, Illinois. The Anderson Ferry is exactly halfway from Pittsburgh to Cairo. At the time of the Teays River (that came north in the location of the Licking River and then up through what is now the basin of the Mill Creek), much of what is now Cincinnati was underwater in a series of lakes. Where the Anderson Ferry is located was dry land and so was a popular crossing and hunting point for Native Americans. European settlers followed the Native American paths in this location, just as they did elsewhere. Dry Creek enters into the Ohio River on the Kentucky side not too far from the ferry landing as well, adding to the geographical significance of the area.[2]

Before bridges, trains, and automobiles, ferries were an efficient and essential means of crossing the Ohio River. Keep in mind, though, that the Ohio River older ferries operated on was different than the Ohio River today. The modern system of locks and dams has significantly increased the depth of the river. In the early 1800s the river varied significantly from shallow to deeper areas. In the winter and during low water, people could walk across the river in many places. In addition, the Ohio River has slowly gotten wider over time. There used to be multiple ferries just in Boone County, Kentucky, alone (where the Anderson Ferry is located), including one in Rabbit Hash. Across the United States, there are approximately three hundred ferry businesses still operating. Some are small, like the Anderson Ferry; others are very large and haul cars and several hundred people. There are five ferries that still operate on the Ohio River from West Virginia through Ohio and Kentucky.[3]

George Anderson, who founded the ferry company that still operates three ferries today, was born in Maryland in 1765 and died in Constance in 1839. His wife, Sarah Brooks, was from North Carolina. All of the early White settlers to Kentucky came from the original thirteen colonies and sought more land and opportunity in these areas that were opening up in the late 1700s and early 1800s. Burlington, Kentucky, and Boone County had been growing and were important areas of settlement in the emerging West.[4]

Anderson was part of a team that was directed by the Boone County Court in Burlington, Kentucky, to build a trail from Burlington to the mouth of Dry Creek at the ferry crossing. It was one of dozens of ferry bonds issued by Boone County to help transport livestock and goods between Boone County and Indiana and Ohio.[5] Burlington's history is tied to different forms of transportation, beginning with ferries and steamboats on the river, then horse and wagon or buggy, and finally automobiles, on land. While traveling through Burlington, you will see the old courthouse that dates from 1898 and the old Boone County clerk's office as well. The courthouse is still used for other functions.

In 1800 Cincinnati's population was half of Boone County's population, but as Cincinnati grew, the desire to cross the Ohio River and travel from Kentucky to the city increased, boosting the ferry's business. The town of Constance, at the ferry landing site in Kentucky, was thriving in the last half of the nineteenth century and the early twentieth century. It boasted tollhouses to help pay for the road, a post office, wagon makers, blacksmiths, and grocers. All of these are gone now, including the post office, but a cyclist can see an old cemetery and a few remaining houses. Like Rabbit Hash, the flood of 1937 devastated the community of Constance. A rider can imagine what it would have been like to bicycle through this area in the early 1900s, passing by one small town after another, each boasting the necessary amenities for daily life, such as a post office, a blacksmith to make horseshoes and tools, and a grocery at minimum.[6]

In 1801 it cost nine pence to cross for both people and larger livestock. Fees varied depending on the animal, as they continue to vary to this day, now by vehicle size (car, bicycle, etc.).[7] The Andersons owned the ferry until 1841, after which it changed owners more than a dozen times until the end of the Civil War. Then Charles Kottmyer bought the ferry. He had been a stagecoach driver but was bothered by the dust so found ferry operating much less threatening to his health. He operated the first ferry by the name of Boone: *Boone I*. Today, *Boone 7* is still in operation. The newest ferry is *Boone 9*.[8]

Originally, the ferries were flatboats with oars and poles. After that, blindfolded horses operated the ferry, one on each side walked on a treadmill to make the paddlewheels rotate. To turn the ferry around, the horses went in reverse to make the ferry go the opposite way. In 1867 Kottmyer built a steam-powered ferry out of wood. In 1947 the ferries began using diesel electric engines. Ten years before that, the company built its first steel-bottomed ferry. Operations with a keel took place on the same deck as the passengers.[9]

Two hundred years after the Anderson Ferry began, it is still a popular means of crossing the river, partly because of its proximity to the Cincinnati Regional Airport, about three miles away. Anderson Ferry is about ten miles west of downtown Cincinnati and the only way to get across the river between downtown Cincinnati and the 1–275 West bridge. The three ferries take an average of 600 cars across the river every day in about 140 trips.[10] Stop and think about this for a minute, that the most efficient means of transportation we have today—air travel—is supporting a much older means of transportation just a few miles away. This is the wonderful thing about human societies: they boast the integration of and dependence on a wide variety of technologies and tools at any given moment. In fact, in a recent television news piece about the ferry's longtime service, one ferry rider called the experience peaceful, suggesting that the few minutes of relatively serene travel by ferry is much preferred to the noise and congestion of car traffic in nearby downtown Cincinnati.[11] The vocation of ferry operator is also a bit of a throwback to the past, as it requires apprenticeship. It takes three years to become a ferryboat captain, and each boat has a captain and a deckhand. Paul Anderson, who currently owns the ferry company, started working as a deckhand while he was still in school in 1961. He bought the ferry in 1986.[12] As of 2020, the ferry has an all-female crew for the first time in its history.[13]

Ferry operators today no longer need worry about ice as did earlier operators when the weather was colder in the winter. But they still need to worry about flooding. When the Ohio River gets above sixty-two feet of flooding, the ferry has to stop operation because they no longer have access to any landing area. Horses no longer power the ferries nor are they carried across the river as they used to be but the next two stops to be highlighted carry even stronger connections to animals.

## Dinsmore Homestead

Just as intellectuals were trying to make sense of the colossal bones found in the salty springs on the Big Bone Lick River, two children were born, Martha Macomb and James Dinsmore, who would come to live near the Ohio River on an eight-hundred-acre farm in the early 1840s. Biking to Dinsmore in the twenty-first century, it would be easy to underestimate the stature of the estate and the family that built it. Today, rural Boone County is peripheral to the much larger city of Cincinnati to the north, but in the late 1700s and early 1800s, as noted earlier, the area was booming, particularly along the river (which was just a mile from the Homestead). The Dinsmore Homestead website, a volume of poetry by Julia Dinsmore, and a conversation with Homestead curator, Cathy Collopy, provides detailed information about the Dinsmore family.[14]

The Dinsmore estate was in the top 5 percent of landholdings in the county, and they were in the top 1 percent of slaveholding families. As these statistics

Dinsmore Homestead

suggest, the Dinsmores were American elite, highly educated and connected to multiple American presidents and manufacturing magnates. Macomb and Dinsmore came from the East and maintained connections across the growing country. They educated their daughters, hiring tutors for them at home and, as they became teens, sending them to boarding school in Cincinnati. President Theodore Roosevelt called Julia Dinsmore, one of the daughters, "One of the best-informed women in the United States." Julia Dinsmore knew Greek and Latin, was fluent in French, and learned German later in her life.

The Dinsmores came from Louisiana, where James Dinsmore had been running a sugar plantation with a partner prior to his marriage in 1829. In 1831 the couple settled on Bayou Black Plantation in Louisiana with about fifty slaves raising sugarcane and cotton. It was difficult business and he worried about losing his children, three daughters, to yellow fever. When an uncle sent James Dinsmore barrels of wine from Boone County, inviting him to come to Kentucky, he did. Julia Dinsmore was nine years old. The agricultural opportunities were much more diverse here, and Dinsmore raised sheep and goats, grew food crops, had a huge orchard (one thousand peach and apple trees), and made wine. Fifteen slaves, tenants, and wage laborers all worked on the Dinsmore land. Some of the German-born immigrant tenants (who lived in Over-the-Rhine in Cincinnati featured in the *Party* tour) operated a basket factory on the farm. All of these goods made their way to Cincinnati or New

Orleans via the Ohio River. The land route was called "the mud road," and that is probably all you need to know about how useful it was as a transportation corridor. It was far easier to travel the mile to the river and to load goods on the ferry. Like residents of Rabbit Hash, the Dinsmores and others in the area often traveled to Rising Sun, Indiana, for goods and services.

Two of the daughters died as young women, leaving Julia Dinsmore the lone heir after her father's death in 1872. A photograph in the home portrays a good-looking, solidly built woman with dark hair. While Julia Dinsmore was apparently betrothed to a Confederate officer, little is known about his identity or fate. But her poetry leaves little doubt as to the mark he left on her heart:

> *Once when he held my hand, along my wrist*
> *With slow caressing finger tip he traced*
> *A blue vein's current till it interlaced*
> *With other wandering streamlets and he missed*
> *The one he followed, then he laughed and kissed*
> *The azure network, saying – "Let it go.*
> *I own the source from which these rivers flow*
> *And need not cavil at a turn or twist."*
> *How often now the words come back again,*
> *Lightly and fondly said so long ago!*
> *None seek among the poor wrist's tangled skein*
> *The thread he sought, his little lost blue vein,*
> *And though the kiss is cold, the laughter flown,*
> *While the pulse beats, the heart is still his own.*[15]

The challenges that Julia Dinsmore faced, including the premature death of animals on her farm, is recorded in her diary after 1872 as she struggled to carry on the operation after her father's death. For example, on February 24, 1875, she recorded, "Found two new lambs and one old ewe down to die apparently." And at the end of that year, "One of 7 little pigs dead." With the death of her older sister, Isabella, Julia Dinsmore raised her nieces on the farm— Patty and Sally. Her nieces fared better marriage-wise. In the family home are two buck deer heads, trophies presented to these young women by their suitors: deer antlers as a means of expressing affection.[16]

Julia Dinsmore's home was one she and her nieces and grandnieces returned to over and over again, as a sanctuary. Even as Julia struggled to keep the farm surviving in the early 1900s, as agriculture became more mechanized, it continued to provide a bucolic respite for family and friends. It also was the source of inspiration for a tremendous amount of poetry by Julia, including sonnets. In 1910 Theodore Roosevelt wrote to Julia that his wife had put several of her poems in her scrapbook—a book that the Roosevelt family considered the most important in their house.[17] Julia Dinsmore is buried in the graveyard on the hillside above the home. Interestingly, on the way there, one crosses a hiking trail that is covered in buffalo clover, a larger-leaved and-flowered clover than the more typical one, and one that requires the stamping of buffalo feet to flourish. The buffalo clover marks the ancient trail of Buffalo to Big Bone Lick. The homestead can be seen from the road and cyclists are encouraged to take a break or hike (behind the house head uphill on the stone steps).

## Rabbit Hash

Founded in the late 1700s, the small settlement of Rabbit Hash has had a general store in operation since 1831. In 1894 it had a population of about one hundred residents. Today, the store is a destination for cyclists (of the motor and nonmotor kind). With a wide selection of snacks and beverages as well as handmade crafts, such as brooms and pottery, the trip along the Ohio River to the general store is a popular one. In addition, there is a small hostel for lodging, a barbecue that is cranked up on the weekends, and live music. Sitting opposite Rising Sun, Indiana, on the Ohio River, one can easily spend several hours watching the river and barges float slowly by.

How the settlement got its name is not known for sure.[18] The lore is that Rabbit Hash was named from the events after the flood of 1847, when the rabbits were pushed to higher ground and became a staple in the locals' diet in a stew. The post office in Rabbit Hash was once called Carlton and mail was often confused with the Carrollton Post Office further downriver. In order to avoid the confusion, the name was changed in 1879 to the name already in circulation, Rabbit Hash. During this period, the town was much like many other small river towns in Kentucky. But today it has a population of just one.

In addition to being named for an animal, Rabbit Hash has had a dog as its mayor for the last three elections, making national news as a result.

In 1830 some Rabbit Hash farmers at a Grange meeting decided to build a storehouse for their goods as they awaited being loaded onto a ferry. Farmers, taking turns, were responsible for opening the store and loading the ferry. But often on a good farming day, the storehouse was left abandoned and goods never got loaded for the ferry crossing, so in 1831, to remedy the situation, James Alexander Wilson became the store proprietor, and it remained in his family until 1919. The produce store was to become the soul of the Rabbit Hash community, even as the community dwindled by the end of the twentieth century. It doubled as a post office until 1913. The grandson of James Alexander Wilson remarked, "Why, on Saturdays they would all meet down to the store and argue about religion, and then on Sundays, they'd stand outside the church doors and argue politics."[19]

There is limited history available about the settlement because of devastating losses from multiple floods. Storeowners and residents battled every flood, clearing the store of goods and taking them to higher ground, and then returning to clean and restore the building after the flooding ended. The store was totally submerged during the flood of 1939, when the river reached 79.9 feet (normal height is about 25 feet). The only reason that it remained in place was because it is anchored to the ground. Several residences and outbuildings, a creamery, tobacco warehouse, and blacksmith shop were washed away in the flood. The ironworks is now a wine shop and tasting room and a bed-and-breakfast, and the blacksmith shop is an antiques store. The Ohio River giveth and taketh away.

The history of Rabbit Hash is tied to the history of Rising Sun, across the river in Indiana. Before locks and dams, the main channel of the Ohio River was along the Indiana side. On the Kentucky side were long sand bars near the shoreline. Steamboats could not land there, so they landed in Indiana, and ferries carried goods across. In low water, people could walk across from one town to the other. For a hundred years or so, Rabbit Hash residents attended school and church in Rising Sun. Rising Sun residents came to Rabbit Hash as well, but much of the traffic crossed the other way. In 1945 an ice storm destroyed the ferry. Locks and dams constructed to facilitate modern riverboat traffic in the 1960s permanently deepened the Ohio River and made crossing by foot impossible. A new ferry makes crossing to Rising Sun possible again.

## Big Bone Lick

If you had been alive in the late 1700s and early 1800s in the eastern United States or Europe, you likely would have heard of Big Bone Lick. The lives of extinct animals, curious travelers, and intellectuals converged at the salt springs on the Big Bone Lick River, a tributary of the Ohio River. Long before this time, though, during the last Ice Age, huge ice sheets covered much of the North American continent, the southern reaches often being in or around Cincinnati. The last ice was present in the region about twelve thousand years ago and had driven many large mammals over the last eight thousand years away from their typical northern homes south to regions like this area of Kentucky. Some of these animals included the ancient stag-moose, bison antiques, the Columbian mammoth, and the American mastodon. Many of these animals weighed over ten thousand pounds and were over nine feet tall, thus having huge needs for salt and water. These massive animals' weight and activity at the site created a depression that was at least three to four feet below the valley floor. Most likely, animals were hunted at the site, though some likely died of natural causes. As such, there was and remains a treasure trove of bones at the site.

Flooding and silting over time kept some of the bones more accessible than at another site with less erosion and silting. The first large animal bones were collected from the site in 1739, including tusks and a femur.[20] Naturalists discussed the significance of the bones for decades without reaching any concrete conclusions. For example, the only animal they knew of that was still alive with tusks was the elephant, so they assumed it had to be some kind of elephant. In terms of its shape, however, it looked nothing like an elephant tusk. But to suggest that the animal that bore this tusk was no longer alive flew in the face of religious and scientific thought at the time. It would not be until the turn of the nineteenth century that many accepted the notion of extinction. Along the way, people like Thomas Jefferson, Meriwether Lewis, and other intellectuals would become engaged in the scientific discussions about the fossils found. Many of the fossils found their way to Monticello (Jefferson's home in Virginia) and to France, where they were studied and the subject of great debate.[21] Among many other things, Big Bone Lick is a reminder of the profound ways in which those of us alive now think very differently about the world than many, including the highly educated, did several hundred years ago.

The site was also a desirable one for humans, both for its salt as well as for the frequency of animal visits. For Native Americans and early settlers, a salt spring would be even more attractive than it was to the animals that had been visiting it for tens of thousands of years. The earliest mention of salt manufacture is in 1755, in the historically fictive account based on John Ingles's memories of his mother, Mary Ingles (see the *Following the River* tour).[22] Surely, though, Native Americans were boiling the water to obtain the solid salts long before this time. Settlers would have continued to do so because they needed salt both for themselves and their domesticated animals. The salts also were believed to have numerous health benefits, either taken internally or applied externally through bathing. The ecologist Stan Hedeen's account of the site enumerated these benefits of external application: prevention and treatment of tuberculosis, rheumatism, uterine trouble, hemorrhoids, lead poisoning, and boils. External application of the water was believed to cure parasitic skin diseases and wash off chemical pollutants.[23]

The American bison (and other animals) got to Big Bone Lick either on foot alone or by swimming and walking. Hedeen reports four bison roads, each up to fifteen feet wide, leading to the Big Bone Lick. From the north and the west, the animals swam across the river before picking up the land trace that would take them the rest of the way to the spring.[24] Stan Hedeen calls the site "the cradle of American paleontology." It continues to be an active site for researchers at the Cincinnati Museum Center and reveals new discoveries on a regular basis. A new museum at the state park covers much of the history of the area and is worth a visit. And all of this in rural Kentucky.

## Walton

Geographically, Walton sat on the road, "the Lexington Turnpike," between Cincinnati and Georgetown/Lexington (a thirty-four-hour trip) in the late 1700s and 1800s.[25] Before automobiles, Karl Kron cycled from Covington to Lexington, passing through Walton, Kentucky, stating: "In the next hour and a half I covered the nine miles, ending at a wretched little inn at Walton, where I stopped for lunch."[26] It is likely that Kron stopped at the Gaines House, which operated as a stopping point for stagecoaches and other travelers since 1814. Another building in the same location had offered similar services since 1795. The Gaines House was being considered for demolition in 1897, but still exists as an historical site and the oldest home in Walton and will be visited on this tour.[27]

Walton was also home to a Civilian Conservation Corps (CCC) camp between 1935 and 1942. The Camp, called "Bean Ridge," eventually housed up to two hundred men, who traveled to work, returning to the camp at night for supper, recreation, and, in some cases, a chance for some education. The location is now the site of the Walton-Verona Middle and High Schools.[28]

The CCC was one of Franklin Delano Roosevelt's first projects in the New Deal, and the one he was the most excited about.[29] The CCC had camps in all fifty states under the auspices of four different federal agencies. The CCC transformed the nation on a number of levels: it reduced unemployment levels, it transformed the men and their families, and it preserved and protected a wide range of public and private lands for future use and enjoyment. It is a remarkable story with a unique Kentucky angle. In Connie Huddleston's account of Kentucky's CCC, she noted an article in the *Cincinnati Enquirer* in June 1935 extolling the program:

> Most popular of all the New Deal ideas is that of the Civilian Conservation Corps. One reason for this is that it had so few brass ornaments. It is a relief plan but not on an extravagant scale...This plan has saved many a young man from being a tramp...If all other New Deal programs were as good as is the Civilian Conservation Corp the country would have reason to rejoice, for it is a success.[30]

The CCC was born of the multiple problems of infrastructure decline, loss of farmland, need for public works, and high unemployment and poverty rates several years after the Great Depression. There were a quarter million young people under or unemployed in the early 1930s.[31] Many of them had given up hope of finding work and staying with their families and had taken to the roads and railroads and were referred to as "teenage tramps." The young men who enrolled in the CCC gained weight and height after six months, a clear sign of their previous malnourishment. They were transformed by their CCC experience in other ways as well. The experience offered dignity, skills, nutritious and plentiful food, camaraderie, and education. The young men could earn a high school diploma, take college courses, or learn a trade skill. Occasional lectures and a library offered further educational opportunities. They were paid a dollar a day for a total of $30/month. They kept $5 for their own maintenance at the camp and the rest was sent to their families. For most families, the influx of cash was an essential part of their subsistence.[32]

The work of the CCC is most visible at state and national parks, where CCC men worked on infrastructure projects. On other rides in this book, you can see their work at places like the picnic shelter and cement slide in Burnet Woods in Clifton (*Crosstown Missions* tour) and the comfort station in Eden Park near the overlook (*Floodplains and Hilltops* tour), and some of the buildings in Mt. Airy Forest. In fact, there was a Black CCC camp in Mt. Airy Forest, as noted in the *Town and Country* tour. The architectural philosophy that guided much of this construction was minimalist. Buildings were to intrude as little as possible on the setting and they were made well with limited materials (mostly stone and wood) and hand tools.

Soil erosion was a global concern from the 1930s on. In the United States, the Dust Bowl storms across the western United States were a visible sign of devastating loss of soil and fertility. A combination of farming mechanization and drought made the plains particularly vulnerable to erosion. Elsewhere, though, particularly in the East, erosion, both in terms of soil loss and landscape alteration, had been a concern for more than a century. Without proper attention to covering bare fields when not planted or contouring on hillsides, soil and its nutrients are easily washed away in rains or blown away with winds.

President Roosevelt had a personal interest in soil erosion, as his family farm was only half as productive as it had been several decades earlier due to loss of topsoil. Under his leadership, the Soil Erosion Service was created in 1933 and two years later renamed the Soil Conservation Service.[33]

The men at Camp Bean Ridge worked for the Soil Conservation Service (SCS), helping farmers with erosion and crop problems on private land. Men worked on controlling gullies by building dams and fences and planting trees. They also removed rocks from fields and drained marshy areas to create more tillable land. In later years, the SCS taught farmers about terracing, contouring, crop rotation, and the use of fallow field cover crops.[34]

Most of the enrollees at Camp Bean Ridge were from nearby areas, and many were disappointed to be assigned to a local camp rather than a National Park out west.[35] Administrators hoped that men from the region would return home after learning about soil conservation measures for six months and use the techniques on their own farms and encourage others to do the same. The young men who were sent to CCC camps to work with the SCS helped to build this federal agency and to set a tone that still exists to this day about the value of stewarding our soils.[36]

The CCC involved massive coordination between the US Army, the Department of Labor, the Department of Agriculture, and the Department of the Interior. The Department of Labor recruited young men from the neediest families first, using unemployment and welfare rolls. The army set up and organized the camps and the Agriculture and Interior Departments chose and directed the work projects. Soil conservation work took place within a number of government agencies as well.[37] There were also local experienced men who worked with the CCC. These men were often unemployed themselves—foresters, lumbermen, farmers, and masons who lived on or near the land where the projects were taking place. They were hired to supervise groups of eight to twelve men in their work.[38]

The CCC's popularity and long-term success can be measured in the stone and other infrastructure still standing but also in the activities of its veterans, who have formed alumni groups and written accounts of their experiences. Huddleston writes:

Generally, the CCC developed a well-rounded man who worked, played and learned with equal enthusiasm. Listening to oral histories collected by the Kentucky Historical Society and attending reunions of former CCC men, one gains an immediate appreciation for who these men were when they joined the CCC and who they became. Most joined out of necessity—their families desperately needed the twenty-five dollars per month that they would be sending home.[39]

For many men, including Paul French (b. 1916), who was interviewed for an oral history project in Kentucky in the 1980s, the opportunity to work and earn money for his family and to learn a skill was single-handedly responsible for changing his life course. He was assigned to a SCS camp fifteen miles from his home in Elizabethtown, Kentucky. After the working day, he taught himself to type and was able to type up to one hundred words per minute after his yearlong stint. He notes that "he was might proud of himself." He took a civil service job with the Social Security Administration after leaving another CCC camp in Kentucky and had a lifelong career with them. He also said that one of his friends used the mapping skills required for completing work on the farms and became a professional draftsman after the CCC.[40]

In Walton, Kentucky, was one of more than one thousand CCC camps full of enthusiastic workers in one of the most impressive and successful massive federal peacetime undertakings of the twentieth century. A recruiting brochure for the CCC in Ohio concluded with: "Thus, in summing up, it may be said that the Civilian Conservation Corps is a molder of men, offering a program which is good for Mother Nature and in which Mother Nature is good to men."[41] We wonder if such a massive project could be undertaken successfully today; it might be we need it as much now as then.

## CHAPTER 16

Scan to visit the
"Schoolhouses
and Scholars"
route

# SCHOOLHOUSES AND SCHOLARS

## Cozaddale, Edenton, Blanchester, Harveysburg, and Waynesville

Along the back roads and small towns northeast of Cincinnati, there are historic sites that reveal the development of public education. Especially interesting is the Harveysburg Free School, built in 1831, and the earliest known schoolhouse for Black children in Ohio. The buildings that we will see hint at two yet-unresolved questions: what kind of education do we want public schools to provide, and how do we want to pay for that?

### The Tour

More detailed information on this route is available on the *Bicycling through Paradise* community page. We invite you to leave additional information on

Harveysburg Free School

route updates, detours, and establishments that will be helpful to future cyclists of this route. Here is the general idea.

Our tour will start in Loveland, Ohio, and head east and then north through small towns connected by rural roads. Terrain is generally flat to rolling. Most of the roads are fairly quiet, but there are some traffic-y stretches where extra caution is required. The tour ends in Waynesville, Ohio.

The tour is composed of five segments. Total one-way distance is over fifty-six miles, but each segment is fun to ride independently. Each segment begins and ends in places where you can find parking, food, and bathrooms. Overnight accommodations are available at Waynesville for anyone planning a weekend trip.

**Segment 1** goes from Loveland to Goshen (9.4 miles, rolling to hilly). We'll start in Loveland, where there is ample parking (because it's also an access point for the Little Miami Scenic Trail). We'll head west on E. Loveland Avenue/O'Bannonville Road and then take Cozaddale-Murdock Road south until we reach Cozaddale, home to the Cozaddale General Store, and the birthplace of the painter and art educator Robert Henri. From there, we'll head south on Cozaddale Road, Stumpy Lane, and Dallasburg Road. The segment ends in Goshen, where there are fast-food places and a convenience store.

**Segment 2** goes from Goshen to Blanchester (15.6 miles, flat to rolling). We'll head southwest on Goshen Road, passing the Kathryn Stagge-Marr Park. We'll take Woodville Pike east to Highway 727, riding along the edge of Stonelick State Park, until we reach Edenton, a beautiful historic town with several buildings dating to the mid-nineteenth century. We'll pass the 1917 Edenton Public School (now private property), and then we'll take a series of back roads east, running generally parallel to Highway 133. We'll pass the Woodville Cemetery, burial place of the schoolteacher Artemus C. Morrow, who in 1851 was murdered in his schoolhouse by one of his students. The segment ends at Blanchester, where there is a convenience store and a McDonald's.

**Segment 3** goes from Blanchester to Clarksville (9.6 miles, rolling terrain). We'll head northeast on Main Street. We'll wind our way up Penquite/Watkins-Bowman Road, Irwin Road, Edwardsville Road, and Pansy Road until we reach Clarksville, a cute historic town where there's a convenience store.

**Segment 4** goes from Clarksville to Harveysburg (11.3 miles, flat to rolling). Don't try this segment on any day when the Ohio Renaissance Festival is in operation, because there will be too much traffic. Any other day, this is an especially beautiful and quiet, rural ride. We'll head north on Spring Hill Road, east on McGwinn Road and Hiatt Road, then north again on Hadley Road. We'll cross over I-71 on Doster Road and then take Branstrator Road, Brooks-Carroll Road, and Harveysburg Road. At Harveysburg we will see the 1831 Harveysburg Free School. We'll also pass the abandoned Massie Township School. Harveysburg has a convenience store.

**Segment 5** goes from Harveysburg to Waynesville (11.0 miles, flat to rolling). Like the previous segment, don't ride this on any day when the Ohio Renaissance Festival is in operation, because there will be too much traffic. Any other time, this is a nice ride. We'll head south and then west on Oregonia Road, skirting the edge of Caesar's Creek State Park. We'll visit the Caesar Creek Pioneer Village, where there are more than a dozen historic buildings, including a log schoolhouse. We'll take North Clarksville Road, crossing over the dam that forms Caesar Creek Lake, and passing the Caesar Creek Visitor's Center. We'll continue on North Clarksville Road into Corwin, where we'll cross the Little Miami Scenic Trail. Then we'll head into Waynesville to visit the Museum at the Friends Home, built in 1905 as housing for elderly Quakers and unmarried schoolteachers. Waynesville is also a stop on the *Visions and Dreams* tour, and it has multiple options for dining and lodging. Try the fried chicken on the porch of the Hammel House.

## Public Lands, Public Schools

In 1785 the Continental Congress established a system for surveying western lands, including the area that would become the state of Ohio. The basic unit of the survey was the township—a square, six miles on each side, containing thirty-six square miles. Each township was gridded into thirty-six sections, each one square mile. (Rivers and streams were also used as township boundaries, so not every township was exactly square, but that was the general idea.)

Once an area had been surveyed, the land would become available for purchase by settlers. The proceeds from each sale would go into the federal treasury, with an exception: within each township, one section was designated as the school section. When land was leased or sold inside the one-square-mile school section, the proceeds were earmarked to pay for common schools—what we would call elementary schools—within that township. This was the beginning of public education funding in Ohio, eighteen years before Ohio was granted statehood.[1]

Because land was still cheap, however, school-section funding was badly insufficient. Parents had to pay tuition, or barter, for their children to attend school. Parents also needed their children to help with farm chores, so most schools were open just a few months each year.

In 1825 the Ohio legislature passed a statewide property tax to fund common schools.[2] The 1825 law also required the trustees of each township to divide the township into school districts, and it provided for the annual election of school directors in each district.[3] Districts were kept small enough so all children could walk to school.[4]

## The One-Room Schoolhouse

A typical early schoolhouse was built of logs, with sections cut out to admit light, with the openings covered with oiled paper in lieu of windows. There were benches of hewn timber. Until writing paper became widely available, the children wrote on slates.[5] Instruction was rudimentary.

Because children came and went depending on their farm schedules, there was only a loose correlation between age and educational attainment, and no effort was made to separate children into grades. William Henry Venable (who was born in 1836 and became a schoolteacher outside Waynesville) later said that in the early days, "There were as many classes in a subject as there were students studying it."[6]

Eventually, school reformers began to argue that different classes of students should be separated by age. Cincinnati introduced graded schools in 1840;[7] Akron and Cleveland in 1846. But in rural areas, one-room schoolhouses remained the norm for decades to come.[8]

So, in a one-room schoolhouse, everyone was lumped together. Everyone, that is, who was White. In 1829 the Ohio legislature passed a law specifically excluding Black children from public schools created for White children.[9]

## School Discipline and the Case of Artemus Morrow

School discipline was harsh and direct. Flogging—"the ancient system of imparting knowledge," as one schoolmaster later put it[10]—was used for both correction and motivation. Venable described the typical schoolmaster standing in front of his class "with the ferule in one hand and Dillworth's Spelling Book in the other, like the genius of education holding up the emblems of power and knowledge."[11]

Students occasionally got even with a despotic schoolmaster, by barring him out of the schoolhouse, or by ducking him in a pond.[12] In his book *Democracy's Schools*, Johann M. Neem tells the story of Warren Burton, a student in an early Massachusetts school. Burton recalled a day one winter when a schoolmaster struck a child on the head with a ruler hard enough to draw blood. The larger students rose up, took hold of the schoolmaster, carried him outside, and threw him down an ice-encrusted hillside. "Down, down he went," Burton recalled, "until he fairly came to the climax, or rather anti-climax, of his pedagogical career."[13]

Usually, these student mutinies had a playful quality. But not always. In 1851 a teacher named Artemus Morrow was holding class in his schoolhouse near Woodville, Ohio, two miles east of Edenton. He had "undertaken to correct" a twelve-year-old boy whose last name was Dale. The boy's elder brother, John Dale, age twenty and also a student, objected, and started to fight with the teacher.

The fight became bad enough that most of the students ran out of the school. With difficulty, Artemus Morrow pinned John Dale to the floor. Morrow assumed that the fight was over, and he went to the window to call the students back. At this point, Dale picked up a billet of stove wood, came up from behind, and struck Morrow three times on the head. Morrow lingered in a delirious state for hours before dying at eight o'clock that evening.[14]

The next day, when the sheriff visited the Dale residence, John Dale was gone. "He was a big strong boy," said Dale's father, "and he's gone to the land of milk and honey." By which the father seems to have meant California.[15]

Artemus Morrow's tombstone is small, containing only his name and his dates of birth and death. It's in the back part of the Woodville Cemetery, on the west side of Washington Street, near Lucas Road.

## Elizabeth Harvey and the Harveysburg Free School

With this background, it's possible to see how remarkable the Harveysburg Free School really was. The school opened in 1831 and was devoted to the education of Black children. The schoolhouse was a good, frame building with plenty of light and ventilation.

The school's founder was Elizabeth Burgess Harvey, a devoted Quaker who was the wife of Dr. Jesse Harvey (a cousin to William Harvey, who had laid out the village). In his 1939 book, *Ohio Builds a Nation*, Samuel Stille wrote of Elizabeth Burgess Harvey, "She was the first woman to devote her life to the advancement and education of the Negro race. Her name should be entered on the roll of honor of those noble people who gave their lives to a great cause."[16]

Tradition says that in addition to black children, the school also educated Native American children. This may be true. There had been a four-acre Shawnee camp outside Harveysburg as late as 1812–14. And note that Elizabeth Harvey and her husband were closely allied with the Quaker mission to the Native Americans at Wapakoneta: a mission that treated Native Americans with kindness and did not try to convert them to Christianity.[17]

Much of the area around Harveysburg and Waynesville had been settled by Quakers, who as a group were deeply devoted to nonviolence. Quaker schoolteachers did occasionally use corporal punishment, but the practice was viewed with suspicion, and as early as 1780 a leading Quaker school in England had decided that the rod could be used only after consultation with another teacher, and only "with due caution, not exceeding three strokes, to be done by one of the masters not offended."[18]

Within the Quaker community, Elizabeth and Jesse Harvey were regarded as moderates. They wanted to see African Americans treated well, but they did not insist on immediate the abolition of slavery, and they accepted, for the moment, that Ohio law required schools to be segregated.[19]

We don't know the names of the earliest students at the Harveysburg Free School. We do know that when the school had been in operation for several years, a slaveholder named Steven Wall visited from North Carolina, bringing with him an eleven-year-old mixed-race boy named Orindatus Simon Bolivar Wall, to be enrolled in the school. Over the next few years, Wall brought five more enslaved children to Harveysburg—Caroline, Benjamin, Sarah, Napoleon, and John.[20]

On his plantation in North Carolina, Wall held more than a hundred enslaved persons, and his reason for wanting to educate just these six was simple: they were his children. Wall never married, but he is known to have forced his sexual attentions on at least three enslaved women—Priscilla, Jane, and Rhody. Priscilla is reported to have said later that Wall "should have been burned at the stake a long time ago."[21]

Elizabeth Harvey pleaded with Wall to emancipate all of the enslaved people on his plantation. Wall promised that he would. But he appears to have reneged on this promise.[22]

In the late 1830s, just as Wall's children were beginning to arrive in Harveysburg, Jesse Harvey decided to create a new high school, called the Harveysburg Academy, to provide instruction beyond the common-school level. He invested substantial money of his own in this venture.

Jesse Harvey announced that Black children would be permitted to attend the new high school but would be kept in separate classes. In this way, he managed to offend nearly everyone in Harveysburg. The radical reformers thought that the school should be fully integrated, while everyone else was offended that the new school would accept African Americans under any circumstances.

This partly-integrated private academy seems to have lasted until 1852. A successor private academy was later rolled over into the public high school system. (On Main Street in Harveysburg is the abandoned Massie Township School.[23] The front part is Art Deco, but the rear was built in 1891, and was a successor to the academy founded by Jesse Harvey.)

Segregated education was highly discriminatory, but it was better than no education at all. By 1850, more than a quarter of Ohio's Black children between the ages of six and twenty were attending school. Then in 1853, a new Ohio law required school boards to establish one or more separate schools for Black children if there were more than thirty of them in the district.[24]

The greatest legacy of the Harveysburg Free School was the career of its most prominent alumnus, Orindatus S. B. Wall—the child of Steven Wall and the enslaved woman Priscilla. Orindatus S. B. Wall attended school in Harveysburg for several years. He later studied at Oberlin College, where he became part of a group called the Oberlin Rescuers, assisting a fugitive slave named John Price (and possibly others).

During the Civil War, Orindatus S. B. Wall became the first commissioned Black captain in the US Army. He was a successful recruiter of African Americans and organized the 127th Ohio Volunteer Infantry. After the war, he became an attorney, and he also worked as a quartermaster in the Freedmen's Bureau, which assisted emancipated slaves. Orindatus S. B. Wall died in Washington, DC, in 1891, and is buried in Arlington National Cemetery.[25]

## High Schools and the Mission of Education

In the nineteenth century, there was a general consensus about the proper curriculum of common schools: reading, writing, and arithmetic. Further education was available, of course, at academies and colleges, but these were tuition-based. By mid-century, however, some people began to feel that education beyond the common school level should be accessible to everyone.

The first tuition-free public high school in Ohio was established in Cleveland in 1846. Akron passed a law requiring high schools in 1847. The Ohio School Law of 1849 provided statewide funding for high schools, but local school boards were not required to create high schools unless they felt that there was sufficient demand.

The idea of public funding for high schools met widespread resistance. Many people felt that the liberal arts courses offered in high schools—literature, history, natural science, and ancient and modern languages—were disconnected from everyday experience. High schools were also seen as a giveaway to the rich, because having a son or daughter in high school meant that you were wealthy enough not to need their labor.[26] Charles Smart, Ohio's state school superintendent in the 1870s, called the high school a "palace of extravagance."[27]

Advocates of high schools insisted that a truly democratic society could be attained only if all students had access to an educational system that promoted culture, critical thinking, and the use of imagination. To this end, they argued, it would be necessary to have professional expertise in decision-making and statewide standards for school administration.

Opponents of high schools, however, also claimed the mantle of democracy. A democratic system, they said, should provide students only with the knowledge and skills required to get good jobs and become patriotic citizens. Anything more was elitist and should not be taxpayer funded. Furthermore, they believed, a democratic school system had to be responsible to local parents, with all decisions made at the level of the local school board, and without state interference.[28]

The historian Johann N. Neem points out that high schools remained on the margins of American education for decades. By 1890, only 6.7% of fourteen-to seventeen-year-olds nationally were enrolled.[29]

## The Twentieth Century

At the time of Ohio's centennial in 1903, the education picture was mixed. Large school districts had graded schools, but some rural areas still had one-room schoolhouses. Teacher training was spotty.[30] State law no longer allowed districts to maintain racially segregated schools, but in practice, many schools were still segregated, and would remain so for many years.[31] And there was still no law requiring children to attend school.

Finally, in 1921 the Bing Act required children between the ages of six and eighteen to attend school. An exception was that a child who was sixteen years old and had completed the seventh grade could quit school to work as a farmer.[32]

A typical schoolhouse from this era is the Edenton Rural School, built in 1917, and still standing (though currently abandoned). The building is small

Edenton Rural School

by today's standards. Tom Irons went to elementary school there in the early 1950s, and he later wrote an article about his experiences in an article for the *Clermont Sun.*

Irons recalled that corporal punishment was still common at the Edenton Rural School in the 1950s, and that the school taught eight grades but only had four schoolrooms, so there were still two grades to a room. (He also recalled that one icy winter, he got his tongue stuck to the flagpole, just like Flick in the film *A Christmas Story.*) Mostly, Irons had fond memories of the school. "It may have held some dangers," he writes, "but it also offered the lessons for youngsters to learn how to flap their small growing wings in the airfoil of this thing we call life."[33]

## School Funding and Equal Opportunity

School buildings have changed over the years, but questions remain about whether the facilities are good enough, and about whether all children have equal access to good schools. Responding to these concerns, Ohio has repeatedly changed its school funding formula. Beginning in 1853, the state collected a uniform property tax across the state, which it then redistributed to each school district based on the number of students enrolled. During the Great

Depression, when many people could not pay their property taxes, the state switched to a sales tax, but the state later switched back to using property taxes for school funding.[34]

In 1975 the Ohio Lottery was created, and the income was earmarked for the schools. But at the same time, some of the property tax income previously allocated to schools was diverted to the general fund. For the schools, it was a wash—dollars in, dollars out.

Today, Ohio public schools receive some money from federal and state sources (including from the lottery, and, now, casinos). But in each school district, most of the funding comes from property taxes collected in that district. This means that wealthy districts have good schools, while poor districts tend to have inadequate schools.[35] And because income and race are still correlated, the school funding formula shortchanges minority children.

Recent fights have focused on the issue of charter schools, which are privately run but receive government money. Many educators feel that by drawing away the better students, and some of the funding, from public schools, charter schools weaken the public education system.[36] It's still true, however, that many students are better off at a charter school. Debate continues, because policies that benefit a particular school, or a particular type of school, may not always benefit all students in a district.

## Robert Henri and the Value of Self-Education

Some of the best observers of American education have come from outside the mainstream of public school teachers and administrators. Robert Henri is known today as an American impressionist painter, and one of the finest artists that the United States has ever produced. But he was also an influential art educator who wrote and taught widely. And he has an interesting personal history.

Robert Henri was born Robert Henry Cozad in 1865, in the village that is now called Cozaddale, Ohio. He was the son of the town's founder, John Jackson Cozad, a real estate developer and professional gambler. John J. Cozad married Theresa Gatewood in 1857, and they moved to Cincinnati in 1865. John J. Cozad decided to establish a manufacturing town outside Cincinnati, hoping to attract Union Army veterans. He began purchasing land in 1867, and the town was named Cozaddale in 1871.[37]

In 1876 young Robert Henry Cozad wrote in his diary, "I am eleven years old, I leave my ma tomorrow to go alone for the first time to school in Cincinnati." His mother had enrolled him in the Chickering Institute, a college-preparatory academy in downtown Cincinnati.[38]

By this time, however, Robert's father, John J. Cozad, had realized that Cozaddale was not working out, and he was buying land out west, at what would become Cozad, Nebraska. For several years, Robert Henry Cozad spent his school terms in Cincinnati and his summers in Nebraska.

Everything changed in 1882, when Robert was seventeen. In Cozad, Nebraska, John J. Cozad went into a store, where he got into a business dispute with a man named Alfred Pearson. Pearson pushed Cozad, who fell against a pile of boxes. As Cozad fell, he pulled a small pistol out of his boot and fired. Pearson dropped to the floor with a bullet hole in his forehead.

To escape law enforcement, the Cozad family moved away and adopted new identities. Seventeen-year-old Robert Henry Cozad became Robert Henri. He spent some time at a boarding school in New York and then joined his parents in Atlantic City. In his letters to other family members during this period, Robert avoided mentioning specific places or dates, and he mailed his letters on trains to avoid an Atlantic City postmark.

In 1886, when Robert Henri was twenty-one, he traveled to Philadelphia and enrolled in the Pennsylvania Academy of Fine Arts to study painting. Here, he showed remarkable talent, and he found his calling. Henri's talent and hard work took him to Paris and Venice.[39] He returned to the United States and taught painting in New York City, where he developed a passionate following of students.[40] "Art," he later wrote, "when really understood is the province of every human being. It is simply a question of doing things, anything, well. It is not an outside, extra thing."[41]

A collection of Robert Henri's writings on art education was eventually published under the title *The Art Spirit*. Henri writes, "Let a student enter the school with this advice. No matter how good the school is, his education is in his own hands. All education must be self-education."[42]

Henri is discussing art schools. But his comments have wider applicability, and it's easy to be reminded of some current debates when he writes:

> The school is a thing of the period. It has the faults and the virtues of the period. It either uses the student for its own success, or the self-educating student uses it for his success. This is generally true of all schools and students of our time.[43]

The 230-year history of education in Ohio is a story of partial success and partial failure. Today, Ohio continues to (partly) fail in its obligation to provide equal educational opportunity to all students, across the lines of income and race. At the same time, as Robert Henri observes, "All education must be self-education." As students begin to mature and have more autonomy, each student must gradually assume the responsibility to seek out, and make the most of, the best educational opportunities that society is willing to provide.

# CROSSTOWN MISSIONS

## Xavier University, University of Cincinnati, and Hebrew Union College

Cincinnati is home to more than a dozen colleges and universities that provide cultural, athletic, and educational opportunities. Three of them are located within a few miles of each other, making for a shorter tour. Xavier University, the University of Cincinnati, and Hebrew Union College are distinct educational institutions. A liberal rabbi, a rabble-rouser turned priest, and an early vision of a need for medical and hands-on training have been influential in the trajectories of these three institutions. That they are products of their times and places sometimes makes for interesting histories.

It would be straightforward and probably even expected to describe the educational value of the three institutions from an historical standpoint, but while the history is important, the missions (sometimes stated, sometimes evolving, sometimes subtle) of these institutions are the glue that bind students to their teachers, teachers to their students, and all to the institution that becomes an important part of their life for several years, if not decades. But historic visions and missions only remain salient by active embrace and adaptation by those responsible for imparting them as the years go by.

### The Tour

More detailed information on the route is available on the *Bicycling through Paradise* community page. We invite you to leave additional information on route updates, detours, and establishments that will be helpful to future cyclists of this route. Here's a general idea of the route.

This tour is 9.7 miles each way, with rolling terrain. Like the Path Dependency tour, this tour starts and ends in the Clifton neighborhood, this time in Burnet Woods by the Nature Center. When the Nature Center is open, there are bathrooms and drinking water inside. Parking is available along Brookline Avenue. Burnet Woods has hiking trails, a lake, and a planetarium. Nearby on Ludlow Avenue are a number of restaurants and shops.

This tour passes the Cincinnati Zoo (the second oldest zoo in the country, and one with an international reputation for the captive breeding of rare animals) and takes in several sites at Xavier University, including Bellarmine Chapel and the Center for Mission and Identity that features the artist Holly Schapker's depictions of the life of St. Ignatius, founder of the Society of Jesus. We then return to Clifton via the same route to cycle through two areas of the University of Cincinnati: the medical campus and West Campus, noting a number of signature buildings by world-class architects and its distinctive topography. Hebrew Union College is the last stop and has a public museum open limited weekday hours and a clock tower with Hebraic numbers.

## Overview

Xavier, a Jesuit, Catholic university, is a medium-sized institution with a five-hundred-year-old educational tradition that guides its holistic, religious, and ethical approach to higher education. It is located between the communities of Evanston, Norwood, and North Avondale. It offers a broad liberal arts curriculum to all of its students and has a Montessori education training program.

The University of Cincinnati is a public university with a number of highly regarded programs, including a Conservatory of Music, a design and architecture school, and medical research and teaching facilities. It has award-winning campus infrastructure dedicated to critical thinking and open access. The cooperative model of education pioneered by the University of Cincinnati was developed to meet the needs of Cincinnati metal and tool industry bosses in the first years of the 1900s. The university provided them with well-trained workers in the rapidly growing industries, and, according to one scholar, freed employers from union control. Students would work for six months and attend classes for six months in a rotating basis for several

Bellarmine Chapel, Xavier University

years. The university, known as the birthplace of co-op education continues to be a leader in the field, broadening from its early efforts with engineering students to a campus wide endeavor in over 50 disciplines. Through careful analysis and discussion of its origins, the university has begun make changes that sensitively and accurately depict the involvement of economic institution of slavery during its early years.

Hebrew Union College, like the University of Cincinnati, is located in Clifton. Hebrew Union College is the intellectual heart of the Reform movement in Judaism. The school educates rabbis, Jewish teachers, pastoral counselors, and scholars. The Cincinnati campus has one of the world's largest Jewish libraries, the Jacob Rader Marcus Center of the American Jewish Archives, and a large museum—academic resources that are at the heart of the school's educational work. Hebrew Union College stands out among the three Cincinnati institutions because it is the oldest continuously existing institution of higher Jewish learning in the Americas, founded in 1875. Today it also has campuses in New York, Los Angeles, and Jerusalem—all of which have much larger Jewish populations than Cincinnati. Still, it is a point of pride and history that this school remains firmly rooted in the city of its origins.

## St. Ignatius's Vision: Xavier University

St. Ignatius of Loyola, Spain, founded the order of the Society of Jesus in 1540. Within twenty-five years, there were one thousand members of the society and thirty-five schools. Born in Spain to a wealthy family, Ignatius became accustomed to a life of pleasure. As a young man, he became a soldier. While bravely defending his small town, he was wounded and, while convalescing, read about the lives of the saints. Their dedication to others and the world around them was in sharp contrast to the rather hedonistic life St. Ignatius had led to that point. He noted that his previous ways and thoughts tended to leave him dissatisfied, but his spiritual dreams and thoughts left him far more satisfied. He began a pilgrimage to Jerusalem and, along the way, gave up his sword and dagger and most of his belongings.[1]

St. Ignatius sought a spiritual path, and continued to pay attention to how he felt about his own experiences and thoughts. He came to think of the strongest ones in two ways, as contentment (or consolation) or dissatisfaction (desolation). He had an epiphany outside Manresa, Spain, where he sat by the River Cardoner and realized that he could not control his relationship with God. He slowly attracted companions, including an "unnamed Manresa woman" who provided financial support. In his thirties, St. Ignatius went back to school, eventually earning a master's degree from the University of Paris.[2]

At the heart of his personal experience, and thus vision for the order, was a spiritual journey between an individual and God. The Spiritual Exercises, a daily set of queries about one's actions and experiences, invest each person with the capacity to get in touch with their deepest desires, as means of learning about God's love and will in their lives. This personal transformation can be a guide to an individual's capacity to be in service and solidarity with others, particularly the less well-off in society. The Spiritual Exercises are accessible to individuals from a wide variety of faith traditions and even those without a religious background may find them transformative. St. Ignatius shared these exercises with some of his peers at the University of Paris, one among them was Francis Xavier. The group called themselves "Friends in the Lord." This group became the foundation of the religious order.[3]

Most students and many faculty and staff at Jesuit institutions, like Xavier, have not necessarily undergone the Spiritual Exercises, even though they might know the story of St. Ignatius and know about the Spiritual Exercises. What they do know, though, is that the Jesuits are open to people of a wide variety of faith backgrounds and committed to intellectual inquiry. Of all the Catholic orders, Jesuits are known for their educational projects worldwide. These educational institutions have a particular spiritual and philosophical foundation that differentiates them from most other educational institutions, secular or religious. First, Jesuit institutions build on a much older, longer-standing tradition of humanistic education that arose in the ancient world. This pattern of education, emphasizing rhetoric and persuasion, literature, and history, was eclipsed in the medieval world by the university. Universities aimed to teach technical skills for a life of vocation. Jesuits' study of humanity sought to prepare students for a meaningful and constructive life, as much avocation as vocation.[4] Even though the Jesuits were deeply invested in Catholicism and individual spiritual journeys, much of the reading they did early on in their schools focused on secular texts interested in civic good. This impulse for engagement is another characteristic of Jesuit schools. There are now more than 180 Jesuit institutions of higher education worldwide (a third in India alone) and double that number of high schools.[5]

Xavier offers a large core curriculum to all students, no matter their major, that focuses on ethics, religion, and society. The heritage of humanistic education, civic good, or community engagement, and attention to the whole person are essential parts of the Xavier (and Jesuit) educational model. One can find this mission exhibited in a wide variety of ways on Xavier's campus. You will see two of those ways on this tour. The first is available during regular business hours: the paintings of Holly Schapker, Xavier graduate. The series that she painted and that is now on display in the Center for Mission and Identity is titled *Adsum* (Latin for "Here I am"). They include depictions of many stages on St. Ignatius' journey toward God.[6]

The second stop is Bellarmine Chapel, home to a Catholic parish and to Catholic students on campus. The 1962 building is simple and modern in its design. Cyclists who are so inclined can dismount and enter the building and sit quietly to experience the peace and spirit of the space, particularly in light of the institution's mission.

## The Cincinnati Zoo

The Zoological Society of Cincinnati opened in 1875, becoming the second oldest zoo in the United States. The zoo has distinguished itself internationally through its breeding and protection of endangered animals, starting with trumpeter swans almost 150 years ago, to western lowland gorillas in the 1970s, and highly endangered Sumatran rhinos just a few years ago.[7] It also has a long track record of promoting comprehensive sustainable practices, such as large-scale solar arrays, green buildings, and storm-water management. The zoo has its own farm, where it grows food for the animals to reduce the amount of processed foods in the animals' diet.[8]

## Space, Place, and Architecture: University of Cincinnati

In 1991 the University of Cincinnati's (UC) master plan called for a Signature Architect program to reshape the campus to make it a more attractive place to work and study, and to raise design awareness in Cincinnati. In 2012 the University of Cincinnati had four buildings on the list of "50 Most Amazing Examples of College Architecture," more than any other school in the country.[9] A 2005 review article in *Places* about the campus' architectural achievements noted that "Cincinnati has emerged as a standard-setting case study in contemporary academic planning, which increasingly integrates intellectual resources with other strategic priorities."[10] A 2015 *New York Times* picture story about University of Cincinnati's star-power architecture captures some of the beauty, expense and originality of the campus' infrastructure. One example is the Albert H. Vontz Center for Molecular Studies. Home to neurological scientists and cancer researchers, it was designed by Frank Gehry. Known for his irregular forms, Gehry's best-known building is the Guggenheim Museum in Bilboa, Spain. The Vontz Center sits on Martin Luther King Drive and is the front door to the UC medical campus. The building is set off by distinctive, mounded green space. The tour will take you by the CARE/Crawley Building, which added 240,000 square feet of research facilities to the medical campus and connects to an older research building through light-filled atriums and color-coded areas.[11] Park your bike and walk up the steps and into the building and explore the juxtaposition of new and old architecture.

Other notable buildings include the Richard E. Lindner Center (a kidney-shaped building sitting behind the Schott Stadium) and the Recreation Center. The Recreation Center, designed by the 2005 Pritzker Prize–winner Thom Mayne, sits behind the Lindner Center and Nippert Stadium on UC's Main Street. The Recreation Center is also an unusual shape due to space limitations. Inside, you will find a climbing wall, lazy river, restaurants, and a convenience store if you need something to eat or drink. As you pass to the right of Nippert Stadium, Tangeman University Center is on the left, designed by the same firm that overhauled the Guggenheim in New York. Inside are restaurants as well. Finally, as you exit campus and travel toward Hebrew Union College on Martin Luther King Drive, you will pass by the blocky, pastel-colored Aronoff Center, which houses the College of Design, Architecture, Art and Planning designed by Peter Eisenman. Inside, hallways and corridors are maze-like rather than linear, making navigating the interior space challenging, if not exciting, at first.[12]

For those who work and study at the University of Cincinnati, the glitzy architecture is part of a much deeper vision and mission that has two significant elements. The first is a commitment to democracy in the sense of making

CARE/Crawley Facility, University of Cincinnati

sure that the university is open and accessible to all comers, both students and the general public. The second is to communicate an intensive sense of space and place.[13]

Let's take this one up first. The natural environment and the built environment upon which it sits are actively incorporated into the education offered at this public school. The university is located in a relatively dense urban area and thus faces significant restrictions in terms of renovation and building. Returning to some of the signature buildings, for example, the Vontz Center for Molecular Studies sits in a natural depression and the mounds in front of it suggest the undulating nature of the terrain of the university campus. There are mounds at many of the vehicular entrance points to campus, reminding visitors and students alike of the terrain immediately around them but also in the greater Cincinnati region. These entrances are also green and inviting, welcoming visitors and the public (part of the first element of the vision). Similarly, the stadium sits in a natural depression as well. The Aronoff Center can be a bewildering maze to a onetime visitor, but for the students who spend years studying there, it becomes a home—a quirky home with inviting nooks and passageways and ever-changing light, a reminder of the power of design to shape the human experience.[14]

In a breathtaking number of ways, the university engages with the community around it, sharing expertise, inviting ideas for research and co-op projects of students, and trying to ensure that the university is a citizen of its region. As the first university to offer a cooperative educational model to university students in 1906, it has a long history of engagement with the community and offering experiential education. Cooperative engineering programs are very popular across the country now but owe their existence to the combination of professor Henry Schneider's vision for combining theoretical and practical experience, industry leaders' willingness to give college students a chance, and the University president's willingness to take a risk. He was so uncertain about the scheme that President Charles Dabney only gave Schneider a year to prove success. Fortunately, he did.[15] More about the industry side of cooperative education in the *Industry and Redevelopment* tour.

Nippert Stadium University of Cincinnati

Moving from space and place to democracy, Nippert Stadium also exemplifies the university's commitment to democracy; it is the only publicly accessible university stadium in the country. The skyboxes, normally the exclusive purview of those who rent them, are available for university use at times other than football games, reinforcing the educational mission and accessibility of the institution. The Vocal Arts Center, overlooking the stadium, is a 150-year-old, lovely acoustic space, and has hosted world-class opera singers. But one can also find opera singers practicing at the southeast corner of the stadium because the acoustics are excellent. McMicken Circle, off of Clifton Avenue, is the historic gateway to the campus, but there is no gate, no booth, no barrier to entry.[16]

## American Judaism: Hebrew Union College

Isaac Mayer Wise founded Hebrew Union College (HUC) in 1875. Wise was born on the Bohemian-Saxon-Bavarian frontier in 1819. At age twenty-seven, he left for the United States, seeking religious freedom, wanting to be the equal of Catholics and Protestants. He fell in love with the United States even before arriving and believed that Judaism was a religion that would flourish on US soil. He was convinced that the United States would embrace Judaism in a way that Jewish communities in other parts of the world would never

243

experience. Wise, like the vast majority of his coreligionists in nineteenth-century America, believed that their adopted nation offered them a genuine opportunity to live fully as Americans and Jews. Evidence of Wise's conviction about American Jewish identity can be seen in the Plum Street Temple (featured on the *Holy City* tour). There in front of the Holy Ark (wherein the Torah scrolls are kept) at the front of the temple are high-backed chairs with five-pointed stars, like those on the American flag. Today a flag sits to the left, for those in the pews, in the front of the synagogue.[17]

Despite his initial enthusiasm for the relative freedoms that the United States offered, Wise encountered numerous obstacles. The small Jewish enclaves he encountered in the United States upon his arrival in 1846 were not well integrated into their broader communities or with each other. Shortly after immigrating to the United States, Wise accepted a pulpit in Albany, New York, where he remained until 1854, when he was invited to become the rabbi of Cincinnati's B'nai Jeshurun Congregation. In the same year, he published the first edition of the *American Israelite*, the oldest Anglo-Jewish newspaper in the world. In 1855 he founded Zion College in Cincinnati, his first attempt to establish an institution of higher learning. The school closed after a few years because it had little financial support. Some years later, in 1867, one of Wise's contemporaries sought to establish a rabbinical seminary in Philadelphia: Maimonides College. Two students went on to serve as American rabbis but it closed before any other students graduated. As this school was closing, efforts to establish a rabbinical seminary were solidifying in Cincinnati. In 1873 Wise and his supporters managed to create a congregational union, the members of which pledged to contribute annual funding to support a Hebrew Theological Institute. The Hebrew Union College opened its doors in October 1875.

In the school's early years, students attended nearby University of Cincinnati in the morning hours and HUC in the evening hours. The first class of rabbis graduated in 1883. One of the graduates described the ceremony thus:

> The faith and trust of Isaac M. Wise were justified. His life work reached its apogee when he laid the hand of blessing upon the heads of his four disciples—Israel Aaron, Henry Berkowitz, Joseph Krauskopf, and David Philipson—and declared them to be rabbis in Israel. It was a strangely

thrilling moment when he pressed the kiss of consecration upon their foreheads. These four young men embodied the hopes of thousands of loyal American Jewish souls. They were setting forth upon a great adventure in the spiritual world. They were to blaze a new path. Upon their success or failure the welfare of the institution hung.[18]

In a neat link with another one of this book's tours, the ordination was concluded with a dinner at the Highland House (the resort at the top of the Mount Adams Incline, see the *Party* tour). One historian, Samuel S. Cohon, has written that Wise was "a towering personality. By his faith, vision, and determination, he became the master builder of American Judaism and the creator of an American Rabbinate."[19] By the early decades of the twentieth century, HUC had grown into a leading center of scholarship. Up to the present day, this school serves as a magnet for attracting important Jewish scholars and hard-working students from across the country and, indeed, from around the world.

The school's name, Hebrew Union College, records the school's original ambition: to serve as an institute of higher Jewish learning for all of American Jewry. Kaufmann Kohler, the second president of Hebrew Union College, convened a group of like-minded rabbis in Pittsburgh in 1885 to articulate the principles of Reform Judaism. "The Guiding Principles of Reform Judaism" are better known as the "Pittsburgh Platform." This famous statement expressed the principles that defined Reform Judaism organized in eight planks. According to Gary P. Zola, executive director of the American Jewish Archives, the eighth plank in that famous platform, declares that Reform Judaism calls upon its adherents to involve themselves in work that will bring a fairer, more just society into existence. According to Zola, this ideal continues to inspire the school's rabbinical students today. It states:

> In the spirit of Mosaic legislation, which strives to regulate the relations between rich and poor, we deem it our duty to participate in the great task of modern times, to solve, on the basis of justice and righteousness, the problems presented by the contrasts and evils of the present organization of society.[20]

This commitment to social action and social justice is shared across all three Cincinnati campuses on this tour and rabbinical alumni continue to embody such concerns. The Pittsburgh Platform, as Wise noted at the time, was essentially a "declaration of independence" for Reform Judaism. In 1886 the Jewish Theological Seminary of New York City was organized to educate traditional rabbis for American leadership. It opened a year later. It would later become the seminary of the Conservative movement in Judaism.[21]

Today, HUC's Cincinnati campus hosts two graduate programs of study: a rabbinical school of about sixty-five students and a graduate school offering a master's and doctorate in subjects relating to the expertise of the faculty of which about twenty-five students avail themselves at any given time. A number of the students who pursue doctoral degrees in areas such as Bible, Rabbinical Literature, etc., are non-Jewish. The campus is also home to the American Jewish Archives (AJA), generally believed to be the world's largest catalogued collection of documentary evidence on the history of a Jewish community.[22]

As one might expect of a Reform religious tradition, there were more opportunities for women to study at HUC than at other schools. Wise took great pride in being a proponent of gender equality, though his words were stronger than his actions. When the HUC opened in 1875, there was a woman in the school, Julia Ettlinger, the niece of an assistant teacher. Ettlinger was likely enrolled to fill a spot but she did as well if not better than most of the men. The first woman teacher at HUC was Cora Kahn, in the late 1920s and 1930s. She was an elocution teacher and taught the men how to orate in a style similar to Protestant ministers so that they could sound more American. She was the first woman to teach in an American rabbinical school.[23]

In 1972 HUC ordained the first female rabbi, Sally Priesand. At first, many thought Priesand had come to HUC to marry a rabbi rather than be one. Priesand recalls her days at HUC with great fondness; both her classmates and teachers were supportive, particularly President Nelson Glueck, a mentor and guide to Priesand. He played an important role in ensuring her ordination, such as leading services the day that the Board of Governors came to town. Unfortunately, Glueck died the year before Priesand was ordained, but he told his wife that there were three things he had still wanted to do before he died and one was to ordain Priesand as a rabbi. As Priesand recalls in a foreword of a book about female rabbis, the fact that Rabbi Alfred Gottschalk, Glueck's successor, maintained Glueck's commitment to her ordination is a testament to his courage as there were those who sought to use the opportunity to not follow through with the ordination.[24]

The historical significance of Cincinnati in nineteenth-century America, Professor Zola noted, helps us to understand the presence of both the college and the AJA—as well as many other cultural institutions that represent a time of greater influence than Cincinnati now wields in the twenty-first century. In the mid-nineteenth century, Cincinnati was the largest city in the western United States and the sixth largest city in the country. Its size and prominence explain the stunning Music Hall and why Cincinnati is home to the second oldest zoo and the oldest baseball team in the country. In the same era, it was also home to the second largest Jewish community in the United States, so was an appropriate location for a rabbinical school. HUC is one of a collection of historic cultural pearls in a city that is far smaller and less significant nationally than it used to be.[25]

# ART DECO ARCHITECTURE IN CINCINNATI

## Lunken Airport, Union Terminal, Downtown, and the Mount Washington Water Tower

The Art Deco style gets its name from an exhibition held in Paris in 1925: the *Exposition Internationale des Arts Décoratifs et Industriels Modernes*. The new style was strongly geometrical, with a sleek elegance that suggested wealth and sophistication, optimism, and dynamism.[1]

In the United States, what we now call Art Deco appeared first in product design and interior design, and especially in film sets. It became the backdrop for the world of Fred Astaire and Ginger Rogers: a cosmopolitan world of strong geometry and high contrasts of black and white; a world of curving staircases, sharp lapels, platinum blonde hair, and gleaming silver cocktail shakers.[2]

After the stock market crash in 1929, Art Deco stayed on as an emotional counterpoint to the Great Depression, a very particular sort of imagined paradise.

By 1930, Art Deco was moving into American architecture, and nearly every major American city has an Art Deco skyscraper or two. Cincinnati has an Art Deco train station, a small Art Deco airport, a water tower, a department store, a telephone exchange, and two of the best Art Deco skyscrapers anyplace: Carew Tower and the Cincinnati Times-Star Building. Most of these buildings are too far apart for a walking tour, but on a bike, the distances are perfect.

Cincinnati Times-Star Building

## The Tour

More detailed information on this route is available on the *Bicycling through Paradise* community page. We invite you to leave additional information on route updates, detours, and establishments that will be helpful to future cyclists of this route. Here is the general idea.

This tour begins and ends at Lunken Airport, a modest-but-good example of Art Deco, designed in 1936. Lunken is a good place to start because it's on the Ohio-to-Erie Trail; there's convenient parking at the Wilmer Trailhead and the airport has public bathrooms. From Lunken, we'll head downtown and to the West End, visiting half a dozen fabulous Art Deco buildings. From there we will loop back to Lunken. Total out-and-back distance of this loop is a little over nineteen miles. Once we get back to Lunken, there's a spur out to see the Mount Washington Water Tower, a great example of late Deco style, completed in 1940.

**Segment 1** goes from Lunken Airport to Union Terminal (8.1 miles, mostly flat). We'll head west on the Ohio River Trail and then pick up the dedicated bike lane on Riverside Drive heading into downtown. At Eggleston Avenue, we'll head north on the Canal Bikeway, which will take us up to the Cincinnati Times-Star Building, built in 1933 and now on the National Register of Historic Places. We'll ride through downtown on Ninth Street, head north alongside Washington Park, and then take Ezzard Charles Drive west to Cincinnati Museum Center at Union Terminal—Cincinnati's most iconic building, and a world-class example of Art Deco style.

**Segment 2** returns from Union Terminal to Lunken Airport (10.2 miles, mostly flat, but including an optional climb up Delta Avenue). On the return trip, we'll go to the corner of Seventh and Elm Streets, where you can see two Art Deco buildings next to each other: the 1931 Cincinnati Bell Telephone Exchange and the 1937 Shillito's Department Store façade. After that, we'll see the 1931 Netherland Plaza Hotel at Carew Tower. Then for comparison, we'll take a quick detour past a post–Art Deco building—the Terrace Plaza Hotel on Sixth Street. On the way back to Lunken Airport, we'll have a chance (if you want) to climb up Delta Avenue to Mount Lookout Square so that we can see Our Lord Christ the King Church, built in 1957 in a modified Art Deco/Moderne style. We'll then head back down Delta Avenue and return to our original starting place at Lunken Airport.

Segment 3 is the Mount Washington Spur (4.9 miles one-way, with one gradual but very long climb). From Lunken Airport, we will head south on the Ohio-to-Erie Trail, crossing the Little Miami River. We'll join Salem Road near the Magrish Trailhead and climb up Salem all the way to Sutton Avenue. We'll head north on Sutton, passing the historic Salem Community Methodist Church (built in 1863), until we get to Campus Lane, which will take us a few blocks east to the Mount Washington Water Tower. At Mount Washington there are several places to eat, including the Mount Washington Creamy Whip and Bakery.

On this tour we'll see some great architecture, and we'll get to think about what it is exactly that makes Art Deco, Art Deco.

## Lunken Municipal Airport

The Lunken Airport terminal was designed in 1936. (The architects were Kruckemeyer & Strong, a local firm.)[3] The interior was designed to be much more lavish than it is today, but it ended up more plain, for reasons explained in in the *Floodplains and Hilltops* tour. It's still worth going inside to see the fine murals, painted for the Works Progress Administration, on the themes of gravity and flight.

Mainly we want to focus on the exterior, on the entrance side facing Wilmer Avenue. Art Deco is often associated with extravagance, and the Lunken

Airport terminal is rather simple. So what marks this as an Art Deco building? There are a number of factors.[4]

First, Lunken has a strong, formal geometry, with a composition that is generally symmetrical, especially around the entrance bay.

Second, the roofline is not flat but is highest in the center and steps down toward the edges. Third, the wall planes are very flat and do not have the rough stone texture that we see at Cincinnati City Hall, for example, or the wood shingle textures on some Victorian houses. In Art Deco buildings, these flat, planar surfaces are often made out of limestone or concrete, and sometimes out of yellowish brick. (Lunken is yellow brick with limestone trim.)

A fourth characteristic of Art Deco architecture is the use of spandrel panels to join windows on different floor levels, creating vertical continuity. At Lunken, we see stacked windows on either side of the entrance bay.

A fifth characteristic is the use of decorative metal grille panels set close to the wall surface. Sometimes, these are at the window spandrels, but they can appear in other places as well. At Lunken, notice the greenish metal panels on either side of the front door, between the upper and lower bands of windows. Here, these panels are very restrained, but they can be much more decorative.

Sixth, the wall surfaces often have shallow, incised decorations. At Lunken, notice the incised vertical lines in the spandrel panels. In more elaborate buildings, this decoration can take the form of bas-relief sculptures. These

Front façade of Lunken Airport Terminal

sculptures might depict animals, plants, or people, but they are always geo-metrically stylized, instead of being naturalistic.

Seventh, Art Deco is also often characterized by what is called "reeding and fluting." Reeding means that you have a surface that looks like the face of a bundle of reeds, a series of convex curves. Fluting means that the curves are concave, like the curved surfaces running up the sides of a Greek column. At Lunken, this motif only occurs in a flattened way at the incised vertical lines that we already discussed, but this is usually three-dimensional.

An eighth characteristic of Art Deco is the use of zigzag or stair-step decoration. We see this at Lunken in the stepped decoration around the entrance doors.

A ninth characteristic is the use of decorative lines radiating out from a single point. At Lunken, the lines in the spandrel panels come together at the base in an inverted $v$ shape—a chevron. Sunburst shapes (which occur in the metal panels inside Lunken) are another common expression of this motif.

Finally, Art Deco buildings sometime feature clocks prominently, as symbols of progress and efficiency. The one at Lunken is on the rear facade, facing the airfield.

We'll see all of these elements again, in more robust form, along our tour.

## The Cincinnati Times-Star Building

The Cincinnati Times-Star newspaper was owned by Charles P. Taft and his wife, Anna Sinton Taft, part of a Cincinnati business and political dynasty. The *Times-Star* had its first offices on Sixth Street, but in the late 1920s, the Tafts commissioned a new sixteen-story headquarters at 800 Broadway. The cornerstone was laid in 1931. (The design firm was Samuel Hannaford and Sons, but Samuel Hannaford had already died, so the sons did the work.)[5]

The exterior is more exuberant and detailed than Lunken Airport, but the basic elements are the same: the bold geometry and symmetry, the roofline steeping down from the center, the flat wall planes, the vertical spandrel panels between windows, the metal grilles, the shallow bas-reliefs, the reeding, zig-zags, and radiating lines—all of it is here. (The building is now county-owned and is used for offices of the juvenile court, so you can go inside the lobby, where the decorative scheme continues.)

Art Deco was an architecture of style, but it was also an architecture of values. Near the top of the Cincinnati Times-Star Building, there are four huge, allegorical figures representing truth, progress, patriotism, and speed. All of these were favorite themes of Art Deco designers (though you wouldn't necessarily be able to figure out what those sculptures represented unless someone told you). In addition to those explicit values, there are other values that are implicit to the architecture itself. Craftsmanship, beauty, and intricate decoration are central to Art Deco.

Art Deco designers also believed that a building's decoration should symbolize the building's use. At the Cincinnati Times-Star Building, many of the small, exterior sculptural elements relate to printing and publishing. There are depictions of Benjamin Franklin, Johannes Gutenberg, and William Caxton, among others. The building tells a story about itself.[6]

## Union Terminal

During the nineteenth and early twentieth centuries, Cincinnati was a major hub of rail traffic. Cincinnati's early train stations were too close to the river and were subject to flooding, so in the late 1920s, a decision was made to change the location. There was land available at a park on the West End. Construction began just two months after the stock market crash of 1929,[7] but nothing was going to slow down the new Union Terminal. The facility opened in 1933. (The architect was Alfred T. Fellheimer of New York, and the principal design consultant was Paul Cret.)[8] This is Cincinnati's most iconic building. You can scarcely open a book about Art Deco without seeing a photo of this building.

Everything at Union Terminal suggests movement and speed. Out front, the transportation concourse was designed for the efficient movement of taxis and busses.[9] Inside, the curving public spaces and long ramps urge every visitor toward a destination.

Themes of transportation and industry occur throughout the decorative scheme. Outside, there are two huge bas-relief sculptures on either side of the main arch. One depicts Hermes, god of commerce and messenger of the gods. The other is an allegorical figure of Transportation, with a winged globe on her back. Inside, the mosaic murals show additional scenes of industry.[10]

But the entire project was a huge mistake. Automobiles, not railroads, were the wave of the future. By the time the ribbon was cut, everyone knew that the era of mass train transit was essentially over. Within a few years, Union Terminal, though an architectural masterpiece, had become a white elephant.

Troop movements during World War II gave a burst of life to the facility, and this is where many soldiers hugged their families and sweethearts good-bye, and there were many joyful

Interior of Union Terminal

reunions at the war's end.[11] But once the war was over, use declined again.

By 1971, there were only two trains a day, and in 1972, Union Terminal was formally abandoned. (You can still take an Amtrak train from this location, but you won't go through the main terminal building.) During the early 1980s, Union Terminal was briefly turned into a downscale shopping mall of off-brand stores. The building was deteriorating, and there was talk of demolition. Then, in 1986, Hamilton County voters approved a bond levy to save the building and turn it into the Cincinnati Museum Center.[12] It now houses a children's museum, an Omnimax theater, a museum of natural history, and the Cincinnati History Museum.

One other thing about Union Terminal. During the 1970s and 1980s, there was a Saturday morning animated cartoon series called *Super Friends*. It was about the Justice League: Wonder Woman, Superman, Batman, and so on. As every comics fan knows, the Justice League meets in a big building called the Hall of Justice. And when you see the cartoon version of the Hall of Justice—it's Union Terminal. To a tee. The show's producer, Hanna-Barbera, was at the time owned by Cincinnati–based Taft Broadcasting—part of Cincinnati's Taft dynasty. So now we've got the Hall of Justice.[13]

## The Cincinnati Bell Telephone Building and the Shillito's Façade

The Cincinnati Bell Telephone Building, at 209 W. Seventh Street, is an example of classic Art Deco, and it's on the National Register of Historic Places. But it's no masterpiece, and it shows the limitations of the style. The building is blocky and staid. The decorations are jarring and busy and don't convey any real sense of movement or hierarchy. (The building was designed by the Cincinnati architect Harry Hake.)[14]

This building can best be appreciated for the small, delightful details—such as the bas-relief sculptures of rotary telephones. The theme of communications continues in the rest of the decorations, too—there are nautical signal flags, figures of a message runner, and a depiction of Alexander Graham Bell.

Right next door to the Bell Telephone building is the old Shillito's department store (now condominiums called the Lofts at Shillito Place) at 151 W. Seventh Street. The bulk of the Shillito's building dates to the 1870s. But in 1928, the store was purchased by the Lazarus family, who decided to modernize. The old, red brick façade of Shillito's was replaced by a new, limestone exterior. (The architects were Potter, Tyler, and Martin, a local firm).[15]

The new façade was completed in 1937, just a few years after the Bell Telephone Building. The new Shillito's facade was a variation of Art Deco called Art Moderne, sometimes called Streamline Moderne. There is not always a clear or useful distinction between Art Deco and Art Moderne. But here, the side-by-side comparison is illuminating.

Unlike the typical vertical emphasis of classic Art Deco buildings (like the Bell Telephone Building), Art Moderne has a more horizontal emphasis.[16] The square corners of Art Deco have given way to curved corners. There is less symmetry. The whole façade has a swoopy, streamlined energy very different from the jazzy, angular lines of the Bell Telephone Building.

Many of the elements of classic Art Deco are still present at Shillito's, including the prominent clocks. And the old style of reeded decoration is here (now at a larger scale), placed in a horizontal band between the windows on the upper stories. Even with these elements, the Shillito's façade is something new, heading in the direction of other buildings yet to come.

## Carew Tower and the Netherland Plaza Hotel

The Carew Tower complex, home to the Netherland Plaza Hotel (now the Hilton Netherland Plaza) is located at 35 W. Fifth Street. It's forty-nine stories tall. For many years—until the Great American Tower was built—it was the tallest building in Cincinnati. (The architect was Walter W. Ahlschlager, in association with Delano & Aldrich.)[17]

Carew Tower was the brainchild of John J. Emery (1898–1976), grandson of the industrialist Thomas Emery. In the late 1920s, Emery had a vision for a new downtown complex, "a city within a city."[18] Emery wanted his complex to include a lavish hotel skyscraper plus shops and offices, including a replacement for the old Mabley and Carew department store.

Early in 1929, Emery approached a group of bank officials about financing for a hotel complex. The bankers refused the loan. Undeterred, Emery decided to fund the project by selling off his entire stock holding—a huge fortune—against the advice of his financial advisers. Soon afterward, the stock market crashed. Emery's holdings would have been worthless if he had stayed in the market.[19] So Carew Tower saved the Emery fortune from ruin. Emery's decision helped Cincinnati, too. During the early years of the Depression, construction work made the tower one of the city's largest employers.[20]

The exterior of the building is handsome, but you have to go inside to appreciate the lavish decoration. Inside the lobby, you can peek into the Palm Court Restaurant (now Orchids at Palm Court), and on the second floor, you may be able to peek into the Hall of Mirrors ballroom.

When the Netherland Plaza opened in 1931, The *Cincinnati Times-Star* compared the new hotel to "the splendors of Solomon's Temple."[21] It was the tallest building west of the Alleghenies and an immediate, prestigious destination for visitors. The guest register includes the names Harry Truman, Eleanor Roosevelt, Dwight Eisenhower, Cary Grant, Anthony Quinn, Gene Autry, the Mills Brothers, Bing Crosby, Elvin Presley, and Queen Wilhelmina of the Netherlands.[22]

In 1932 Winston Churchill checked into the Netherland Plaza. The hotel manager was giving Churchill a tour of the best suite, when Churchill rushed from the bathroom and grabbed a telephone. The manager thought that perhaps some world crisis was afoot. In fact, Churchill was calling his interior designer at home in England, telling him to stop work on the bathroom, because he'd just seen something he liked better.[23]

John J. Emery, scion of the Emery family, became one of the best patrons of the arts that Cincinnati ever had. He was a major benefactor of the Cincinnati Art Museum. And fifteen years after the completion of Carew Tower, he built another downtown hotel—the Terrace Plaza.

In 1947 Emery hired the New York firm Skidmore, Owings, and Merrill for his new hotel. The designer was Natalie de Blois. For the interior, Emery commissioned large murals by Joan Miro and Saul Steinberg,[24] murals that can now be seen at the Cincinnati Art Museum.

After visiting Carew Tower, it's worth circling the block to run by the Terrace Plaza building, on 6th Street (taking up the whole block between Vine and Race Streets), because this would be the shape of things to come. (The building is now closed, but you can see the exterior.) This is an International Style building, so there is no surface ornamentation. The roofline is flat, and the lines are simple throughout. Those unadorned walls and flat roofs would be the death of Art Deco, though Art Deco didn't quite know it yet.

## Our Lord Christ the King Church

Edward J. Schulte was a prolific Cincinnati architect, best known for his projects for the Catholic Church: churches, seminaries, convents, rectories, and schools. Schulte worked both in Cincinnati and around the nation, beginning in the early 1920s.

By the late 1930s, Schulte was working on the design of a new church, school, and rectory for the parish of Our Lord Christ the King on Mount Lookout Square in Cincinnati, at the corner of Linwood and Ellison Avenues. The church sanctuary was intended to replace an older church on the same site. Construction was held up by World War II and then by postwar increases in labor and material costs. The congregation continued meeting in the older building until the replacement (now redesigned in a slightly more modest style) could finally be built, in 1956–57.[25]

At the street corner, the church has a tower with a large sculpture depicting Christ the King. At the base of the tower is the baptistery, which is separated from the sanctuary by a canopied entry drive, providing a streamlined flow of traffic.

Schulte's tastes had been formed in the Art Moderne era, and his personal style reflects this influence. The flat, limestone wall planes are here, and the curved corners, and the bas-relief sculptures. The reeding is here, too, at a huge scale, on the tower. Everything is elegantly crafted, full of rich detail. Schulte wrote that architecture needed to be "the fusing of art, philosophy, citizenship, and engineering, and, quite frequently, economics."[26]

Schulte's work can be seen in many other places around Cincinnati. One of his masterpieces was the interior renovation of St. Peter in Chains Cathedral in downtown Cincinnati. Schulte completed the renovation in 1957, the same year as Christ the King. The *Homeland Insecurity* tour will take us past another of Schulte's churches: St. Catherine Church in Fort Thomas, Kentucky.

## The Mount Washington Water Tower

Old water towers in Cincinnati often look like castles. They're made of textured stone, or stone and brick, and they have crenelated tops—stepping up and down, as if archers are going to be shooting at you through the openings. The 1892 water tower at Fort Thomas looks like this, and so does the standpipe at the top of Eden Park, just up the hill from Krohn Conservatory. The huge water tank structure at Mount Airy, built in 1926–27, follows the same formula.

The Mount Washington Water Tower doesn't look like a castle. It looks, if anything, like a rocket ship. (This is most noticeable if you step back far enough to see the beacon on top. Planes take off from Lunken nearby, and the beacon is illuminated to keep them from flying into the tower.) The structure is streamlined and symmetrical, and it's clearly a product of the machine age, not the Middle Ages. With its flat wall surfaces (at the base) and fluted decoration (on the shaft), the Mount Washington Water Tower is a fine example of Art Deco style. (The architects were Kruckemeyer & Strong, same as Lunken Airport.)[27]

There aren't many Art Deco water towers, so we should appreciate the one we have. It's 143 feet tall. When it was completed in 1940, it was "said to be the highest all-concrete tower of its nature," with walls three and a half feet thick at the base and two and a half feet thick at the top. It was designed to hold three million gallons of water,[28] and was later changed to function purely as an emergency supply.[29] The tower has become a symbol of the Mount Washington community.

## After Art Deco

After 1940 or so, the popularity of Art Deco declined, not only in architecture but also in product design and film set design. There are lots of reasons why. It may not be a coincidence that the great period of Art Deco interior design coincided with the last decade in which movies were shot in black and white. The sharp contrasts and strong geometry of Art Deco fitted beautifully with the white-tie-and-tails aesthetic of 1920s and 1930s film. But when Technicolor arrived, and the silver screen was no longer just silver, film had a different expressive potential.

World War II, and then the postwar housing crisis, demanded more innovation and efficiency. And, once again, Americans looked to Europe for inspiration. Designers like Walter Gropius and Ludwig Mies van der Rohe promoted the new, international style of modernism, with straight, clean lines and no surface decoration, symbolic or otherwise. Not coincidentally, the new style was cheaper to build.

The modern movement came in so powerfully that it swept every previous design trend into the basement, the antique shop, and the junkyard. Some of the values of the Art Deco movement—including speed and progress—survived the jump to modernism. Other values—including decoration and skilled craftsmanship—were left behind. By the 1960s, modern architecture was everywhere.[30]

Not everyone was happy about the change. Edward Schulte was still at the top of his game when it became clear that no one wanted his work anymore. Schulte had been able to keep producing his highly sculptural and craft-based buildings into the 1950s and early 1960s, mainly because his chief client was the Catholic Church, which was still flush with cash and had a long tradition of building elaborate churches. But the ground was shifting.

In 1972 Edward Schulte wrote his autobiography: *The Lord Was My Client*. He didn't try to hide his contempt for what was happening around him:

> It became obvious to me that architecture had relinquished its position as a leader and custodian of the fine arts; concerning itself with tricky solutions, and indulging in "cute" phrases such as "less is more," which can be interpreted as "nothing is the most."...The realization of the ugliness of our visual surroundings, coupled with the many evidences of moral decline, plus the general loss of aesthetic values, influenced my decision to retire.[31]

As Schulte contemplated the modern city, he dropped some of his attitude and became more wistful:

> I must admit that at my advanced age I frequently wonder why I thoughtfully consider spending the remainder of my life in a small town, where the pace is slower, where tensions are minimized, and a more even balance between culture and technology exists. Perhaps this is a dream impossible of accomplishment, but I cannot refrain from wondering why, despite great expenditure of money and exertion of political power, our cities continue to decay. Evidently our values are oriented toward goals other than beauty...We accept the taxes resulting from vast expenditures for super highways, but one wonders why they are extended through the heart of our cities, forever destroying parks, the historic buildings, and landmarks.[32]

The modern movement was indeed indifferent or hostile toward previous design styles and toward historic preservation. It took a long time before Americans could appreciate again the buildings of the past and the values that those buildings had embodied.

Scan to visit the
"Industry, Rust Belt,
and Redevelopment"
route

# INDUSTRY, RUST BELT, AND REDEVELOPMENT

## Norwood, Oakley, and Madisonville

Three communities in close proximity demonstrate that commerce and industry are particularly subject to flux and often enter and exit communities with a tremendous amount of energy and consequences. Unlike other tours, this tour is about how large-scale enterprises can almost completely disappear from a landscape. This one will require imagination. But it is also about how communities and their businesses adapt and respond. The landmarks of today sit atop those of days gone by. And our sense of belonging must include the dreams and aspirations of those whose labor and leisure marked our communities not so long ago.

## The Tour

More detailed information on the route is available on the *Bicycling through Paradise* community page. We invite you to leave additional information on route updates, detours, and establishments that will be helpful to future cyclists of this route. Here's a general idea of the route.

This is a mostly flat route, nine miles each way. The tour begins at University Station in Norwood, the site of the BASF chemical plant, and then continues through Norwood to Lower Millcrest Park, then to the site of the old General Motors (GM) plant near Montgomery Rd and Sherman Ave, and the old United States Playing Card Company complex at the end of Park Ave with its still majestic clock tower. Traveling on Robertson Avenue through Oakley, we will parallel the southern end of the former Cincinnati Milling Machine complex and some worker housing before turning to the newly redesigned Oakley Square. From there we will turn to Oakley's Centre of Cincinnati complex and return to Robertson for a ride to Madisonville and the corner of Whetsel and Madison Road to see the new development and envision the commercial shopping district that once existed there.

At the beginning and end of the tour are coffee shops and parking. In Norwood and Oakley there are also several restaurants to choose from.

## Camaros and Firebirds

On August 26, 1987, at 8:30 p.m., a $22,000 red Camaro rolled off the GM Norwood assembly line and was given to nineteen-year-old Wendell Spurlock, a GM employee, for free. He probably wished he had not been given it. He had won it in a raffle and he was not the only one. GM held a raffle to give away a number of cars in the hopes that the raffle would distract from the bitter reality of plant closure. Spurlock and 1,600 others were laid off that day. The closure made no sense to those in Norwood. The city of Norwood unsuccessfully sued GM in an effort to try to get money to rebuild rather than close the plant. The plant was a citizen of Norwood—providing jobs and tax revenue but also a sense of identity and purpose to individuals and the community alike. Spurlock and others would have preferred that it had stayed that way.[1]

The Norwood plant was the first of ten that GM closed to reduce costs in order to better face global automobile competition. GM closed this plant rather than one in California that manufactured the same cars because it was an aging facility, GM's second oldest, and difficult to modify for newer production systems. Flint, Michigan, would be another plant to close. In light of what has since happened in Flint, including municipal deficits and lead in their municipal water, the community of Norwood has weathered the closure better.

It was not only the workers and their families that faced life-altering circumstances as a result of the plant closure. The city of Norwood had to figure out how to replace the 28 percent of its budget that would no longer be coming from GM taxes. As a result, the city laid off twenty-six municipal workers and did not replace twenty-two others. The city closed an elementary school and laid off 11 percent of its teachers. The plant had been in Norwood since 1923, and of the four thousand employees, about a quarter lived in Norwood.

The Norwood plant had been critical to GM's success, helping the firm expand its car distribution south and east via the I-75 manufacturing corridor. In the 1920s, Norwood was already an independent city with infrastructure to support the plant. GM purchased a tract of land known as Norwood Park, south of the railroad tracks (and the Norwood Lateral now) and east of Smith Road, home to a traveling circus and a regional baseball team. Now a series of complexes, stores and offices now occupy the same land. A parking structure on the corner of Elm and Smith Roads is all that remains from the old factory.

Just a few years before the closing, GM had invested heavily in the plant to modernize its production, including building an elevated assembly line so that workers could work at arm height rather than off the floor. Between 1967 and 1987, Norwood was one of only two plants that made the popular Camaros and Firebirds.

The Norwood shop also had a reputation for innovation, such as the Turbo Bell painting technique and the F-car platform (for making Firebirds in pieces). Turbo Bells were high-speed turbines that atomized electrically charged paint and solvent near an oppositely charged vehicle, so that the paint particles would attract and stick. The technique involved volatile organic solvents that were not allowed in the only other factory where Firebirds were made—Van Nuys, California. Turbo Bell painting was of superior quality—shinier, thicker, and far less prone to peeling and other problems.

But the plant also had a reputation for contentious labor-management relations and was landlocked so could not expand. Still, it took a new CEO who sought automation and cared less for worker's welfare to make the call to close. In a hundred years, circus elephants and lions, low-slung sexy cars, and medical offices have existed in the same small area of Cincinnati, but there are no signs to mark the passing of cars or lions. Instead, uninspired retail architecture that looks like it could be anywhere in the suburban United States is all that is visible.

## Norwood

The reverberations of the closed GM plant and others are still visible in Norwood in a struggling business district along Montgomery Avenue and in crumbling infrastructure. But Norwood has suffered from far more than a car manufacturing facility closing in the last several decades. As a result of these closures and others, several thousand jobs were lost and thirty-five acres of brown fields, sites of previous commercial or industrial use that leave behind contaminants, were created. In addition to declining revenues, the city has experienced a nearly 40 percent decline in population between 2010 and 2015. All of Norwood's residents are living within a quarter mile of a known or potential brownfield. Due to its severe circumstances, the city has been recognized by the state as one of only five "Situational Distressed Communities" since 2010.[2]

In July 1990, the BASF chemical plant, located a few blocks from Xavier University exploded, killing one worker and injuring more than ninety. Workers made linings for cans and coatings for paper cups. A vapor cloud of highly flammable cleaning solvent leaked from a chemical reactor and caused the fire and explosions. The explosion sent fireballs fifty feet into the air. Thick

Former US Playing Card plant

black smoke poured from the building into nearby areas. The five-alarm fire took more than two hours, eighteen engine companies, and all six Cincinnati life squads and heavy rescue units to put out and assist the injured. The blast's sound and reverberations impacted as many as twenty-five thousand people, who lived within a four-to five-mile radius of the factory. It caused an estimated $50 million in property damage in Evanston and Norwood. The factory shut down and the area became another brownfield. In 2010 BASF donated the two-and-a-half acre site to Xavier University. The university contracted with a developer to build apartments, retail, medical, and other services on the corner in what has become University Station.[3]

LeBlond Machine Tools closed its factory near Hyde Park in 1989 and moved it to Mason. In many ways similar to Cincinnati Milling detailed below, this factory site sought to create a good working environment. The factory had lots of natural lighting, locker rooms with showers, and free coffee. There was a dining hall, infirmary, and training classrooms. Outside there was a lake, fountain, and pavilion. Rookwood Pavilion (1993) and Rookwood Commons (2000) have both become premier shopping destinations in that same location.[4]

In 2009 Norwood suffered another loss when the United States Playing Card Company, which had been based there since 1900, relocated to Erlanger, Kentucky. The departing firm left behind over six hundred thousand square feet of manufacturing space in a group of buildings instantly recognizable by its iconic clock tower. Even more iconic than the clock tower are the Bicycle playing cards, among many other brands, that were manufactured there. It was the largest playing cards manufacturer in the world. Part of the complex is now occupied by the Multi-Color Corporation, a custom label provider. In the summer of 2020, the complex was slated for mixed-use development.[5]

The Norwood Lateral construction began in 1962 and was finished by 1977. Two hundred Norwood homes were razed, decreasing the community's population and tax revenues. Norwood also had to pay 5 percent of the cost of the project. If one has not lived through these changes, it is hard to see them except in the lingering effects that look like another "has-been community."[6]

But there are heroes and successes. The northern portion of the Rookwood complex, which now straddles Smith Road just east of I–71, was acquired only after a long battle between property owners and the city of Norwood. A neighborhood of ninety-nine well-maintained homes and businesses, all of which had paid their taxes on time, was in the way of Jeffrey R. Anderson and his expanding plans for Rookwood.[7]

Anderson's plans were attractive to Norwood's leaders because they sought to redress some of the economic downturn described above. Mayor Tom Williams believed that the development would help all of Norwood. The city felt eminent domain was justified, given their economic straits.[8]

Most of the homeowners sold out to the development company, but a handful of homeowners refused to sell. The developer asked Norwood to take their homes by eminent domain. The Institute for Justice, which helped to support the homeowners, described two of its residents. Carl and Joy Gamble had lived in the neighborhood for thirty-four years and raised their children in their home. They owned a family grocery store until 2001, when they retired, and looked forward to relaxing at home and in their yard. Mary Beth Wilker and Nick Motz had recently bought a house and renovated it for Wilker's graphic design business. A third homeowner, Joe Horney, rented homes in the area.[9]

The neighborhood was economically diversified, with small business (a wine shop, a couple of lounges, and a hairdresser), some rental homes, and many others owner-occupied. A study commissioned by the developer claimed that the homes were in a "deteriorating area." Some of the justification for the neighborhood as a deteriorating area was that different people owned different homes, that there were cul-de-sacs, and some people had to back out of their driveways.[10]

A deteriorating area was the argument that the city of Norwood used to justify the neighborhood's elimination for redevelopment. A trial at the Hamilton County Common Pleas Court in June 2004 and the 1st District Court of Appeals both affirmed Norwood's position. And the highlight, according to one of the plaintiff's lawyers, Scott Bullock, was Joy Gamble's testimony. She was asked why she wanted to keep her home and said: "All of our memories are there. We're rooted there. We do not want to be uprooted. We want to stay right here until we're carried out feet first."[11] They lost. And Joy and Carl had to leave their home and move into the basement of their daughter's home in Kentucky.[12]

The Gambles and Horney appealed the 1st District's decision to the Ohio Supreme Court in *Norwood v. Horney.* The Ohio Supreme Court found in the plaintiffs' favor in late July 2006. It was the first ruling from a state high court since a controversial ruling from the Supreme Court the year before that allowed governments to seize private property for development. But Ohio said that economic benefit alone was insufficient cause for eminent domain action. The ruling attracted national attention.[13]

In 2008 Joe Horney sold his house to the developer for $1.25 million. The Gambles had sold theirs earlier. But, far more importantly, he and his neighbors were responsible for significantly reining in the power of Ohio's eminent domain law. He noted in an article in the *Libertarian News* from September 2006 that "it was a long road to get to this point, but it was worth it. What really sits well with me is that this is a good thing for every homeowner and small business owner in Ohio."[14] It is important to know that as you eat at Taste of Belgium or any of the other restaurants in the area, that this location has a history, a David and Goliath story, if you will. Citizens of Norwood, seeking a better life for themselves and their families, ironically, found themselves as both David and Goliath.

Norwood remains a diverse community that supports a variety of businesses as well as its own infrastructure. At the corner of Carter Avenue and Mills Avenue is an innovative enterprise, Moriah Pie, which seeks to serve up hope and nourishment to children and families alike. Run by members of a Vineyard faith community, the Friday night pay-as-you-can pizza parlor uses fruits and vegetables grown in Norwood (including in Millcrest Park) as the main ingredients in its soups, salads, pizzas, pies, and cakes.

Moriah Pie's location in Norwood is not an accident. A small group of people, both staff and volunteers, seek to redress some of the consequences of company executives' decisions in previous decades. The resulting lack of opportunity and attraction of drink and drugs create a cycle that is hard to break. Area children and youth are encouraged to participate in the gardening and in Friday night pizza. The gardens are open and sometimes suffer from vandalism, but the Moriah Pie community is committed to allowing neighbors access to the gardens and enterprise. Those who run the Friday night restaurant believe that community is something that must be created and re-created, enacted and reenacted out of hard work and a deep faith, no matter the larger economic choices that seem largely out of their control. The result is a vibrant scene on one corner of Norwood where a diverse group of people gather weekly for great tasting food and to linger as the evening cools.[15]

## Oakley

The Cincinnati Milling Company was the partner in the University of Cincinnati's experiment in cooperative education discussed in the *Crosstown Missions* tour. The Cincinnati Milling Machine Company (it became known as Milacron in 1970) began in 1874 as Cincinnati Screw and Tap Co., a small machine shop on Vine Street in Cincinnati that manufactured parts for and repaired sewing machines. Within two years, the firm also made machines to produce screws and the taps and dies that cut threads for them.[16]

In 1887 they were planning to make a new milling machine when Frederick A. Geier returned to Cincinnati to settle his father's estate. His father had been a woodworker, specializing in bungs (conical closures) for barrels. Collecting a debt from the machine company, he heard about the new milling machine they sought to make and bought an interest in the small shop. Neither an engineer nor a machinist, Geier thought milling machinery was far more promising than barrel making. Shortly, he was to become a world leader in machine tooling. In 1889 the company leaders and stockholders decided to concentrate on the machines for tool making (milling machines) rather than the screw and tap and die-making machines. By 1890, they were selling their machines as far away as Germany.[17]

In 1893 the US economy collapsed. Sales for the company evaporated, as did money and credit. The machine company limped along for more than a year. Geier saw that bicycles were one of the few things still in demand. A bicycle manufacturing company in Indianapolis needed twelve milling machines to produce bicycles but could not get credit or pay up front for them. So Geier called the Mill's employees together and explained the situation, saying that it would take about nine months before the company employees would get paid for their labor, if they took the contract. During that time, the Mill could pay them twenty-five cents for every dollar and give them the balance in scrip. The workers accepted the deal and area bakers and butchers accepted the scrip. The company was able to pay off its scrip and pay a shareholder dividend in 1894.[18]

In 1911 Geier sought to expand his business into the suburbs (from the Spring Grove Avenue location in the Mill Creek Valley) and chose a one-hundred-acre site in Oakley, a community with

Monument to the Cincinnati Machine Tool Company

a population of five hundred, for his "factory colony." Just to the east of Norwood, Oakley had recently been joined to Cincinnati by electric streetcar (having previously been linked by horse-drawn streetcars). A racetrack opened there in the 1890s, making it an entertainment destination. But Oakley had little by way of industry beyond a blacksmith shop serving wagon traffic on the Madisonville Turnpike, which linked Cincinnati to Madisonville (now Madison Road) and a wood-planing mill.[19]

Geier envisioned not just one factory but multiple factories to supply the chain of goods that were needed as inputs for the milling machines and to make use of a central power plant that was going to be expensive to build. An onsite foundry manufactured iron that went into the machine tools and a local power plant provided energy for the industry. He also convinced other businesses to locate near the colony, including Cincinnati Lathe and Tool Co., and Cincinnati Planer Co. Geier's vision was one of stability both for his company but also for the workers and the community that made it possible.

Cincinnati Milling became a tight-knit community and earned a reputation for taking care of its workers. Workers had access to lockers and showers, innovative medical care (thanks to Frederick's brother, Otto) and insurance, and later dental care, a cafeteria, sports teams, and garden plots. The company had its own Boy Scout troop and recreational space. Former worker housing can be seen along Appleton Avenue, but few factory workers could initially afford to live in Oakley. Many commuted to work from tenements in the city. A social reformer of the time, Graham Taylor wrote, "The suburbanite who leaves business behind at nightfall for the cool green rim of the city, would think the world had gone topsy-turvy if at 5:30 he rushed out of a factory set in a landscape of open fields and wooded hillsides, scrambled for a seat in a street-car or grimy train and clattered back to the region of brick and pavement, of soot and noise and jostle."[20] And yet thousands of factory workers did just this. By the 1920s, Geier was working to ensure adequate housing for his factory employees.

The company began providing the milling machines that budding automobile companies needed. In the 1920s, the company began building grinding machines as well. Henry Ford's first machine tool came from Cincinnati Milling. Ford would continue to purchase machines from Cincinnati Milling throughout the 1920s as he built not just cars but economies.[21]

By World War II, Cincinnati Milling operated the world's largest machine tool factory, occupying six acres of floor space. During the war, Cincinnati's machines played an important role in supplying Allied armies across the world. Employment peaked in the 1960s, and then competition from Japan and other overseas companies in the 1970s required the company to diversify to stay profitable. The company began making plastics machinery, robots, computer controls, minicomputers, and metal-cutting fluids. But new milling machines could replace three or four old ones, and mass production required keeping costs at a minimum, so they were, in some ways, victims of their own success. Milacron sold the machine tool business to Unova in 1998, closing the Oakley complex in 2002.[22]

This change, like the one in Norwood and to a lesser extent in Madisonville, is part of a larger historical trend, as Fairfield has written, one that is marked by an abandonment of commitment to place and an embrace of flexibility in production that in turn leads to temporary labor regimes, outsourcing, overseas investment, and relocation for lower taxes.

Since that time, the Oakley industrial complex has transitioned, like many other sites in Ohio, to service-oriented businesses, particularly shopping malls. Over a hundred acres, a series of sprawling developments, including Oakley Station, now occupy the area. The juxtaposition of the residential and commercial developments around Oakley Station that are automobile-centered and the older Oakley Square, once served by a streetcar and far more pedestrian friendly, is stark. Big box stores, a large movie theater, and a grocery store are swimming in a sea of parking lots. As the tour takes you through the complex, feel free to explore and return to Madison Road via any route.

Across the street, Mad Tree Brewing is located in the old Rock-Tenn paperboard production factory. The paper facility opened in the 1940s and was closed in 2014 because it was one of the company's oldest facilities and was out of compliance with the Environmental Protection Agency's clean air standards.[23] Mad Tree opened in 2013 and was the first Ohio craft brewery to can its beer. It moved to the Rock-Tenn building in 2017.

Graham Taylor, the social critic who earlier commented on commuting, worried in the early 1900s about gentrification, loss of walkability, and lack of opportunity for recreation and neighborliness as all would erode public spirit and civic engagement. Why, he wondered, were modern science and technology applied to industrial building and arrangement but not to community planning, housing, and health? Not doing so, Taylor called a "civic stupidity." Like Norwood, there is not much left of the not-so-distant industrial past of Oakley.[24] A monument to the perfection milling machines produced stands in one small corner of the Kroger parking lot and a derivative enterprise of Milacron still operates in a corner of the shopping complex. Other than that, one would have little idea that a world leader in precision tool machines contributed mightily to the welfare of Oakley and many families for decades.

But, just like in Norwood, if you know where to look, there are people who seek to rebuild community and to pay homage to the efforts of those who have gone before. Not far from Oakley Station, in an old tool and die company building that provided supplies to Milacron, local entrepreneurs have adapted the building to accommodate a glass fusing workshop, artists' studios, and a gallery and glass shop, known as Brazee Street Studios. Solar panels (which account for about one-third of the building's energy use), bioswales (to capture rainwater and keep it out of the sewers), native plants, and beehives complement the values of the enterprise.

## Madisonville

Our tour ends in Madisonville, where it is easier to see some of the transitions we have been describing in Norwood and Oakley. Here, previous storefronts are still visible, for example.[25]

Madisonville's industries were largely clustered around Corsica Hollow on both sides of Red Bank Road (then called Dunbar Place) between Madison Road and the B&O (now CSX) railroad tracks and the corner of Whetsel Avenue and Madison Road. Starting in 1919, the Cooper Battery Company had a large automobile battery manufacturing plant on the east side of Dunbar Place just north of the railroad tracks. Another local business was the Deerfield Service Garage, a large brick building at the southeast corner of Madison Road and Dunbar Place (Red Bank Road), where UDF is now located. And the Prest-O-Lite Electric Company had a factory just a little further south, approaching Brotherton Road.

Many decades ago, through the 1950s, the corner of Madison Avenue and Whetsel Road was a thriving shopping district, both for people from Cincinnati and from outlying areas to the east. Drug stores, a meat market and grocery, barber shops, a floral shop, a hardware store, a newspaper office, and a car repair shop all served Cincinnati residents. An interurban streetcar carried people from downtown along Madison Road to the shopping area.

Madisonville celebrated its 150th anniversary in 1959, and there was a huge public celebration with a parade, outdoor vendors, and other events.

After the 1950s, with growing popularity of the automobile, Madisonville's shopping district faced competition from further afield, Hyde Park and Oakley shopping districts, and the Kenwood Mall. What had been a walkable community with all the amenities nearby lost customers to stores further away.

But major building projects have been taking place in Madisonville since the early 2000s at the corner of Redbank and Madison Roads. Where the John P. Parker School now stands there once was Ward (apple) Orchards. Across Madison Road was Nu-Tone, manufacturer of doorbells, intercoms, built-in stereos, and kitchen exhaust fans, among other items, founded by J. Ralph and Patricia Corbett. Nu-Tone's facility spread across thirty acres in Madisonville for fifty-nine years.

The Corbetts are familiar to Cincinnati residents for their generous arts philanthropy. Before founding the company, Ralph Corbett was a lawyer and radio producer. It was through his *Notes on Business* show that he came into contact with a man who wanted to replace doorbell buzzers with musical chimes. The company started in 1936 with four employees and one room and grew by 1967 to fourteen plants in the United States and Canada. The international headquarters were built in 1949 in Madisonville. Mr. Corbett marketed the chimes and Mrs. Corbett designed them. Nu-Tone sold the site to MedPace, a global clinical research organization, and they moved from Madisonville in 2008. An entire campus development is under way, including a hotel, 250 multifamily housing units, 250,000 square feet of office space, 100,000 square feet of retail and commercial space, and green space open for community use.

And, now, as this chapter is completed, combined retail and housing complexes are being constructed on the corner of Madison and Whetsel and a beautiful historic building on another corner is now the home to Bad Tom Smith Brewing.

GM Firebirds, Bicycle playing cards, door chimes, machines to manufacture parts for cars, and other goods were all made within a few miles of each other earlier this century. For various reasons, they are all completely gone. Places where we eat and drink sit on top of the hard work and dreams of those who have come before us. They might not have always had the interests of those in their surrounding communities as their top priorities, but they were part of the success of these communities for some time. Lest we become too high-minded about our own priorities, this tour serves to remind that today's shopping, manufacturing, and research centers will give way to something else in the next decades that few of us can likely predict and with consequences that will undoubtedly be mixed.

# Notes

## Introduction

1   Stanley Hedeen, *Little Miami: Wild & Scenic, River Ecology & History*, 20, https://little miamistatepark.org/images/stories/history/riverecologyhistory.pdf.

2   Hedeen, *Little Miami*, 3.

3   Charles Cist, *Cincinnati in 1841, Its Early Annals and Future Prospects* (Cincinnati: n.p., 1841), 13–14.

4   Mikael Hard and Andrew Jamison, *Hubris and Hybrids: A Cultural History of Technology and Science* (New York: Routledge, 2005), 176–80.

5   Hard and Jamison, *Hubris and Hybrids*, 177.

6   Wolfgang Schivelbusch, "Railroad Space and Railroad Time," in *The Railway Journey: The Industrialization of Time and Space in the Nineteenth Century* (Berkeley: University of California Press, 1977), 33–44.

7   Robert McFarlane, *The Old Ways: A Journey on Foot* (New York: Viking, 2012), 322.

8   Stan Hedeen used this expression on a tour of the Mill Creek with Xavier students, September 2015.

9   McFarlane, *Old Ways*, 147.

10   Rachel Carson, *The Sense of Wonder* (New York: Perennial Library, 1965), 54.

11   Carson, *Sense of Wonder*, 88–89.

12   Eva M. Selhub and Alan C. Logan, *Your Brain on Nature: The Science of Nature's Influence on your Health, Happiness, and Vitality* (Mississauga, Ontario: John Wiley and Sons, 2012), 21.

## Chapter 1

1   Stanley Hedeen, *The Mill Creek: An Unnatural History of an Urban Stream* (Cincinnati, OH: Blue Heron Press, 1994), ix.

2   "But First, What Is a Watershed?" Mill Creek Alliance, http://www.millcreekwater shed.org/whatiswatershed/.

3   "Symmes Purchase," Ohio History Central, https://ohiohistorycentral.org/w/Sym mes_Purchase.

4   "Little Miami River," *Wikipedia*, https://en.wikipedia.org/wiki/Little_Miami_River.

5   "But First, What Is a Watershed?

6   "Ohio River Basin," Ohio River Basin Consortium for Research and Education, https://www.ohio.edu/orbcre/basin/index.html.

7   Hedeen, *Mill Creek*, 44–51.

8   Uwe Lubken, "Rivers and Risk in the City: The Urban Floodplain as a Contested Space," in *Urban Rivers: Remaking Rivers, Cities, and Space in Europe and North America*, ed. Stephane Castonguay and Matthew Evenden (Pittsburgh: University of Pittsburgh Press, 2012), 132.

9   Hedeen, *Mill Creek*, 10.

10  Scott Russell Sanders, *Staying Put: Making a Home in a Restless World* (Boston: Beacon Press, 1993), 27.

11  Skip Tate, "Patron Saint of Lost Causes," *Cincinnati Magazine*, September 1988, 66.

12  Hedeen, *Mill Creek*, 11.

13  Hedeen, *Mill Creek*, 12–13; Scamyhorn and Steinle, 63–64.

14  Scamyhorn and Steinle, 105–10.

15  Scamyhorn and Steinle, 150–55.

16  Scamyhorn and Steinle, 20.

17  Hedeen, *Mill Creek*, 11–16; Scamyhorn and Steinle, 107–9.

18  Roxanne Dunbar-Ortiz, *An Indigenous Peoples' History of the United States* (Boston: Beacon Press, 2014), 22.

19  Hedeen, 11–16; Scamyhorn and Steinle, 107–9.

20  Hedeen, 29–38.

21  Hedeen, 71–91.

22  "P&G: A Company History," https://www.pg.com/translations/history_pdf/english _history.pdf; Sue Ann Painter, Alice Weston, and Beth Sullebarger, *Architecture in Cincinnati: An Illustrated History of Building and Designing an American City* (Athens: Ohio University Press, 2007), 111–13.

23  Hedeen, *Mill Creek*, 56–59.

24  Hedeen, 72–73.

25  Hedeen, 64–70.

26  Hedeen, 95–127.

27  Hedeen, 95–127.

28  Hedeen, 95–140.

29  John Tallmadge, *The Cincinnati Arch: Learning from Nature in the City* (Athens: University of Georgia Press, 2004), 200.

30  Jen Kinney, "How to Pay America's Big Sewer Bill," NextCity.org, February 26, 2016, https://nextcity.org/daily/entry/cities-combined-sewer-overflow-upgrade-green -infrastructure.

31  Hedeen, *Mill Creek*, 126–27.

32  Lubken, *Rivers and Risk in the City*, 131.

33  Stanley Hedeen, "Waterproofing the Mill Creek Flood Plain," *Queen City Heritage* (Spring 1998): 15.

34  Lubken, *Rivers and Risk in the City*, 138.

35  George P. Stimson, "River on a Rampage: An Account of the Ohio River Flood of 1937," *Bulletin of Cincinnati Historical Society* 22, no. 2 (April 1964): 101–2.

36  Hedeen, *Mill Creek*, 151–58.

37  Todd Dykes, "Little-Known Cincinnati Dam Needs Millions in Repairs," WLWT, July 19, 2016, https://www.wlwt.com/article/little-known-cincinnati-dam-needs -millions-in-repairs/3567794.

38  Hedeen, *Mill Creek*, 168.

39  Hedeen, 163–76.

40  "The Mill Creek Alliance," https://www.themillcreekalliance.org.

41  "Crown," Tri-State Trails, https://tristatetrails.org/crown/.

## *Chapter 2*

1  Colin G. Calloway, *The Shawnees and the War for America* (New York: Penguin, 2007), xxiv–xxv.

2  "The Queen's Crown Jewels: J. Fitzhugh Thornton Memorial," Queen City Survey, February 18, 2008, http://queencitysurvey.blogspot.com/2008/02/queens-crown -jewels.html.

3  Charles River Editors, *Native American Tribes: The History and Culture of the Shawnee* (Ann Arbor, MI: Charles River, n.d.).

4  Calloway, *Shawnees and the War for America*, 79-84.

5  Calloway, 79–84.

6  Calloway, 85–94.

7  Robert M. Owens, *Mr. Jefferson's Hammer: William Henry Harrison and the Origins of American Indian Policy* (Norman: University of Oklahoma Press, 2007), 16–17.

8  Owens, *Mr. Jefferson's Hammer*, 21–25.

9  Owens, 31–35.

10  Owens, 39–50.

11  Owens, 79–92.

12  Owens, 68, 72; see also "Former Slave Burned," *Cincinnati Commercial Tribune*, October 28, 1899, 2.

13  Calloway, *Shawnees and the War for America*, 129–31.

14  Edward Eggleston and Lillie Eggleston Seelve, *Tecumseh and the Shawnee Prophet* (New York: Dodd, Mead & Co., 1878), 118–20.

15 Aymen Ibrahem and Bill Cramer, "Tecumseh and the Eclipse of 1806," Eclipse-Chasers, April 18, 2015, https://www.eclipse-chasers.com/article/history/tse1806.shtml.

16 Calloway, *Shawnees and the War for America*, 134.

17 Calloway, 139–44.

18 Calloway, 145–52.

19 Jeff Suess, "William Henry Harrison's Presidential Campaign Changed Politics," Cincinnati.com, May 23, 2015, https://www.cincinnati.com/story/news/2015/05/22/william-henry-harrisons-bid-presidency-changed-campaigns-run/27774087/.

20 "William Henry Harrison and the Cincinnati & Whitewater Canal," Historical Marker Database, https://www.hmdb.org/m.asp?m=78769.

21 Betty Kamuf, "Problems Plagued Canal Projects," Cincinnati.com, March 24, 2014, https://www.cincinnati.com/story/news/2014/03/24/problems-plagued-canal-projects/6833875/.

22 William Henry Harrison, *A Discourse on the Aborigines of the Ohio Valley* (Chicago: Fergus Printing Company, 1883), 10.

23 Harrison, *Discourse on the Aborigines*, 10–11.

24 Harrison, 11.

25 Robert Silverberg, *The Mound Builders* (Greenwich, CT: New York Graphic Society, 1970), 48.

26 Carey Hoffman, "Ancient Connection: Evidence from Summer Digs Points to Shawnee Lookout as Oldest Continuously Occupied Site," ScienceBlog, September 1, 2009, https://scienceblog.com/24769/ancient-connection-new-evidence-points-to-shawnee-lookout-as-oldest-continuously-occupied-site/.

27 Hoffman, "Ancient Connection."

28 "John Tyler," History.com, July 9, 2019, https://www.history.com/topics/us-presidents/john-tyler.

29 "John Tyler."

## Chapter 3

1 "Camp Dennison Settled by German Pietist Refugees," *Cincinnati Enquirer*, June 26, 1960, 33.

2 "Pietism," *Wikipedia*, https://en.wikipedia.org/wiki/Pietism.

3 Stanley Hedeen, *The Little Miami: Wild and Scenic, River Ecology & History*, 41, https://littlemiamistatepark.org/park-and-trail/history-park-trail/19-uncategorised/little-miami-scenic-trail-and-river/31-the-little-miami-wild-and-scenic-river-ecology-and-history.

4 "Christian Waldschmidt," Indian Hill Historical Society, https://www.indianhill.org/history/people-indian-hill-history/christian-waldschmidt/.

5 Josiah Morrow, "Jeremiah Morrow," *"Old Northwest" Genealogical Quarterly*, January 1906, 131.

6 Morrow, "Jeremiah Morrow," 244–45.

7   Morrow, 122–23.

8   Morrow, 132–33.

9   Morrow, 245.

10  William Henry Smith, *A Sketch of Governor Jeremiah Morrow, or, A Familiar Talk about Monarchists and Jacobins* (Cincinnati: Ohio Archaeological and Historical Society, 1888), 200.

11  Jeremiah Morrow, "Address of Governor Morrow," in *Annual Report of the Superintendent of State House to the Governor of the State of Ohio for the Year 1863* (Columbus: Richard Nevins, 1864), 14.

12  Morrow, "Jeremiah Morrow," 249–50.

13  Hedeen, *Little Miami*, 50.

14  Joan Baxter, "Some History on the Little Miami Railroad," *Xenia Daily Gazette*, April 6, 2018, https://www.xeniagazette.com/opinion/28412/some-history-on-the-little-miami-railroad.

15  Hedeen, *Little Miami*, 52.

16  Hedeen, 52.

17  Morrow, "Jeremiah Morrow," 245.

18  Chapman Brothers, "Hon. Isaac M. Barrett," in *Portrait and Biographical Album of Greene and Clark Counties, Ohio* (Chicago: Chapman Bros., 1890), 181.

19  Lorrie Owen, ed., "Barret, George, Concrete House," in *Ohio Historic Places Dictionary*, vol. 2 (St. Claire Shores, MI: Somerset Publishers, 1999), 535.

20  Ohio State Board of Agriculture, *Annual Report*, vol. 5 (Columbus: S. Medary, 1850), 179.

21  George Barrett, *The Poor Man's Home, and Rich Man's Palace, Or, the Application of Gravel Wall Cement to the Purposes of Building* (Cincinnati: Applegate & Co., 1854), 7.

22  Benjamin Kline, "Durable Housing: 19th Century Miller Had Concrete Ideas on Building," *Dayton Daily News*, Sunday, January 27, 1985, 1-B.

23  "Orson Squire Fowler," *Wikipedia*, https://en.wikipedia.org/wiki/Orson_Squire_Fowler.

24  Barrett, *Poor Man's Home*, 12–13.

25  Barrett, 60.

26  Barrett, 57.

27  Howard Burba, "Remember when the Powder Mills Exploded," *Dayton Daily News*, March 5, 1933, https://www.daytonhistorybooks.com/powdermill.html.

28  Renee Wilde, "WYSO Curious Investigates the Explosive History of Buildings along the Bike Path," WYSO, July 27, 2017, https://www.wyso.org/post/wyso-curious-investigates-explosive-history-buildings-along-bike-path.

29  Thomas D. Schiffer, *Peters and King* (Iola, WI: Krause Publications, 2002), 14.

30  Gregory P. Davis, "Gershom Peters Changes the World from Warren County, Ohio," https://www.gregorydavisdds.com/blog/2017/01/05/gershom-peters-changes-the-world-178549.

31  Schiffer, *Peters and King*, 29–44.

32  "G. M. Peters, LLD," *Journal and Messenger: The Central National Baptist Paper*, October 9, 1919, 10.

33  Gershom M. Peters, *The Master, Or, The Story of Stories Retold* (New York: Fleming H. Revell Co., 1911), 7.

34  John Beardsley, *Gardens of Revelation: Environments by Visionary Artists* (New York: Abbveville Press, 1995), 139–40.

35  Thomas A. Michel, "Harry Andrews and His Castle," in *Personal Places: Perspectives on Informal Art Environments*, ed. Daniel Franklin Ward (Bowling Green, OH: Bowling Green State University Popular Press, 1984), 121.

36  Beardsley, *Gardens of Revelation*, 140.

37  Michel, "Harry Andrews and His Castle," 116–17.

38  Beardsley, *Gardens of Revelation*, 142.

39  Michel, "Harry Andrews and His Castle," 115.

40  Michel, "Harry Andrews and His Castle," 120.

41  Beardsley, *Gardens of Revelation*, 143.

42  Lori Jareo, "Harry Andrews and the Legend of Chateau La Roche," World War I, http://www.worldwar1.com/sfroche.htm.

43  "Little Miami Scenic Trail," *Wikipedia*, https://en.wikipedia.org/wiki/Little_Miami _Scenic_Trail.

44  Graydon DeCamp, "Railbed Bike Hike Plan Praised Here," *Cincinnati Enquirer*, March 18, 1975, 10.

45  Sue McDonald, "Along the River," *Cincinnati Enquirer*, May 12, 1984, 9.

46  Alice Hornbaker, "Little Miami Bike Trail Extends its Reach," *Cincinnati Enquirer*, August 2, 1991, EXTRA-1.

47  "Honton Gets State Biking Post," *Telegraph-Forum* (Bucyrus, OH), June 11, 1985, 11.

48  "Erie, Ohio Trail Aim," *Coshocton Tribune*, November 27, 1991, 1.

49  "Ed Honton," *Columbus Dispatch*, October 16, 2005, https://www.legacy.com/obi tuaries/dispatch/obituary.aspx?n=ed-honton&pid=15384370.

## Chapter 4

1  Richard Scamyhorn and John Steinle, *Stockades in the Wilderness: The Frontier Defenses and Settlements of Southwestern Ohio* (Cincinnati: Commonwealth Book Company, 2015), 13–14.

2  Stanley Hedeen, *Little Miami River: Wild and Scenic, River Ecology and History*, https://littlemiamistatepark.org/park-and-trail/history-park-trail/19-uncategorised/ little-miami-scenic-trail-and-river/31-the-little-miami-wild-and-scenic-river -ecology-and-history, 9–12.

3  Scamyhorn and Steinle, *Stockades in the Wilderness*, 14.

4  "History of Columbia Tusculum," Columbia Tusculum, Cincinnati, https://www .columbiatusculum.org/history.

5  "History of Columbia Tusculum."

6    Scamyhorn and Steinle, *Stockades in the Wilderness*, 15.

7    Scamyhorn and Steinle, 15–20.

8    Ann Thompson, "Pioneer Cemetery Is Clue to Cincinnati Founders," WVXU, August 27, 2013, https://www.wvxu.org/post/pioneer-cemetery-clue-cincinnati -founders#stream/0; "History of Columbia Tusculum."

9    "Images of Historical Cincinnati," Cincinnati Museum Center, 234, http://library .cincymuseum.org/topics/a/files/artists/ima-233.pdf.

10   Richard C. Wade, *The Urban Frontier: The Rise of Western Cities, 1790–1830* (Urbana: University of Illinois Press, 1959), 23.

11   "History of Columbia Tusculum."

12   Works Progress Administration, *Cincinnati: A Guide to the Queen City and Its Neighbors* (N.p.: US History Publishers, 1979), 242.

13   Michael C. Robinson, "History of Navigation of the Ohio River Basin," (Institute for Water Resources, 1938), 8.

14   Hedeen, *Little Miami River*, 51–55.

15   "Current Statistics of Women in Aviation Careers in the U.S.," *Women in Aviation International*, https://www.wai.org/resources/waistats.

16   Jim Milner, "High Flying with Martha Lunken," *Cincinnati Magazine*, February 16, 2015, https://www.cincinnatimagazine.com/article/high-flying-martha-lunken/.

17   "Lunken Airport's History," City of Cincinnati, https://www.cincinnati-oh.gov/dote/ lunken-airport/history/.

18   Walt Schaefer, "Airport Murals Need Repair," *Cincinnati Enquirer*, June 19, 1999, 15.

19   Clara Longworth de Chambrun, *The Making of Nicholas Longworth: Annals of an American Family* (New York: Ray Long and Richard R. Smith, 1933), 29.

20   Longworth de Chambrun, *Making of Nicholas Longworth*, 47.

21   "Our History," Cincinnati Observatory, https://www.cincinnatiobservatory.org/ about/our-history/.

22   Marian Knight, "Historic Mount Adams," Cincinnati Museum Center, 27–28, http:// library.cincymuseum.org/topics/l/files/longworth/chsbull-v28-n1-his-027.pdf.

23   Knight, "Historic Mount Adams," 27–28.

24   Much of this information is drawn from a permanent exhibit at the Cincinnati Art Museum.

25   Oscar Lovell Triggs, *Arts and Crafts Movement* (New York: Parkstone Press International, 2014), 121–25.

26   "Storer, Maria Longworth Nichols," Theodore Roosevelt Center, https://www.theo dorerooseveltcenter.org/Learn-About-TR/TR-Encyclopedia/Family-and-Friends/ Maria-Storer.

27   "First Person Program Series: Maria Longworth Nichols Storer," Heritage Village Museum, https://heritagevillagecincinnati.org/events/first-person-program-series -maria-longworth-nichols-storer/; Ralph P. Locke and Cyrilla Barr, *Cultivating Music in America: Women Patrons and Activists since 1860* (Berkeley: University of California Press, 1997), 72.

28  Michael George, Eden Park History Tour, September 2015; Knight, "Historic Mount Adams."

29  "A Glance at the Garden of Eden," Cincinnati Museum Center, http://library.cincy museum.org/topics/l/files/longworth/chsbull-v28-n2-gla-142.pdf.

30  "Alms Park," https://www.cincinnatiparks.com/parks-venues/east/alms-park/.

## Chapter 5

1  James Alexander Thom, *Follow the River* (New York: Ballantine Books, 1981), 131.

2  Thom, *Follow the River*, 139.

3  Thom, 163.

4  Thom, 362.

5  Daryl Polley, "Bellevue," in *Encyclopedia of Northern Kentucky*, ed. Paul A. Tenkotte and James C. Claypool (Lexington: University Press of Kentucky, 2009), 77.

## Chapter 6

1  "Underground Railroad: Fee Villa," *Breathless Adventurer* (blog), June 27, 2015, https://breathlessadventurer.com/2015/06/27/ur-moscow/.

2  "Franklin Township Looking to Restore Grave," *Clermont Sun*, January 12, 2017, https://www.clermontsun.com/2017/01/12/franklin-township-looking-to-restore -grave/.

3  Alexander Duncan, "Letter from Mr. Duncan of Ohio," *Niles National Register*, January 5, 1839, 292; see also Alexander Duncan, *Speech of Mr. Duncan, of Ohio, on the Subject of the New Jersey Election, Delivered in the House of Representatives, U.S. January 9, 1840* (Baltimore: Office of the Post, 1840), 23.

4  Marie Pollitt Bethanie, "The Antislavery Movement in Clermont County" (master's thesis, Northern Kentucky University, 2005), 1–19, 73–75.

5  Alexander Duncan, *Remarks of Mr. Duncan of Ohio on the Right of Partition, Delivered in the House of Representatives, January 6, 1844* (Washington, DC: Globe Office, 1844), 4.

6  Alexander Duncan, *Remarks of Mr. Duncan of Ohio*, 8.

7  Ann Hagedorn, *Beyond the River* (New York: Simon & Schuster, 2004), 127.

8  Jeff Suess, "1836 Cincinnati Riots Couldn't Stop Anti-Slavery Newspaper," Cincinnati.com, May 11, 2017, https://www.cincinnati.com/story/news/2017/05/11/ 1836-cincinnati-riots-couldnt-stop-anti-slavery-newspaper/101497562/.

9  Hagedorn, *Beyond the River*, 114.

10  "The Fugitive Slave Law of 1850," Constitutional Rights Foundation, https://www .crf-usa.org/images/pdf/Fugitive-Slave-Law-1850.pdf.

11  Hagedorn, *Beyond the River*, 135.

12  John Henry Tibbets, "Reminiscences of Slavery Times," Tibbets Family Antislavery History, https://fordwebtech.com/tibbets-history/JohnTibbetsLetter.php.

13  Tibbets, "Reminiscences of Slavery Times."

14  Tibbets.

15  Randy McNutt, "New Richmond Marker Recalls Slavery Opposition," *Cincinnati Enquirer*, February 8, 2003, 13.

16  McNutt, "New Richmond Marker Recalls Slavery Opposition."

17  Pension File of Leroy Lee, National Archives and Records Administration, "Federal Military Pension Application, Civil War and Later Complete File," Application 463231, Certificate 513815.

18  "Caleb Swan Walker House," New Richmond Underground Railroad Tour, http://newrichmondugrrtour.weebly.com/about.html.

19  "Cranston Presbyterian Church," New Richmond Underground Railroad Tour, http://newrichmondugrrtour.weebly.com/about.html.

20  "Second Baptist Church," New Richmond Underground Railroad Tour, http://newrichmondugrrtour.weebly.com/about.html.

21  John P. Parker, *His Promised Land*, ed. Stuart Seely Sprague (New York: W. W. Norton, 1996) 7–16.

22  Parker, *His Promised Land*, 7–16.

23  Parker, 102–3.

24  Parker, 103–4.

25  Hagedorn, *Beyond the River*, 135–37.

26  Hagedorn, 138.

27  Hagedorn, 138.

28  Hagedorn, 139.

29  Hagedorn, 139.

30  Parker, *His Promised Land*, 86.

31  *Williams Hamilton County Directory for 1907–8* (Cincinnati: Williams Directory Co.), 254.

32  "Officials in Quandary Due to Objections of Norwood Residents to Negro Colony," *Cincinnati Enquirer*, July 4, 1922, 24.

33  "Park to be Located in Norwood to Prevent Threatened Formation of Negro Colony," *Cincinnati Enquirer*, July 18, 1922, 10; "Park Is Solution of Puzzle," *Cincinnati Enquirer*, September 6, 1922, 20.

34  "Would Enjoin Health Officer," *Cincinnati Enquirer*, March 27, 1914, 10.

35  "Verschiedenes" [Sundries], *Tagliches Cincinnatier Volksblatt*, March 27, 1914, 5.

36  Death Certificate of Miranda Parker, Ohio Bureau of Vital Statistics, Certificate 3693, June 27, 1920.

37  "Park Is Solution of Puzzle."

38  "Norwood Mayor Praised," *Cincinnati Enquirer*, September 19, 1922, 20.

## Chapter 7

1  Donald M. Burden, "Whitewater Canal Historical Corridor Guide" (master's thesis, Ball State University, 2006), 19–22.

2   "Major Canals Built in the 19th Century, American Northeast," Geography of Transportation Systems, https://transportgeography.org/?page_id=1128.

3   Boone Triplett, *Canals of Ohio: A History and Tour Guide* (Wadsworth, OH: Silver Sassafras Publications, 2011), 134–52.

4   Phillip Anderson, "Whitewater Canal Scenic Byway," ISSUU, May 21, 2012, 15. https://issuu.com/ruralphil/docs/wcsb_canal_route_5.22.12.

5   Burden, "Whitewater Canal Historical Corridor Guide," 41.

6   Freed D. Cavinder, *More Amazing Tales from Indiana* (Bloomington: Indiana University Press, 2003), 92–93.

7   "National Historic Landmark Nomination: Duck Creek Aqueduct," National Register of Historic Places, https://www.nps.gov/hdp/project/coveredbridges/nhls/Duck Creek.pdf.

8   "James Brown Ray (1794–1848)," Governors' History Site, https://www.in.gov/gover norhistory/2374.htm.

9   James M. Miller, "An Early Criminal Case: Samuel Fields," *Indiana Magazine of History* 1, no. 4 (1905): 201–3.

10  Miller, "Early Criminal Case," 202.

11  Miller, 202.

12  Miller, 203.

13  Miller, 203.

14  Miller, 203.

15  Miller, 203.

16  Doug Masson, "Bicentennial Installment 2: Indiana as a Young State," *A Citizen's Guide to Indiana* (blog), January 11, 2016, https://www.masson.us/blog/bicentennial -installment-2-indiana-as-a-young-state/.

17  Masson, "Bicentennial Installment 2."

18  Andrew Olson, "Mammoth Internal Improvements Act: The Bee Line Railroad Facing Dilemma: Loss of Local Control," *Indiana History Blog*, March 13, 2017, https://blog.history.in.gov/the-bee-line-railroad-financing-dilemma-loss-of-local -control/.

19  Burden, "Whitewater Canal Historical Corridor Guide," 7.

20  Paul Fatout, "Canalling in the Whitewater Valley," *Indiana Magazine of History* 60, no. 1, (March 1964): 59.

21  Burden, "Whitewater Canal Historical Corridor Guide," 1.

22  Burden, 11.

23  Brian Gauvin, "Erie Canal Tugboats Push on through Two Centuries of Change," *Professional Mariner*, February 28, 2018, http://www.professionalmariner.com/ March-2018/Erie-Canal-tugboats-push-on-through-two-centuries-of-change/.

24  "Whitewater Canal," *Moment of Indiana History*, June 13, 2005, https://indianapublic media.org/momentofindianahistory/whitewater-canal/.

25  Fatout, "Canalling in the Whitewater Valley," 76.

26  Geoff Hobson, "A Return to City's Canal Days, with a Twist," *Cincinnati Enquirer*, November 14, 1992, A-1, A-4.

27  Fatout, "Canalling in the Whitewater Valley," 39, 76–78.

28  "James B. Ray," *Wikipedia*, https://en.wikipedia.org/wiki/James_B._Ray.

## Chapter 8

1   Millard F. Rogers Jr., *Rich in Good Works: Mary M. Emery of Cincinnati* (Akron, OH: University of Akron Press, 2001), 78.

2   Bradley D. Cross, "On a Business Basis: An American Garden City," *Planning Perspectives* 19, no. 1 (2004), https://www.tandfonline.com/doi/abs/10.1080/0266543042000177913.

3   Tom Callarco et al., *Places of the Underground Railroad, a Geographical Guide* (Santa Barbara, CA: ABC-CLIO, LLC, 2011), 77.

4   Millard F. Rogers Jr., *John Nolen and Mariemont* (Baltimore, MD: Johns Hopkins University Press, 2001), 16–18.

5   Rogers, *Rich in Good Works*, 81.

6   Rogers, *John Nolen and Mariemont*, 177.

7   "Mariemont to Be Model City," *Cincinnati Enquirer*, April 23, 1922, 15.

8   Rogers, *Rich in Good Works*, 86.

9   Rogers, *Rich in Good Works*, 87.

10  Archibald Rutledge, "I Got a Glory," *Syracuse Herald-American*, August 29, 1965, 20.

11  James T. Lloyd, *Lloyd's Steamboat Directory, and Disasters on the Western Waters* (Cincinnati: James T. Lloyd & Co., 1856), 89.

12  *History of Clermont County, Ohio, with Illustrations and Biographical Sketches* (Philadelphia: Louis H. Everts, 1880), 483–85.

13  "John Perin," Find-A-Grave, https://www.findagrave.com/memorial/150078624.

14  Lloyd, *Lloyd's Steamboat Directory*, 89.

15  Lloyd, 89.

16  Betty Kamuf, "Problems Plagued Canal Projects," Cincinnati.com, March 24, 2014, https://www.cincinnati.com/story/news/2014/03/24/problems-plagued-canal-projects/6833875/.

17  Lloyd, *Lloyd's Steamboat Directory*, 89–91.

18  Lloyd, 91.

19  Lloyd, 91.

20  Lloyd, 91–92.

21  Ballard C. Campbell, *Disasters, Accidents, and Crises in American History* (New York: Facts on File, 2008), 80.

22  William Lytle, "Personal Narrative of William Lytle," *Quarterly Publication of the Historical and Philosophical Society of Ohio* 1, no. 1 (January–March 1906): 4.

23  Byron Williams, *History of Clermont and Brown Counties, Ohio*, vol. 2 (Milford, OH: Hobart Publishing, 1913), 193.

24 Williams, *History of Clermont and Brown Counties*, 197.

25 Linda Smith Walker, *Williamsburg and Batavia: Images of America* (Charleston, SC: Arcadia Publishing, 2012), 13–15.

26 Williams, *History of Clermont and Brown Counties*, 279.

27 Walker, *Williamsburg and Batavia*, 13–15.

28 Williams, *History of Clermont and Brown Counties*, 317.

29 Lytle, "Personal Narrative," 3.

30 Ruth C. Carter, ed., *For Honor, Glory, and Union: The Mexican & Civil War Letters of Brig. Gen. William Haines Lytle* (Lexington: University Press of Kentucky), 2–6.

31 William Haines Lytle, *Poems of William Haines Lytle*, ed. William Henry Venable (Cincinnati: Stewart & Kidd, 1912), 135–36.

32 Carter, *For Honor, Glory, and Union*, 19, 23.

33 Lytle, *Poems of William Haines Lytle*, 113–14.

34 William Bailie, *Josiah Warren: The First American Anarchist* (Boston: Small, Maynard & Co., 1906), 51.

35 "Utopia, Ohio," History Collection, https://historycollection.com/10-american-uto pian-communities-rose-perfection-dramatically-collapse/5/.

36 John Cunliffe and Guido Erreygers, "The Enigmatic Legacy of Charles Fourier: Joseph Charlier and Basic Income," *History of Political Economy* 33, no. 3 (Fall 2001), https://muse.jhu.edu/article/13304.

37 "A Surprising Fact about Feminism," *Chicago Tribune*, January 7, 2016, https://www .chicagotribune.com/redeye/redeye-a-surprising-fact-about-feminism-20160107 -story.html.

38 "Phalange," *Encyclopedia Britannica*, https://www.britannica.com/topic/phalange -government.

39 Bailie, *Josiah Warren*, 50.

40 Josiah Warren, *Equitable Commerce: A New Development of Principles*, ed. Stephen P. Andrews (New York: Burt Franklin, 1852), vi.

41 Bailie, *Josiah Warren*, 50.

42 David S. D'Amato, "Josiah Warren: The Most Practical Anarchist," Libertarian ism.org, March 23, 2020, https://www.libertarianism.org/columns/josiah-warren -practical-anarchist.

43 "Flood Drowned Out Fourierism," *Cincinnati Enquirer*, August 22, 1897, 13.

44 Bailie, *Josiah Warren*, 50.

45 Bailie, 50.

46 Bailie, 9–13.

47 Bailie, 51.

48 *History of Clermont County*, 344.

49 "Letter from H. C. Wright," *Anti-Slavery Bugle* (Lisbon, OH), September 13, 1851, 3.

50 Peter Linebaugh, *Stop, Thief! The Commons, Enclosures, and Resistance* (Oakland, CA: PM Press, 2014), 201

51  Randy McNutt, "Life in Utopia," *Dennison Magazine*, https://denisonmagazine.com/opening_page/life-in-utopia/.

52  William Turner Coggeshall, *The Signs of the Times, Comprising a History of the Spirit-Rappings in Cincinnati and Other Places* (Cincinnati: privately published, 1851), 123.

53  *History of Clermont County*, 343–44.

54  "Heart-Rending Calamity!! Fall of a Building: Seventeen Lives Lost," *Portage Sentinel* (Ravenna, OH), December 29, 1847, 2.

55  "Letter from H. C. Wright," 3.

56  "Augustus Wattles," Following the Trail of the Underground Railroad, http://sgmm.org/plainandsimple/wattles.html.

57  Bailie, *Josiah Warren*, 57.

58  Bailie, 55.

59  James Joseph Martin, *Men against the State* (Auburn, AL: Ludwig von Mises Institute, 2009), 63.

60  Martin, *Men against the State*, 63.

61  Bailie, *Josiah Warren*, 54–55.

62  Martin, *Men against the State*, 100–102.

## Chapter 9

1  Kevin Grace and Tom White, *Cincinnati's Over-the-Rhine* (Charleston, SC: Arcadia, 2003), 29.

2  "Cincinnati, OH Population and Races," USA.com, http://www.usa.com/cincinnati-oh-population-and-races.htm.

3  Melissa Kramer, *The Inclines of Cincinnati* (Charleston, SC: Arcadia, 2009).

4  "The Queen's Drink? Beer," *Cincinnati Magazine*, July 1980, 81.

5  Michael D. Morgan, *Over-the-Rhine: When Beer Was King* (Charleston, SC: History Press, 2010), 56–67.

6  Morgan, *Over-the-Rhine*, 33.

7  P. Christiaan Klieger, *The Fleischmann Yeast Family* (Charleston, SC: Arcadia, 2004).

8  Morgan, *Over-the-Rhine*, 30.

9  Morgan, 14, 68.

10  Greg Noble and Lucy May, "Cincinnati's Rise and Fall as a Brewery Town: From Porkopolis to Beeropolis, How It All Began," WCPO, January 17, 2017, https://www.wcpo.com/entertainment/local-a-e/cincinnatis-rise-and-fall-as-a-brewery-town-part-1-from-porkopolis-to-beeropolis-how-it-all-began.

11  Catherine Cooper, "Happy 100th, Hudepohl," *Cincinnati Magazine*, April 1985, 112.

12  Timothy J. Holian, "The Hudepohl Brewing Company of Cincinnati, Ohio: A Case Study in Regional Brewery Prosperity and Decline," *Journal of Brewery History* 141, no. 201: 12–53.

13  Don Heinrich Tolzmann, *John Hauck: Cincinnati's West End Beer Baron: The Man and His Brewery* (Cincinnati: Little Miami Publishing, 2017).

14 Noble and May, "Cincinnati's Rise and Fall as a Brewery Town."

15 Greg Hand, "Don't Try This at Home: Cincinnati's Legendary Beer Gulpers," *Cincinnati Magazine*, November 21, 2015, https://www.cincinnatimagazine.com/city wiseblog/dont-try-this-at-home-cincinnatis-legendary-beer-gulpers/.

16 Greg Hand, "Cincinnati's Old Breweries Were Death Traps," *Cincinnati Curiosities* (blog), May 2, 2017, https://handeaux.tumblr.com/post/160225399187/cincinnatis -old-breweries-were-bloody-death-traps.

17 Noble and May, "Cincinnati's Rise and Fall as a Brewery Town."

18 Noble and May.

19 Noble and May; "OTR History," http://www.otrfoundation.org/OTR_History.htm.

20 Noble and May.

21 Noble and May.

22 Noble and May.

23 John H. White Jr., "The Cincinnati Inclined Plane Railway Company: The Mount Auburn Incline and the Lookout House," Cincinnati Museum Center, http://library .cincymuseum.org/topics/i/files/inclines/chsbull-v27-n1-cin-007.pdf, 7.

24 Jeff Suess, "Inclines Helped the City Spread Out," *Cincinnati Enquirer*, March 3, 2017, https://www.cincinnati.com/story/news/2017/03/03/inclines-helped-city-spread -out/98577752/.

25 White, "Cincinnati Inclined Plane Railway Company."

26 Kramer, *Inclines of Cincinnati*.

## Chapter 10

1 Calvin Dill Wilson, *Glendale the Beautiful* (N.p.:1931), 1.

2 "History & Master Plan," Cincinnati Parks, https://www.cincinnatiparks.com/ history-and-masterplan/.

3 Kurt Culbertson, "George Edward Kessler: Landscape Architect of the American Renaissance," in *Midwestern Landscape Architecture*, ed. William H. Tishler (Urbana: University of Illinois Press, 2000), 99–116.

4 Philip Pregill and Nancy Volkman, *Landscapes in History: Design and Urban Planning in the Eastern and Western Tradition* (New York: John Wiley and Sons, 1999), 532.

5 Henry B. Teetor, *The Past and Present of the Mill Creek Valley* (Cincinnati: Cohen and Co., 1882), 246–47.

6 The information for this section was drawn from a number of sources, including "Glendale History: A Glimpse into the Past," http://www.glendaleohioarchive.org/ history.html, and "Glendale's Historical Markers, http://www.glendaleohioarchive .org/markers.html.

7 Pregill and Volkman, *Landscapes in History*, 532.

8 Teetor, *Past and Present of the Mill Creek Valley*, 238–307.

9   Teetor, 278–80; Frederick Whitford, Andrew G. Martin, and Phyllis Mattheis, *The Queen of American Agriculture: A Biography of Virginia Claypool Meredith* (West Lafayette, IN: Purdue University Press, 2008), 8–11.

10  Whitford, Martin, and Mattheis, *Queen of American Agriculture*, 8–11.

11  George Ralph Hall, *By George, He Did It! A True Scholar's Autobiography* (N.p.: 2011).

12  "The Eliza House," Glendale's Historical Markers, http://www.glendaleohioarchive .org/markers.html; Frank W. Hale, "Salmon Portland Chase: Rhetorician of Abolition," *Negro History Bulletin* 26, no. 5 (February 1963): 166.

13  Elisha Anderson, "Black Squirrels in Michigan Popping up in More Places," *Detroit Free Press*, January 23, 2016, https://www.freep.com/story/news/local/michigan/ 2016/01/23/black-squirrels-in-michigan/78362460/.

14  Quan Trong, "City's Largest Park Celebrates 100 Years," *Cincinnati Enquirer*, June 4, 2011, S6-S7.

15  "National Register of Historic Places Program: Landscape Architecture Month Feature 2013, Mount Airy Forest, Cincinnati, Ohio," National Park Service, https:// www.nps.gov/NR/feature/landscape/2013/Mount_Airy.htm.

16  Joseph L. Arnold, *The New Deal in the Suburbs: A History of the Greenbelt Town Program, 1935–1954* (Columbus: Ohio University Press, 1971), xii-xiii, 11, 37.

17  Ebenezer Howard, *Garden Cities of Tomorrow* (Cambridge, MA: MIT Press, 1965), 45.

18  Howard, *Garden Cities of Tomorrow*, 142.

19  Arnold, *New Deal in the Suburbs*, 50, 85.

20  Arnold, 58.

21  Arnold, 112.

22  Arnold, 150–85, 244.

23  Arnold, 127–91.

24  Stanley Hedeen, *The Mill Creek: An Unnatural History of an Urban Stream* (Cincinnati: Blue Heron Press, 1994), 159–62.

## Chapter 11

1   Harold W. Turner, *From Temple to Meeting House* (New York: Mouton Publishers, 1979), 18–32.

2   Jonathan D. Sarna, "'A Sort of Paradise for the Hebrews': The Lofty Vision of Cincinnati Jews," in *The Jews of Cincinnati*, ed. Jonathan D. Sarna and Nancy H. Klein (Cincinnati: Center for the Study of the American Jewish Experience on the Campus of Hebrew Union College, Jewish Institute of Religion, 1989), 18.

3   Information for this section was mostly drawn from *The Jews of Cincinnati*; a conversation with Andrea Rapp, Wise Temple librarian, and Alex Burte, director of membership and programming at Isaac M. Wise Temple, summer 2018; and several conversations with Gary Zola, American Jewish Archives Center. See also "History

of Plum Street Temple," Isaac M. Wise Temple, https://www.wisetemple.org/about/our-history/history-of-plum-street-temple/.

4   Sarna, "'A Sort of Paradise,'" 15.

5   Jonathan D. Sarna and Nancy H. Klein, eds., *The Jews of Cincinnati* (Cincinnati: Center for the Study of the American Jewish Experience on the Campus of Hebrew Union College, Jewish Institute of Religion, 1989), 54.

6   Sarna, "'A Sort of Paradise,'" 1.

7   Sarna, "A Sort of Paradise," 14; Sarna and Klein, *The Jews of Cincinnati*, 46.

8   Sarna, "A Sort of Paradise," 14.

9   Sarna, "A Sort of Paradise," 15.

10   Isaac Mayer Wise, *The World of My Books*, trans. and intro by Albert H. Friedlander (Cincinnati: American Jewish Archives), 12.

11   Wise, *World of My Books*.

12   "A History of Old St. Mary's," https://www.oldstmarys.org/about/a-history-of-old-st-marys/.

13   "Roman Catholic Church," Ohio History Central, https://ohiohistorycentral.org/w/Roman_Catholic_Church.

14   "Bluffton Pastor and Party to Tour Europe," *Indianapolis News*, March 29, 1938, 8.

15   "Called Here," *Indianapolis Star*, December 23, 1928, 8; "Call to Bluffton Accepted By Coers," *Indianapolis Star*, August 4, 1935, 10.

16   "Pastor Enters Red Cross Work," *Daily Telegram* (Adrian, MI), June 29, 1942, 1; "Rev. M. H. Coers Arrives in Africa," *Indianapolis Star*, June 6, 1943, 6.

17   James S. Bielo, "'Where Prayers May Be Whispered': Promises of Presence in Protestant Place-Making," *Ethnos* (2019): 4–5.

18   Claude Wolff, "'Garden of Hope' Chapel Being Built in Kenton," *Courier-Journal* (Louisville, KY), August 8, 1956, 17.

19   "Lyman Beecher," Ohio History Central, https://ohiohistorycentral.org/w/Lyman_Beecher.

20   "Debate at the Lane Seminary, Cincinnati, Speech of James A. Thome, of Kentucky," delivered at the Annual Meeting of the American Anti-Slavery Society, May 6, 1834.

21   "Debate at the Lane Seminary," 4.

22   "Debate at the Lane Seminary."

23   Ron Gorman, "From Hopeless Bondage to Lane Rebel," *Oberlin Heritage Center* (blog), http://www.oberlinheritagecenter.org/blog/2013/09/james-bradley-from-hopeless-bondage-to-lane-rebel/.

24   "Union Baptist Church," https://www.union-baptist.net/about-us/our-history/.

25   "George Washington Williams," Union Baptist Church, https://www.union-baptist.net/about-us/our-history/pastors/george-washington-williams/.

26   "Population by Counties—1790-1870, Table 2, State of Ohio," US Census, https://www2.census.gov/library/publications/decennial/1870/population/1870a-09.pdf#.

27  John Hope Franklin, *George Washington Williams: A Biography* (Durham, NC: Duke University Press, 1998), ix.

28  Franklin, *George Washington Williams*, x.

29  Franklin, 38.

30  Franklin, 41.

## Chapter 12

1   "Spring Grove," *Cincinnati Commercial*, April 25, 1870, 7.

2   Brent Coleman, "History: Who Is Buried in Spring Grove's Dexter Mausoleum?" Cincinnati.com, January 14, 2014, https://www.cincinnati.com/story/news/2014/01/13/history-who-is-buried-in-spring-grove-cemeterys-dexter-mausoleum/4455281/

3   "Searching out the 'Old Dexter Whiskey' Three," *Those Pre-Pro Whiskey Men!* (blog), November 26, 2015, http://pre-prowhiskeymen.blogspot.com/2015/11/searching-out-old-dexter-whiskey-three.html.

4   Coleman, "Who Is Buried in Spring Grove's Dexter Mausoleum?"

5   "Freaks of the Lightning," *Cincinnati Commercial*, April 26, 1878, 8.

6   "Harvard University Benefits," *Cincinnati Enquirer*, March 15, 1919, 5; "News of the Courts," *Cincinnati Enquirer*, March 9, 1923, 5.

7   Coleman, "Who Is Buried in Spring Grove's Dexter Mausoleum?"

8   Mike Osborne, "Former US Nuclear Weapons Plant Undergoes Amazing Transformation," VOA News, June 22, 1010, https://www.voanews.com/usa/former-us-nuclear-weapons-plant-undergoes-amazing-transformation.

9   Jenny Wohlfarth, "What Lies beneath Fernald Preserve," *Cincinnati Magazine*, June 7, 2019, https://www.cincinnatimagazine.com/citywiseblog/what-lies-beneath-the-fernald-preserve/.

10  Kenneth R. Feinberg, "In the Shadow of Fernald: Who Should Pay the Victims?" *Brookings Review* 8, no. 90 (Summer 1990): 41.

11  "Uranus," Haggard Hawks: Obscure Words, Language, Facts & Etymology, February 10, 2016, https://www.haggardhawks.com/post/2016/02/10/Uranus.

12  "Uranus," Greek Mythology, https://www.greekmythology.com/Other_Gods/Uranus/uranus.html.

13  "Marie Curie and Lise Meitner," Institute of Physics, https://www.iop.org/resources/topic/archive/curie-meitner/page_65216.html#gref.

14  "Lisa Crawford," Fernald Living History Project Transcript, Tape FLHP0166, August 17, 1999, http://www.fernaldcommunityalliance.org/FLHPinterviews/CrawfordLisa.pdf.

15  Feinberg, "In the Shadow of Fernald," 41–46.

16  "Nature of the Contamination," Museum display panel at Fernald Preserve Visitors' Center, photographed March 28, 2018.

17  Gary Lee, "$20 Million Settlement Reached Between Nuclear Plant Workers, Energy Dept.," *Washington Post*, July 27, 1994, https://www.washingtonpost.com/archive/politics/1994/07/27/20-million-settlement-reached-between-nuclear-plant-workers-energy-dept/e99368ac-7518-4cc2-a352-e778c4345308/.

18  "History of the Fernald Citizens Advisory Board," Fernald Citizens Advisory Board, 1993–2006, https://www.lm.doe.gov/land/sites/oh/FernaldCAB/FCABHistory/history.html.

19  Docent-led group hike at Fernald, April 11, 2015; See also Wohlfarth, "What Lies beneath Fernald Preserve."

20  Kenneth Noble, "U.S., For Decades, Let Uranium Leak at Weapons Plant," *New York Times*, October 15, 1988, 1.

21  "Fissile Material Basics," Institute for Energy and Environmental Research, https://ieer.org/resource/factsheets/fissile-material-basics/.

22  Nardi Reeder Campion, *Mother Ann Lee: Morning Start of the Shakers* (Hanover, NH: University Press of New England), 1990, xv, 1–30.

23  Campion, *Mother Ann Lee*, 23–31.

24  Campion, 45, 61.

25  "Shakers," New World Encyclopedia, https://www.newworldencyclopedia.org/entry/Shakers.

26  Stephen J. Stein, *The Shaker Experience in America: A History of the United Society of Believers* (New Haven, CT: Yale University Press, 1992), 160.

27  Ann Morrow, "Shakers' Many Gifts," HistoryNet, https://www.historynet.com/shakers-many-gifts.htm.

28  J. P. MacLean, *Shakers of Ohio* (Philadelphia: Porcupine Press, 1975), 59–388.

29  Laura A. Hobson, "White Water Shaker Village: A Trip to a Purer, Simpler Time," Cincinnati.com, April 2, 2019, https://www.cincinnati.com/story/news/2019/04/02/white-water-shaker-village-trip-purer-simpler-time/3271749002/.

30  "The Great Disappointment," *Wikipedia*, https://en.wikipedia.org/wiki/Great_Disappointment.

31  Frank Grayson, "Extinct Shaker Colony," *Cincinnati Times Star*, December 20, 1932.

32  "Among the Shakers: A Visit to Whitewater Village," *Cincinnati Commercial*, July 21, 1871.

33  J. P. MacLean, "Origin, Rise, Progress, and Decline of the Whitewater Community of Shakers Located in Hamilton County, Ohio," *Ohio History*, January 1901, 401.

34  "Among the Shakers," in *Whitewater, Ohio, Village of Shakers, 1824–1916: Its History and Its People*, ed. Marjorie Byrnside Burress (Cincinnati: privately printed, 1979), 31.

35  Bob Lynn, "Recalling Life with the Shakers: An interview with Sherman Smith," *Cincinnati Enquirer*, April 7, 1968.

36  Grayson, "Extinct Shaker Colony."

37  *Harrison News*, June 20, 1907.

38 "Whitewater Colony of Shakers Soon Will Disappear," *Cincinnati Times Star*, October 17, 1916.

39 *Harrison News*, February 2, 1882, in Burress, ed., *Whitewater, Ohio, Village*, 38–39.

40 "Paddy's Run," Historical Marker Database, https://www.hmdb.org/m.asp?m=23991.

41 "Victorian Funeral Customs and Superstitions," Friends of Oak Grove Cemetery, https://friendsofoakgrovecemetery.org/victorian-funeral-customs-fears-and-super stitions/.

## Chapter 13

1 Duane A. Griffin, "Hollow and Habitable Within: Symmes' Theory of Earth's Internal Structure and Polar Geography," *Physical Geography* 25, no. 5 (September 2004): 382.

2 John McBride, *Symmes's Theory of Concentric Spheres: Demonstrating that the Earth is Hollow and Habitable Within, and Widely Open about the Poles* (Cincinnati: Morgan, Lodge, and Fisher, 1826, reprinted by Nabu Public Domain Reprints, n.d.), 93–102.

3 Peter W. Sinnema, "10 April 1818: John Cleves Symmes's 'No. 1 Circular.'" BRANCH: Britain, Representation and Nineteenth-Century History, http://www.branchcollec tive.org/?ps_articles=peter-w-sinnema-10-april-1818-john-cleves-symmess-no-1 -circular.

4 McBride, *Symmes's Theory of Concentric Spheres*, 115.

5 McBride, 114–16.

6 McBride, 120–27.

7 McBride, 121.

8 L. I. Chaplow, "Tales of a Hollow Earth: Tracing the Legacy of John Cleves Symmes in Antarctic Exploration and Fiction" (master's thesis, University of Canterbury, 2011), 5–12, https://core.ac.uk/download/pdf/35465577.pdf.

9 McBride, *Symmes's Theory*, 130.

10 "Hamilton Burying Ground," Find-A-Grave.com, https://www.findagrave.com/cemetery/2645918/hamilton-burying-ground.

11 Doris L. Pace and Marie Johns, *The Amish Mennonite Settlement in Butler County, Ohio* (Trenton, OH: Trenton Historical Society, 1983), 7–13.

12 Pace, *Amish Mennonite Settlement*, 29–30.

13 Neil Ann Stucky Levine, ed., *Transplanted German Farmer: The Life and Times of Christian Iutzi...in His Own Words* (Sugar Creek, OH: Carlisle Printing, 2009), 25.

14 Levine, *Transplanted German Farmer*, 30.

15 Levine, *Transplanted German Farmer*, 31.

16 Pace, *Amish Mennonite Settlement*, 45.

17 William Henry Grubb, *History of the Mennonites of Butler County, Ohio* (Trenton: privately published, 1916), 15–16.

18 Pace, *Amish Mennonite Settlement*, 29.

19 "Amish," *Wikipedia*, https://en.wikipedia.org/wiki/Amish.

20  "Mennonites," *Wikipedia*, https://en.wikipedia.org/wiki/Mennonites.

21  "Why the Star City," City of Miamisburg, http://miamisburg200.com/history/.

22  See, for example, "Miamisburg," *Cincinnati Commercial Gazette*, January 9, 1885, 3; and "Silver Jubilee," *Darke County Democratic Advocate* (Greenville, OH), January 7, 1888, 1.

23  Howard Burba, "The Day They Opened Miamisburg Mound," *Dayton Daily News*, February 28, 1932, Dayton History Books Online, https://www.daytonhistorybooks .com/miamisburgmound.html.

24  "Miamisburg Mound," Ohio History Connection, https://www.ohiohistory.org/visit/ museum-and-site-locator/miamisburg-mound.

25  Burba, "The Day They Opened Miamisburg Mound."

26  Marego Athens, "Mysterious Midwest Mounds," *Baltimore Sun*, December 1, 2002, https://www.baltimoresun.com/news/bs-xpm-2002-12-01-0212010302-story.html.

27  "Serpent Mound," History.com, August 21, 2018, https://www.history.com/topics/ landmarks/serpent-mound.

## Chapter 14

1  "Fort Washington," Ohio History Central, https://ohiohistorycentral.org/w/Fort _Washington.

2  Russell Weigley, *History of the United States Army* (New York: MacMillan, 1967), 81.

3  James Madison, *The Writings of James Madison*, vol. 3, ed. Gallard Hunt (New York: G. P. Putnam's Sons, 1902), 317.

4  Weigley, *History of the United States Army*, 75–88.

5  "Newport Barracks," Explore Kentucky History, https://explorekyhistory.ky.gov/ items/show/44.

6  Weigley, *History of the United States Army*, 158-164, 182.

7  "United States Indian Wars, 1780s–1890s," FamilySearch, https://www.familysearch .org/wiki/en/United_States_Indian_Wars,_1780s-1890s.

8  John Kieswetter, "Civil Unrest Woven into City's History," Cincinnati.com, July 15, 2001, https://www.cincinnati.com/story/news/blogs/our-history/2018/06/08/civil-un rest-woven-into-citys-history/685960002/.

9  Kieswetter, "Civil Unrest Woven into City's History."

10  "Ohio in the American Civil War," *Wikipedia*, https://en.wikipedia.org/wiki/Ohio _in_the_American_Civil_War.

11  Lora Schmidt Cahill and David L. Mowery, *Morgan's Raid across Ohio: The Civil War Guidebook of the John Hunt Morgan Heritage Trail* (Columbus: Ohio Historical Society, 2014).

12  Lester Horwitz, *The Longest Raid of the Civil War* (Cincinnati: Farmcourt Publishing, 2001), 2-3.

13  Horwitz, *Longest Raid of the Civil War*, ix-xx, 1–5.

14  Horwitz, 356–76.

15  Albert Vinton Stegman Jr., "Samuel Bigstaff," in *History of Fort Thomas* (Fort Thomas, KY: Optimist Club, n.d.), n.p.

16  "The 'Napoleon of Promoters' Was Early Fort Thomas Developer and Major Promoter," Fort Thomas Matters, February 28, 2017, http://www.fortthomasmatters .com/2017/02/the-napoleon-of-promoters-was-early.html.

17  William R. Stevens, comp., *Fort Thomas Military Reservation 1888–1964* (Fort Thomas, KY: Campbell County Historical Society, n.d.), 17–18.

18  Stegman, "Samuel Bigstaff."

19  Stevens, *Fort Thomas Military Reservation*, 6, 14–22.

20  Stevens, 50.

21  "USS *Maine* (1889)," *Wikipedia*, https://en.wikipedia.org/wiki/USS_Maine_(1889).

22  "The Democratic Peace II: War with Spain," Institute of World Politics, https:// www.iwp.edu/articles/2019/04/17/the-democratic-peace-ii-war-with-spain/.

23  "Spanish-American War," History.com, May 14, 2010, https://www.history.com/ topics/early-20th-century-us/spanish-american-war.

24  "Fort Thomas History," City of Fort Thomas, Kentucky, http://ftthomas.org/ fort-thomas-history/.

25  Owen Findsen, "CSO Conductor Victim of WWI Fear," *Cincinnati Enquirer*, September 21, 1997, E-14.

26  Jeff Suess, "Anti-German Hysteria in City during WWI," Cincinnati.com, March 11, 2017, https://www.cincinnati.com/story/news/2017/03/11/anti-german-hysteria-city -during-wwi/98895422/.

27  Findsen, "CSO Conductor Victim of WWI Fear."

28  "Internment of Japanese Americans," *Wikipedia*, https://en.wikipedia.org/wiki/ Internment_of_Japanese_Americans.

29  Robert Earnest Miller, "The War That Never Came: Civilian Defense in Cincinnati, Ohio, during World War II," *Queen City Heritage* 49, no. 4 (Winter 1991): 6–8.

30  "Nike Missile Locations Ohio," Military Standard, http://www.themilitarystandard .com/missile/nike/locationsoh.php.

31  "Americans: Was Your Town a [Rumored] Cold War Missile Target?" Ask MetaFilter, October 27, 2009, https://ask.metafilter.com/136571/Americans-Was-your-town -a-rumored-Cold-War-missile-target.

32  Jacob R. Mecklenborg, *Cincinnati's Incomplete Subway: The Complete Story* (Charleston, SC: History Press, 2010), 87–89.

33  Gerald White, "Central Parkway 'Subway' Isn't One, U.S. Official Says," *Cincinnati Enquirer*, April 5, 1963, 1.

34  Est Nyboer, comp., "The Complete Bush Quotes: Oceans No Longer Protect Us," Quotes Headquarters, http://estnyboer.com/bush/oceans.htm.

## Chapter 15

1   Paul Anderson, "The History of the Anderson Ferry, Part 1 of 2," YouTube, September 11, 2012, https://www.youtube.com/watch?v=8P_98u1zkCE.

2   Anderson, "History of the Anderson Ferry."

3   Anderson.

4   Anderson.

5   Anderson.

6   Bridget B. Striker, *Lost River Towns of Boone, Kentucky* (Charleston SC: History Press, 2007), 1–5.

7   Anderson, "History of the Anderson Ferry."

8   Striker, *Lost River Towns of Boone, Kentucky*, 6; Anderson, "History of the Anderson Ferry."

9   "Anderson Ferry," https://andersonferry.com/our-story/.

10  Paul Anderson, "The History of the Anderson Ferry, Part 2 of 2," YouTube, September 11, 2012, https://www.youtube.com/watch?v=VCkX6vGTdRw.

11  "Anderson Ferry Can Get You around the Brent Spence Bridge Closure," WCPO, June 23, 2017, https://www.youtube.com/watch?v=TzxGtRcY7RM.

12  Anderson, "History of Anderson Ferry, Part 2."

13  Larry Seward, "The Anderson Ferry Has an All-Female Crew for the First Time 203 Years," WCPO, March 9, 2020, https://www.wcpo.com/news/local-news/the-anderson-ferry-has-an-all-female-crew-for-the-first-time-in-203-years.

14  Cathy Collopy conversation, education and collections coordinator, Dinsmore Homestead, October 2018; "Dinsmore Farm," dinsmorefarm.org; Julia Stockton, *Verses and Sonnets* (London: Forgotten Books, 2015).

15  Stockton, *Verses and Sonnets*, 110.

16  "Julia Stockton Dinsmore Journals," Dinsmore Farm, http://www.dinsmorefarm.org/library/letters-journals-poetry/.

17  "Julia Stockton Dinsmore Journals."

18  The following information is drawn from several sources: Donald E. Clare Jr., "History," Rabbit Hash Historical Society, http://www.rabbithashhistsoc.org/about/history/; Callie Clare, *Potions and Notions: The Legacy of Rabbit Hash, Kentucky* (Union, KY: Rabbit Hash Historical Society, 2011); Donald Clare, *Rabbit Hash, Kentucky: River Born, Kentucky Bred* (Charleston SC: History Press, 2012).

19  Clare, *Rabbit Hash, Kentucky*, chapter 7.

20  Stanley Hedeen, *Big Bone Lick: The Cradle of American Paleontology* (Lexington: University Press of Kentucky, 2008), 33–35.

21  Hedeen, *Big Bone Lick*, 56–82.

22  Hedeen, 9.

23  Hedeen, 15–19.

24  Hedeen, 22.

25  Robin Edwards, "Abner Gaines House," *Kentucky History*, https://explorekyhistory .ky.gov/items/show/671.

26  Karl Kron, "The Hills of Kentucky," *Outing and the Wheelmen: An Illustrated Monthly Magazine of Recreation*, October 1883–March 1884.

27  Edwards, "Abner Gaines House."

28  Thomas Schiffer, "Walton's Camp Bean Ridge a CCC Camp," *Cincinnati Enquirer*, January 27, 2016, https://www.cincinnati.com/story/news/local/boone-county/2016/ 01/27/waltons-camp-bean-ridge-soil-conservation/78949710/.

29  Connie Huddleston, *Kentucky's Civilian Conservation Corps* (Charleston SC: History Press, 2009), 11.

30  Huddleston, *Kentucky's Civilian Conservation Corps*, 113.

31  Robert D. Leighninger Jr., *Long-Range Public Investment: The Forgotten Legacy of the New Deal* (Columbia: University of South Carolina Press, 2007), 11.

32  Neil M. Maher, "Labor: Enrollee Work and the Body Politic," in *Nature's New Deal: The Civilian Conservation Corps and the Roots of the American Environmental Movement* (Oxford: Oxford University Press, 2008), 77–113.

33  Rebecca Smith, "Saving the Dust Bowl: 'Big Hugh' Bennett's Triumph over Tragedy," *Society for History Education* 41, no. 1 (November 2007): 65–95.

34  "Walton CCC Camp Bean Ridge," Historical Marker Database, https://www.hmdb .org/m.asp?m=133269.

35  "Interview with Paul French," William H. Berge Oral History Center, https://oral history.eku.edu/items/show/5.

36  "Soil Conservation in the New Congress," History, Art & Archives, https://history .house.gov/Historical-Highlights/1901-1950/Soil-Conservation-in-the-New-Deal -Congress/.

37  Robert D. Leighninger, *Long Range Public Investment*, 12.

38  Edwin G. Hill, *In the Shadow of the Mountain: The Spirit of the CCC* (Pullman: Washington State University Press, 1990), 11.

39  Huddleston, *Kentucky's Civilian Conservation Corps*, 114.

40  "Interview with Paul French."

41  "CCC in Ohio," Ohio History Connection Selections, 12, https://ohiomemory.org/ digital/collection/p267401coll32/id/28789.

## Chapter 16

1  "Land Ordinance of 1785," *Wikipedia*, https://en.wikipedia.org/wiki/Land_Ordi nance_of_1785.

2  "Public Schools," Ohio History Central, https://ohiohistorycentral.org/w/Public _Schools.

3  Emerson E. White, "History of Public Education in Ohio for Fifty Years," *Ohio Educational Monthly*, August 1897, 395.

4   Johann N. Neem, *Democracy's Schools: The Rise of Public Education in America* (Baltimore, MD: Johns Hopkins University Press, 2007), 68.

5   William Henry Venable, *Beginnings of Literary Culture in the Ohio Valley* (Cincinnati: Robert Clarke & Co., 1891), 188–92.

6   Venable, *Beginnings of Literary Culture*, 192.

7   "Education in Ohio, 1780–1903," Ohio Memory, http://ohiohistoryhost.org/ohio memory/wp-content/uploads/2014/12/TopicEssay_Education.pdf.

8   Neem, *Democracy's Schools*, 122.

9   Paul Finkelman, "The Strange Career of Race Discrimination in Antebellum Ohio," *Case Western Reserve Law Review* 55, no. 2 (2004): 390.

10  Neem, *Democracy's Schools*, 99.

11  Venable, *Beginnings of Literary Culture*, 193.

12  Venable, 195–96.

13  Neem, *Democracy's Schools*, 137.

14  "Shocking Murder of a School Teacher," *Portsmouth Enquirer* (Portsmouth, OH), January 20, 1851, 4.

15  "Wilmington Ohio Main Street 1930," *Uibles Family Blog*, http://uible.blogspot.com/ search?q=Artemus.

16  Samuel Hardin Stille, *Ohio Builds a Nation* (Lower Salem, OH: Arlendale Book House, 1939), 118.

17  Karen S. Campbell, *Quaker Ministry in the Wilderness: The Harvey Family of Harveysburg, Ohio, & Clinton County, Ohio* (Waynesville, OH: Mary L. Cook Public Library, 2006), 42–43, 90–91.

18  W. A. Campbell Stewart, "Punishment in Friends' Schools, 1779–1900," *Journal of the Friends' Historical Society* 42, no. 2 (1950): 52. https://core.ac.uk/download/ pdf/153659671.pdf.

19  Campbell, *Quaker Ministry in the Wilderness*, 89.

20  Campbell, 79–82.

21  Campbell, 82.

22  Campbell, 79-80.

23  Campbell, 92–95.

24  "Education in Ohio, 1780–1903."

25  Campbell, *Quaker Ministry*, 80–86.

26  Neem, *Democracy's Schools*, 29.

27  Neem, 28.

28  Neem, 68–72, 77–79.

29  Neem, 28.

30  White, "History of Public Education in Ohio for Fifty Years," 399.

31  "Cincinnati School Desegregation," Marian Spencer Papers, http://libapps.libraries .uc.edu/exhibits/marian-spencer/cincinnati-school-desegregation/.

32  "Public Schools."

33  Tom Irons, "Memories of Clermont's Edenton Rural School," *Clermont Sun*, March 30, 2012, https://www.clermontsun.com/2012/03/30/memories-of-clermont's -edenton-rural-school/.

34  "History of Ohio School Funding," Cleveland Heights-University Heights City School District, https://www.chuh.org/HistoryofOhioSchoolFunding.aspx.

35  "History of Ohio School Funding," Cleveland Heights-University Heights City School District.

36  Stephanie Simon, "Special Report: Class Struggle: How Charter Schools Get the Students They Want," Reuters, February 23, 2013, https://www.reuters.com/article/ us-usa-charters-admissions/special-report-class-struggle-how-charter-schools-get -students-they-want-idUSBRE91E0HF20130215.

37  Bennard Perlman, *Robert Henri: His Life and Art* (New York: Dover, 1991), 1–2.

38  Perlman, *Robert Henri*, 3.

39  Perlman, 5–22.

40  Robert Henri, *The Art Spirit* (New York: Basic Books, 2007), 1–4.

41  Henri, *Art Spirit*, 11.

42  Henri, 119.

43  Henri, 119.

## Chapter 17

1  "Ignatius of Loyola," Jesuit Resource, https://www.xavier.edu/jesuitresource/jesuit -a-z/terms-i/index; George Traub and Debra Mooney, "A Biography of St. Ignatius Loyola (1491–1556): The Founder of the Jesuits," Xavier University, https://www .xavier.edu/mission-identity/xaviers-mission/who-was-st-ignatius-loyola.php; Fr. Barton T. Geger, "Myths, Misquotes and Misconceptions about St. Ignatius Loyola," *Jesuit Higher Education: A Journal* 5, no. 1 (May 2016).

2  "Ignatius of Loyola"; Traub and Mooney, "Biography of St. Ignatius Loyola"; Geger, "Myths, Misquotes and Misconceptions."

3  "Ignatius of Loyola"; Traub and Mooney, "Biography of St. Ignatius Loyola."

4  John Fairfield, "Honesty, Courage and Resilience: Calvinist Conceptions of Virtue and Education for Sustainability," Jesuit Resource, https://www.xavier.edu/jesuit resource/jesuit-a-z/terms-s/ajcu-ecology-educators.

5  "List of Jesuit Educational Institutions," *Wikipedia*, https://en.wikipedia.org/wiki/ List_of_Jesuit_educational_institutions.

6  For more on Holly Schapker's work, see https://www.xavier.edu/mission-identity/ xaviers-mission/buildings-statues-and-beauty/adsum.

7  "History, Mission and Vision," Cincinnati Zoo & Botanical Garden, http://cincinna tizoo.org/about-us/history-and-vision/.

8  "Go Green," Cincinnati Zoo & Botanical Garden, http://cincinnatizoo.org/con servation/go-green/.

9   M. B. Reilly, "UC Earns Four Top Spots on Amazing Architecture List, More Than Any Other School," UC News, April 24, 2012, https://www.uc.edu/news/articles/legacy/enews/2012/04/e15669.html.

10  Daniel S. Friedman, "Campus Design as Critical Practice," *Places*, January 2005.

11  Ofer Wolberger, "Cincinnati Starchitecture," *New York Times*, September 13, 2015, https://www.nytimes.com/slideshow/2015/09/13/magazine/university-of-cincinnati/s/cincinnati-university-slide-P1KC.html.

12  Wolberger, "Cincinnati Starchitecture."

13  These two elements were identified by Mary Beth McGrew, Eileen Stumpfel, and Amy Townsend-Small of the University of Cincinnati in a conversation on the University of Cincinnati campus in May 2018.

14  McGrew, Stumpfel, and Townsend-Small.

15  Mary Niehaus, "University of Cincinnati Co-op: 100 Years of Success," *UC Magazine*, https://magazine.uc.edu/issues/1205/success1.html.

16  McGrew, Stumpfel, and Townsend-Small.

17  The information for this section came from the following sources: several conversations with Gary Zola, American Jewish Archives Center; a conversation with a conversation with Andrea Rapp, Wise Temple librarian; and Alex Burte, director of membership and programming at Isaac M. Wise Temple, summer 2018; and Jonathan D. Sarna and Nancy H. Klein, eds., *The Jews of Cincinnati* (Cincinnati: Center for the Study of the American Jewish Experience on the Campus of Hebrew Union College, Jewish Institute of Religion, 1989).

18  David Phillipson, *My Life as an American Jew* (Cincinnati: J. G. Kidd and Son, Incorporated, 1941), 22.

19  Samuel S. Cohon, "The History of Hebrew Union College," *Publications of the American Jewish Historical Society* 40, no. 1 (September 1950): 37.

20  "Article Declaration of Principles," Central Conference of American Rabbis, https://www.ccarnet.org/rabbinic-voice/platforms/article-declaration-principles/.

21  Conversations with Gary Zola, 2018.

22  Conversations with Gary Zola, 2018.

23  Conversations with Gary Zola, 2018.

24  Conversation with Sally Priesand, July 2018.

25  Conversations with Gary Zola, 2018.

## *Chapter 18*

1   "French Art Deco," Heilbrunn Timeline of Art History, Metropolitan Museum, https://www.metmuseum.org/toah/hd/frdc/hd_frdc.htm.

2   Philip French, "For Fred and Ginger, Art Deco Was the Magic Moment," *Guardian*, March 29, 2003, https://www.theguardian.com/theobserver/2003/mar/30/features.review77.

3   "Kruckemeyer, Edward H.," Architectural Foundation of Cincinnati, https://www .architecturecincy.org/programs/biographical-dictionary-of-cincinnati-architects/k/.

4   "Art Deco Style 1925–1940," Pennsylvania Historical & Museum Commission, http://www.phmc.state.pa.us/portal/communities/architecture/styles/art-deco.html.

5   Sarah Stephens, "The Times Star Building," *CityBeat*, August 15, 2007, https://www .citybeat.com/home/article/13025688/the-timesstar-building.

6   Steven J. Rolfes and Douglas R Weise, *Cincinnati Art Deco: Images of America* (Charleston, SC: Arcadia, 2014), 71–73.

7   Rolfes, *Cincinnati Art Deco*, 22.

8   "Fellheimer, Alfred," Architectural Foundation of Cincinnati, https://www.architec turecincy.org/programs/biographical-dictionary-of-cincinnati-architects/f/.

9   Rolfes, *Cincinnati Art Deco*, 39.

10  Rolfes, 25, 34.

11  Rolfes, 43.

12  "Cincinnati Union Terminal," *Wikipedia*, https://en.wikipedia.org/wiki/Cincinnati _Union_Terminal.

13  Carol Motsinger, "Justice League Calls Cincinnati's Union Terminal Home," Cincinnati.com, December 5, 2016, https://www.cincinnati.com/story/entertain ment/2016/12/05/union-terminal-inspires-another-superhero-hq/95004910/.

14  Scott L. Gampher, "Harry Hake Architects," *Ohio Valley History* 15, no. 3 (Fall 2015), https://muse.jhu.edu/article/597317.

15  "Potter, Russell, S.," Architectural Foundation of Cincinnati, https://www.architec turecincy.org/programs/biographical-dictionary-of-cincinnati-architects/.

16  "Art Deco and Moderne," Architectural Styles of America and Europe, https://archi tecturestyles.org/art-deco/.

17  Peter Pennoyer and Ann Walker, *The Architecture of Delano & Aldrich* (New York: W. W. Norton, 2003), 156.

18  "Walking Tour & Pocket History, Netherland Plaza," Historic Hotels of America, https://www3.hilton.com/resources/media/hi/CVGNPHF/en_US/pdf/en_CVGNPHF _Walking-Tour-and-History_Dec2016.pdf.

19  Rolfes, *Cincinnati Art Deco*, 49.

20  Rolfes, 51.

21  "Walking Tour & Pocket History."

22  "Walking Tour & Pocket History."

23  Rolfes, *Cincinnati Art Deco*, 61.

24  "The Terrace Plaza Hotel: Recognizing Greatness," *AEQAI*, March 3, 2019, http:// aeqai.com/main/2019/03/the-terrace-plaza-hotel-recognizing-greatness/.

25  Geoffrey J. Giglierano and Deborah A. Overmyer, and Frederic L. Propas, *The Bicen- tennial Guide to Greater Cincinnati* (Cincinnati: Cincinnati Historical Society, 1988), 365.

26  Edward J. Schulte, *The Lord Was My Client* (Cincinnati: privately printed, 1972), ii.

27 "Mount Washington Comprehensive Plan," Mount Washington Community Council, April 2007, 95, http://www.mwcc.org/wpcontent/uploads/2017/02/2007_mt_washington_comprehensive_plan.pdf.

28 "Water Tower Completed," *Cincinnati Enquirer*, September 20, 1940, 24.

29 Steve Hoffman, "Spotlight: Mount Washington," *Cincinnati Enquirer*, May 15, 1992, 85.

30 "The International Style," Art Story, https://www.theartstory.org/movement/international-style/.

31 Schulte, *Lord Was My Client*, i-ii.

32 Schulte, 148.

## Chapter 19

1 Information on the GM plant was drawn from Ann Thompson, "Remembering Norwood's GM Plant 30 Years Later," WVXU, August 25, 2017, https://www.wvxu.org/post/remembering-norwoods-gm-plant-30-years-later#stream/o; Associated Press, "G.M Plant Closing Shakes Ohio Town," *New York Times*, August 27, 1987, https://www.nytimes.com/1987/08/27/us/gm-plant-closing-shakes-ohio-town.html'; *Norwood, Where Legends Were Born*, https://www.norwoodlegends.com; Conversation with Drew Money, August 2018; Philip Borris, *Echoes of Norwood: General Motors Automobile Production During the Twentieth Century* (N.p.: Chev-Star, 2013).

2 Gerry Stoker, "City of Norwood, Ohio, U.S. Environmental Protection Agency Work Plan for Brownfields Assessment Grants," 2. This document used to be accessible through the city of Norwood website but it no longer is.

3 "Blast in Cincinnati Kills at Least 1, Injures Dozens," *Washington Post*, July 20, 1990; "Explosion in Evanston," *Cincinnati Enquirer*, July 20, 1990, A-7.

4 Steven Wright, "R. K. LeBlond's Legacy Lives On," *Cincinnati Business Courier*, March 9, 1998, https://www.bizjournals.com/cincinnati/stories/1998/03/09/focus3.html.

5 "United States Playing Card Company, Cincinnati," Ohio History Collection, https://www.ohiomemory.org/digital/collection/p267401coll34/id/7880; Trina Edwards, "U.S. Playing Card Moves to N. Ky.," Fox 19 Now, August 20, 2009, https://www.fox19.com/story/10963316/us-playing-card-moves-to-n-ky/; Evan Millward, "Massive Mixed-Use Development in the Cards for Former Factory Site in Norwood," WCPO, June 10, 2020, https://www.wcpo.com/news/local-news/hamilton-county/norwood/massive-mixed-use-development-in-the-cards-for-former-factory-site-in-norwood.

6 "Norwood, Ohio," *Wikipedia*, https://en.wikipedia.org/wiki/Norwood,_Ohio.

7 "Norwood, OH Eminent Domain," Institute for Justice, https://ij.org/case/city-of-norwood-v-horney/.

8 "NOW Transcript," PBS, June 24, 2005, http://www.pbs.org/now/transcript/transcriptNOW125_full.html.

9 "Norwood, OH Eminent Domain."

10  "Norwood, OH Eminent Domain."

11  Scott Bullock, "The Norwood, Ohio Eminent Domain Trial," *Institute for Justice*, June 2004, https://ij.org/ll/june-2004-volume-13-number-3/the-norwood-ohio-eminent-domain-trial/.

12  John Kramer, "Norwood Homeowners Carl and Joy Gamble Announce Sale of Home," Institute for Justice, March 30, 2007, https://ij.org/press-release/norwood-oh-eminent-domain-release-3-30-2007/.

13  "Norwood, OH Eminent Domain."

14  Institute for Justice and the Libertarian Party of Ohio, "Ohio Libertarian Party Credited in Eminent Domain Victory," *Libertarian Party News*, September 2006, https://www.lp.org/wp-content/uploads/2016/11/LP-News-September-Final-Walton-web.pdf.

15  One of the authors volunteers at Moriah Pie, and this information is drawn from her experience.

16  The information for this section is drawn from Ed Zdrojewski, "Frederick Geier and the Cincinnati Mill," *Cutting Tool Engineering*, June 1993; L. E. J., "MMS Shop Talk," *Modern Machine Shop* 70, no. 8 (January 1998): 40–43; John D. Fairfield, *Oakley: From Hamlet to the Center of Cincinnati* (Cincinnati: Commonwealth Book Company, 2018).

17  Zdrojewski, "Frederick Geier and the Cincinnati Mill."

18  Zdrojewski.

19  Zdrojewski; Fairfield, *Oakley*, 6–14.

20  Fairfield, 39.

21  Fairfield, 49.

22  Fairfield, 52–57.

23  Bowdeya Tweh, "RockTenn Closing Oakley Plant, Laying off 63," *Cincinnati Enquirer*, October 24, 2014, https://www.cincinnati.com/story/money/2014/10/24/rocktenn-closing-cincinnati-facility/17843825/.

24  Fairfield, *Oakley*, 40.

25  Information for the section on Madisonville was drawn from a variety of newspaper articles held in collection at the Madisonville Historical Society.

# BIBLIOGRAPHY

"Alms Park." Cincinnati Parks, https://www.cincinnatiparks.com/parks-venues/east/alms-park/.

"Americans: Was Your Town a [Rumored] Cold War Missile Target?" Ask MetaFilter, October 27, 2009, https://ask.metafilter.com/136571/Americans-Was-your-town-a-rumored-Cold-War-missile-target.

"Amish." *Wikipedia*, https://en.wikipedia.org/wiki/Amish.

"Among the Shakers." In *Whitewater, Ohio, Village of Shakers, 1824–1916: Its History and Its People*, edited by Marjorie Byrnside Burress (Cincinnati: privately printed, 1979), 31.

Anderson, Elisha. "Black Squirrels in Michigan Popping up in More Places." *Detroit Free Press*, January 23, 2016, https://www.freep.com/story/news/local/michigan/2016/01/23/black-squirrels-in-michigan/78362460/.

Anderson, Paul. "The History of the Anderson Ferry, Part 1 of 2." YouTube, September 11, 2012, https://www.youtube.com/watch?v=8P_98u1zkCE.

———. "The History of the Anderson Ferry, Part 2 of 2." YouTube, September 11, 2012, https://www.youtube.com/watch?v=8P_98u1zkCE.

Anderson, Phillip. "Whitewater Canal Scenic Byway." ISSUU, May 21, 2012, 15. https://issuu.com/ruralphil/docs/wcsb_canal_route_5.22.12.

"Anderson Ferry." https://andersonferry.com/our-story/.

"Anderson Ferry Can Get You around the Brent Spence Bridge Closure." WCPO, June 23, 2017, https://www.youtube.com/watch?v=TzxGtRcY7RM.

Arnold, Joseph L. *The New Deal in the Suburbs: A History of the Greenbelt Town Program, 1935–1954*. Columbus: Ohio University Press, 1971.

"Art Deco and Moderne." Architectural Styles of America and Europe, https://architecturestyles.org/art-deco/.

"Art Deco Style 1925–1940." Pennsylvania Historical & Museum Commission, http://www.phmc.state.pa.us/portal/communities/architecture/styles/art-deco.html.

"Article Declaration of Principles." Central Conference of American Rabbis, https:// www.ccarnet.org/rabbinic-voice/platforms/article-declaration-principles/.

Associated Press. "G.M Plant Closing Shakes Ohio Town." *New York Times*, August 27, 1987, https://www.nytimes.com/1987/08/27/us/gm-plant-closing-shakes-ohio-town .html.

Athens, Marego. "Mysterious Midwest Mounds," *Baltimore Sun*, December 1, 2002, https://www.baltimoresun.com/news/bs-xpm-2002-12-01-0212010302-story .html.

"Augustus Wattles." http://sgmm.org/plainandsimple/wattles.html.

Bailie, William. *Josiah Warren: The First American Anarchist*. Boston: Small, Maynard & Co., 1906.

Barrett, George. *The Poor Man's Home, and Rich Man's Palace, Or, the Application of Gravel Wall Cement to the Purposes of Building*. Cincinnati: Applegate & Co., 1854.

Basso, Keith. *Wisdom Sits in Places: Landscape and Language Among the Western Apache*. Albuquerque: University of New Mexico Press, 1996.

Baxter, Joan. "Some History on the Little Miami Railroad." *Xenia Daily Gazette*, April 6, 2018, https://www.xeniagazette.com/opinion/28412/some-history-on-the-little-mi ami-railroad.

Beardsley, John. *Gardens of Revelation: Environments by Visionary Artists*. New York: Abbeville Press, 1995.

Bielo, James S. "'Where Prayers May be Whispered': Promises of Presence in Protestant Place-Making," *Ethnos* (2019): 4–5.

"Blast in Cincinnati Kills at Least 1, Injures Dozens." *Washington Post*, July 20, 1990.

"Bluffton Pastor and Party to Tour Europe." *Indianapolis News*, March 29, 1938, 8.

Borris, Philip. *Echoes of Norwood: General Motors Automobile Production during the Twentieth Century*. N.p.: Chev-Star, 2013.

Burba, Howard. "The Day They Opened Miamisburg Mound." *Dayton Daily News*, February 28, 1932, Dayton History Books Online, https://www.daytonhistorybooks .com/miamisburgmound.html.

———. "Remember When the Powder Mills Exploded." *Dayton Daily News*, March 5, 1933, Dayton History Books Online, https://www.daytonhistorybooks.com/pow dermill.html.

Burden, Donald M. "Whitewater Canal Historical Corridor Guide." Master's thesis, Ball State University, 2006.

Burress, Marjorie Byrnside, ed. *Whitewater, Ohio, Village of Shakers, 1824–1916: Its History and Its People*. Cincinnati: privately printed, 1979.

"But First, What Is a Watershed?" Mill Creek Alliance, http://www.millcreekwater shed.org/whatiswatershed/.

Cahill, Lora Schmidt, and David L. Mowery. *Morgan's Raid across Ohio: The Civil War Guidebook of the John Hunt Morgan Heritage Trail*. Columbus: Ohio Historical Society, 2014.

"Caleb Swan Walker House." New Richmond Underground Railroad Tour, http://newrichmondugrrtour.weebly.com/caleb-swan-walker-house.html.

Callarco, Tom, et al. *Places of the Underground Railroad, a Geographical Guide.* Santa Barbara, CA: ABC-CLIO, 2011.

"Called Here." *Indianapolis Star*, December 23, 1928, 8.

Calloway, Colin G. *The Shawnees and the War for America.* New York: Penguin, 2007.

"Call to Bluffton Accepted By Coers." *Indianapolis Star*, August 4, 1935, 10.

Campbell, Ballard C. *Disasters, Accidents, and Crises in American History.* New York: Facts on File, 2008.

Campbell, Karen S. *Quaker Ministry in the Wilderness: The Harvey Family of Harveysburg, Ohio, & Clinton County, Ohio.* Waynesville, OH: Mary L. Cook Public Library, 2006.

"Camp Dennison Settled by German Pietist Refugees." *Cincinnati Enquirer*, June 26, 1960, 33.

Campion, Nardi Reeder. *Mother Ann Lee: Morning Start of the Shakers.* Hanover, NH: University Press of New England, 1990.

Carson, Rachel. *The Sense of Wonder.* New York: Perennial Library, 1965.

Carter, Ruth C., ed. *For Honor, Glory, and Union: The Mexican and Civil War Letters of Brig. Gen. William Haines Lytle.* Lexington: University Press of Kentucky, 1999.

Chaplow, L. I. "Tales of a Hollow Earth: Tracing the Legacy of John Cleves Symmes in Antarctic Exploration and Fiction." Master's thesis, University of Canterbury, 2011, https://core.ac.uk/download/pdf/35465577.pdf.

Chapman Brothers. *Portrait and Biographical Album of Greene and Clark Counties, Ohio.* Chicago: Chapman Bros., 1890.

Charles River Editors. *Native American Tribes: The History and Culture of the Shawnee.* Ann Arbor, MI: Charles River, n.d.

Cavinder, Freed D. *More Amazing Tales from Indiana.* Bloomington: Indiana University Press, 2003.

"CCC in Ohio." Ohio History Connection Selections, https://ohiomemory.org/digital/collection/p267401coll32/id/28789.

"Cincinnati School Desegregation." Marian Spencer Papers, http://libapps.libraries.uc.edu/exhibits/marian-spencer/cincinnati-school-desegregation/.

Cheng, Irene. "The Shape of Utopia: The Architecture of Radical Reform in Nineteenth Century America." PhD diss., Columbia University, 2014.

"Christian Waldschmidt." Indian Hill Historical Society, https://www.indianhill.org/history/people-indian-hill-history/christian-waldschmidt/.

"Cincinnati, OH Population and Races." USA.com, http://www.usa.com/cincinnati-oh-population-and-races.htm.

"Cincinnati Union Terminal." *Wikipedia*, https://en.wikipedia.org/wiki/Cincinnati_Union_Terminal.

Cist, Charles. *Cincinnati in 1841, Its Early Annals and Future Prospect.* Cincinnati: n.p., 1841.

Clare, Callie. *Potions and Notions: The Legacy of Rabbit Hash, Kentucky*. Union, KY: Rabbit Hash Historical Society, 2011.

Clare, Donald E., Jr. "History." Rabbit Hash Historical Society, http://www.rabbithash histsoc.org/about/history/.

———. *Rabbit Hash, Kentucky: River Born, Kentucky Bred*. Charleston, SC: History Press, 2012.

Coggeshall, William Turner. *The Signs of the Times, Comprising a History of the Spirit-Rappings in Cincinnati and Other Places*. Cincinnati: privately published, 1851.

Cohon, Samuel S. "The History of Hebrew Union College." *Publications of the American Jewish Historical Society* 40, no. 1 (September 1950): 17–55.

Coleman, Brent. "History: Who Is Buried in Spring Grove's Dexter Mausoleum?" Cincinnati.com, January 14, 2014, https://www.cincinnati.com/story/news/2014/01/13history-who-is-buried-in-spring-grove-cemeterys-dexter-mausoleum/4455281/.

Cooper, Catherine. "Happy 100th, Hudepohl." *Cincinnati Magazine*, April 1985, 112.

"Cranston Presbyterian Church." New Richmond on the Ohio Underground Railroad Tour, http://newrichmondugrrtour.weebly.com/cranston-presbyterian-church.html.

Cross, Bradley D. "On a Business Basis: An American Garden City." *Planning Perspectives* 19, no. 1 (2004), https://www.tandfonline.com/doi/abs/10.1080/0266543042000177913.

"Crown." Tri-State Trails, https://tristatetrails.org/crown/.

Culbertson, Kurt. "George Edward Kessler: Landscape Architect of the American Renaissance." In *Midwestern Landscape Architecture*, edited by William H. Tishler, 99–116. Urbana: University of Illinois Press.

Cunliffe, John, and Guido Erreygers. "The Enigmatic Legacy of Charles Fourier: Joseph Charlier and Basic Income." *History of Political Economy* 33, no. 3 (Fall 2001), https://muse.jhu.edu/article/13304.

"Current Statistics of Women in Aviation Careers in the U.S." Women in Aviation International, https://www.wai.org/resources/waistats.

D'Amato, David S. "Josiah Warren: The Most Practical Anarchist." Libertairanism.org, March 23, 2020, https://www.libertarianism.org/columns/josiah-warren-practical-anarchist.

Death Certificate of Miranda Parker. Ohio Bureau of Vital Statistics, Certificate 3693, June 27, 1920.

"Debate at the Lane Seminary, Cincinnati, Speech of James A. Thome, of Kentucky." Delivered at the Annual Meeting of the American Anti-Slavery Society, May 6, 1834.

DeCamp, Graydon. "Railbed Bike Hike Plan Praised Here." *Cincinnati Enquirer*, March 18, 1975, 10.

"The Democratic Peace II: War with Spain." Institute of World Politics, https://www.iwp.edu/articles/2019/04/17/the-democratic-peace-ii-war-with-spain/.

"Dinsmore Farm." dinsmorefarm.org.

Duncan, Alexander. "Letter from Mr. Duncan of Ohio, September 15, 1838." *Niles National Register*, January 5, 1839, 292–93.

———. *Remarks of Mr. Duncan of Ohio, on the Right of Partition, Delivered in the House of Representatives, January 6, 1844.* Washington, DC: Globe Office, 1844.

———. *Speech of Mr. Duncan, of Ohio, on the Subject of the New Jersey Election, Delivered in the House of Representatives, U.S. January 9, 1840.* Baltimore: Office of the Post, 1840.

Dykes, Todd. "Little-Known Cincinnati Dam Needs Millions in Repairs," WLWT, July 19, 2016, https://www.wlwt.com/article/little-known-cincinnati-dam-needs -millions-in-repairs/3567794.

"Ed Honton." *Columbus Dispatch*, October 16, 2005, https://www.legacy.com/obi tuaries/dispatch/obituary.aspx?n=ed-honton&pid=15384370.

Edwards, Robin. "Abner Gaines House." Kentucky History, https://explorekyhistory .ky.gov/items/show/671.

Edwards, Trina. "U.S. Playing Card Moves to N. Ky." Fox 19 Now, August 20, 2009, https://www.fox19.com/story/10963316/us-playing-card-moves-to-n-ky/.

"Education in Ohio, 1780–1903." Ohio Memory, http://ohiohistoryhost.org/ohio memory/wp-content/uploads/2014/12/TopicEssay_Education.pdf.

Eggleston, Edward, and Lillie Eggleston Seelve. *Tecumseh and the Shawnee Prophet.* New York: Dodd, Meade & Company, 1878.

"The Eliza House." Glendale's Historical Markers, http://www.glendaleohioarchive.org/ markers.html.

"Erie, Ohio Trail Aim." *Coshocton Tribune*, November 27, 1991, 1.

"Explosion in Evanston." *Cincinnati Enquirer*, July 20, 1990, A-7.

Fairfield, John. "Honesty, Courage and Resilience: Calvinist Conceptions of Virtue and Education for Sustainability." Jesuit Resource, https://www.xavier.edu/jesuit resource/jesuit-a-z/terms-s/ajcu-ecology-educators.

Fairfield, John D. *Oakley: From Hamlet to the Center of Cincinnati.* Cincinnati: Common- wealth Book Company, 2018.

Fatout, Paul. "Canalling in the Whitewater Valley." *Indiana Magazine of History* 60, no. 1 (March 1964): 37–78.

Feinberg, Kenneth R., "In the Shadow of Fernald: Who Should Pay the Victims?" *Brook- ings Review* 8, no. 90 (Summer 1990): 41.

"Fellheimer, Alfred." Architectural Foundation of Cincinnati, https://www.architec turecincy.org/programs/biographical-dictionary-of-cincinnati-architects/f/.

Findsen, Owen. "CSO Conductor Victim of WWI Fear." *Cincinnati Enquirer*, Septem- ber 21, 1997, E-14.

Finkelman, Paul. "The Strange Career of Race Discrimination in Antebellum Ohio." *Case Western Reserve Law Review* 55, no. 2 (2004).

"First Person Program Series: Maria Longworth Nichols Storer." Heritage Village Museum, https://heritagevillagecincinnati.org/events/first-person-program-series -maria-longworth-nichols-storer/.

"Fissile Material Basics." Institute for Energy and Environmental Research, https://ieer .org/resource/factsheets/fissile-material-basics/.

"Flood Drowned Out Fourierism." *Cincinnati Enquirer*, August 22, 1897, 13.

"Former Slave Burned." *Cincinnati Commercial Tribune*, October 28, 1899.

"Fort Thomas History." City of Fort Thomas, Kentucky, http://ftthomas.org/ fort-thomas-history/.

"Fort Washington." Ohio History Central, https://ohiohistorycentral.org/w/Fort _Washington.

Franklin, John Hope. *George Washington Williams: A Biography*. Durham, NC: Duke University Press, 1998.

"Franklin Township Looking to Restore Grave." *Clermont Sun*, January 12, 2017, https:// www.clermontsun.com/2017/01/12/franklin-township-looking-to-restore-grave/.

"Freaks of the Lightning." *Cincinnati Commercial*, April 26, 1878, 8.

"French Art Deco." Heilbrunn Timeline of Art History, Metropolitan Museum, https:// www.metmuseum.org/toah/hd/frdc/hd_frdc.htm.

French, Philip. "For Fred and Ginger, Art Deco Was the Magic Moment." *Guardian*, March 29, 2003, https://www.theguardian.com/theobserver/2003/mar/30/features. review77.

Friedman, Daniel S. "Campus Design as Critical Practice." *Places*, January 2005.

"The Fugitive Slave Law of 1850." Constitutional Rights Foundation, https://www .crf-usa.org/images/pdf/Fugitive-Slave-Law-1850.pdf.

"G. M. Peters, LLD." *Journal and Messenger: The Central National Baptist Paper*, October 9, 1919, 10.

Gampher, Scott L. "Harry Hake Architects." *Ohio Valley History* 15, no. 3 (Fall 2015), https://muse.jhu.edu/article/597317.

Gauvin, Brian. "Erie Canal Tugboats Push on through Two Centuries of Change." Professional Mariner, February 28, 2018, http://www.professionalmariner.com/March -2018/Erie-Canal-tugboats-push-on-through-two-centuries-of-change/.

Geger, Fr. Barton T. "Myths, Misquotes and Misconceptions about St. Ignatius Loyola." *Jesuit Higher Education: A Journal* 5, no. 1 (May 2016).

"Gets State Biking Post." *Telegraph-Forum* (Bucyrus, OH), June 11, 1985, 11.

"Glendale History: A Glimpse into the Past." http://www.glendaleohioarchive.org/ history.html.

"George Washington Williams." Union Baptist Church, https://www.union-baptist.net/ about-us/our-history/pastors/george-washington-williams/.

Giglierano Geoffrey J., Deborah A. Overmyer, and Frederic L. Propas. *The Bicentennial Guide to Greater Cincinnati*. Cincinnati: Cincinnati Historical Society, 1988.

"A Glance at the Garden of Eden." Cincinnati Museum Center, http://library.cincymu seum.org/topics/l/files/longworth/chsbull-v28-n2-gla-142.pdf.

Bibliography

"Glendale's Historical Markers." http://www.glendaleohioarchive.org/markers.html.

"Go Green." Cincinnati Zoo & Botanical Garden, http://cincinnatizoo.org/conservation/go-green/.

Gorman, Ron. "From Hopeless Bondage to Lane Rebel." *Oberlin Heritage Center* (blog), http://www.oberlinheritagecenter.org/blog/2013/09/james-bradley-from-hopeless-bondage-to-lane-rebel/.

Grace, Kevin, and Tom White. *Cincinnati's Over-the-Rhine*. Charleston, SC: Arcadia Publishing, 2003.

Grayson, Frank. "Extinct Shaker Colony," *Cincinnati Times Star*, December 20, 1932.

"The Great Disappointment." *Wikipedia*, https://en.wikipedia.org/wiki/Great_Disappointment.

Griffin, Duane A. "Hollow and Habitable Within: Symmes' Theory of Earth's Internal Structure and Polar Geography." *Physical Geography* 25, no. 5 (September 2004), 382–97.

Grubb, William Henry. *History of the Mennonites of Butler County, Ohio*. Trenton: privately published, 1916.

Hagedorn, Ann. *Beyond the River*. New York: Simon & Schuster, 2004.

Hale, Frank W. "Salmon Portland Chase: Rhetorician of Abolition." *Negro History Bulletin* 26, no. 5 (February 1963): 165–68.

Hall, George Ralph. *By George, He Did It! A True Scholar's Autobiography*. N.p., 2011.

"Hamilton Burying Ground." Find-A-Grave.com, https://www.findagrave.com/cemetery/2645918/hamilton-burying-ground.

Hand, Greg. "Cincinnati's Old Breweries were Death Traps." *Cincinnati Curiosities* (blog), May 2, 2017, https://handeaux.tumblr.com/post/160225399187/cincinnatis-old-breweries-were-bloody-death-traps.

———. "Don't Try This at Home: Cincinnati's Legendary Beer Gulpers." *Cincinnati Magazine*, November 21, 2015, https://www.cincinnatimagazine.com/citywiseblog/dont-try-this-at-home-cincinnatis-legendary-beer-gulpers/.

Hard, Mikael, and Andrew Jamison. *Hubris and Hybrids: A Cultural History of Technology and Science*. New York: Routledge, 2005.

Harrison, William Henry. *A Discourse on the Aborigines of the Ohio Valley*. Chicago: Fergus Printing Company, 1883.

"Harvard University Benefits." *Cincinnati Enquirer*, March 15, 1919, 5.

"Heart-Rending Calamity!! Fall of a Building—Seventeen Lives Lost." *Portage Sentinel* (Ravenna, OH), December 29, 1847, 2.

Hedeen, Stanley. *The Little Miami: Wild and Scenic, River Ecology and History*, https://littlemiamistatepark.org/park-and-trail/history-park-trail/19-uncategorised/little-miami-scenic-trail-and-river/31-the-little-miami-wild-and-scenic-river-ecology-and-history.

———. *Big Bone Lick: The Cradle of American Paleontology*. Lexington: University Press of Kentucky, 2008.

———. *The Mill Creek: An Unnatural History of an Urban Stream.* Cincinnati: Mill Creek Restoration Project, 1994.

———. "Waterproofing the Mill Creek Flood Plain." *Queen City Heritage* (Spring 1998): 15–25.

Henri, Robert. *The Art Spirit.* New York: Basic Books, 2007.

Hill, Edwin G. *In the Shadow of the Mountain: The Spirit of the CCC.* Pullman: Washington State University Press, 1990.

"History & Master Plan." Cincinnati Parks, https://www.cincinnatiparks.com/history-and-masterplan/.

"History, Mission and Vision." Cincinnati Zoo & Botanical Garden, http://cincinnatizoo.org/about-us/history-and-vision/.

"History of Cincinnati and Hamilton County, Ohio." Glendale History, http://www.glendaleohioarchive.org/history.html.

*History of Clermont County, Ohio, with Illustrations and Biographical Sketches of its Prominent Men and Pioneers.* Philadelphia: Louis H. Everts, 1880.

"History of Columbia Tusculum." Columbia Tusculum, Cincinnati, https://www.columbiatusculum.org/history.

"History of the Fernald Citizens Advisory Board." Fernald Citizens Advisory Board, 1993–2006, https://www.lm.doe.gov/land/sites/oh/FernaldCAB/FCABHistory/history.html.

"History of Ohio School Funding." Cleveland Heights-University Heights City School District, https://www.chuh.org/HistoryofOhioSchoolFunding.aspx.

"A History of Old St. Mary's." https://www.oldstmarys.org/about/a-history-of-old-st-marys/.

"History of Plum Street Temple." Isaac M. Wise Temple, https://www.wisetemple.org/about/our-history/history-of-plum-street-temple/.

Hobson, Geoff. "A Return to City's Canal Days, with a Twist." *Cincinnati Enquirer,* November 14, 1992, 1, A-4.

Hobson, Laura A. "White Water Shaker Village: A Trip to a Purer, Simpler Time." Cincinnati.com, April 2, 2019, https://www.cincinnati.com/story/news/2019/04/02/white-water-shaker-village-trip-purer-simpler-time/3271749002/.

Hoffman, Carey. "Ancient Connection: Evidence from Summer Digs Points to Shawnee Lookout as Oldest Continuously Occupied Site." ScienceBlog, September 1, 2009, https://scienceblog.com/24769/ancient-connection-new-evidence-points-to-shawnee-lookout-as-oldest-continuously-occupied-site/.

Hoffman, Steve. "Spotlight: Mount Washington." *Cincinnati Enquirer,* May 15, 1992, 85.

Holian, Timothy J. "The Hudepohl Brewing Company of Cincinnati, Ohio: A Case Study in Regional Brewery Prosperity and Decline." *Journal of Brewery History* 141, no. 201: 12–53.

Hornbaker, Alice. "Little Miami Bike Trail Extends its Reach." *Cincinnati Enquirer,* August 2, 1991, EXTRA-1.

Horwitz, Lester. *The Longest Raid of the Civil War*. Cincinnati: Farmcourt Publishing, 2001.

Howard, Ebenezer. *Garden Cities of Tomorrow*. Cambridge, MA: MIT Press, 1965.

Huddleston, Connie. *Kentucky's Civilian Conservation Corps*. Charleston SC: History Press, 2009.

Ibrahem, Aymen, and Bill Cramer. "Tecumseh and the Eclipse of 1806." Eclipse-Chasers, April 18, 2015, https://www.eclipse-chasers.com/article/history/tse1806.shtml.

"Ignatius of Loyola." Jesuit Resource, https://www.xavier.edu/jesuitresource/jesuit-a-z/terms-i/index.

"Images of Historical Cincinnati." Cincinnati Museum Center, http://library.cincymuseum.org/topics/a/files/artists/ima-233.pdf.

Institute for Justice and the Libertarian Party of Ohio. "Ohio Libertarian Party Credited in Eminent Domain Victory." *Libertarian Party News*, September 2006, https://www.lp.org/wp-content/uploads/2016/11/LP-News-September-Final-Walton-web.pdf.

"The International Style." Art Story, https://www.theartstory.org/movement/international-style/.

"Internment of Japanese Americans." *Wikipedia*, https://en.wikipedia.org/wiki/Internment_of_Japanese_Americans.

"Interview with Paul French." William H. Berge Oral History Center, https://oralhistory.eku.edu/items/show/5.

Irons, Tom, "Memories of Clermont's Edenton Rural School." *Clermont Sun*, March 30, 2012, https://www.clermontsun.com/2012/03/30/memories-of-clermont's-edenton-rural-school/.

J., L. E. "MMS Shop Talk." *Modern Machine Shop* 70, no. 8 (January 1998): 40–43.

"James B. Ray." *Wikipedia*, https://en.wikipedia.org/wiki/James_B._Ray.

"James Brown Ray (1794–1848)." Governors' History Site, https://www.in.gov/governorhistory/2374.htm.

Jareo, Lori, "Harry Andrews and the Legend of Chateau La Roche." World War I, http://www.worldwar1.com/sfroche.htm.

"John Perin." Find-A-Grave, https://www.findagrave.com/memorial/150078624.

"John Tyler." History.com, July 9, 2019, https://www.history.com/topics/us-presidents/john-tyler.

"Julia Stockton Dinsmore Journals." Dinsmore Farm, http://www.dinsmorefarm.org/library/letters-journals-poetry/.

Kamuf, Betty. "Problems Plagued Canal Projects." Cincinnati.com, March 24, 2014, https://www.cincinnati.com/story/news/2014/03/24/problems-plagued-canal-projects/6833875/.

Kieswetter, John. "Civil Unrest Woven into City's History." Cincinnati.com, June 8, 2018, https://www.cincinnati.com/story/news/blogs/our-history/2018/06/08/civil-unrest-woven-into-citys-history/685960002/.

Kinney, Jen. "How to Pay America's Big Sewer Bill." Next City, February 26, 2016, https://nextcity.org/daily/entry/cities-combined-sewer-overflow-upgrade-green-infrastructure.

Klieger, P. Christiaan. The Fleischmann Yeast Family. Charleston, SC: Arcadia Publishing, 2004.

Kline, Benjamin. "Durable Housing: 19th Century Miller had Concrete Ideas on Building." Dayton Daily News, January 27, 1985, 1-B.

Knepp, Gary. "Clermont County, Ohio, Freedom Trail." Clermont County, Ohio, Convention & Visitors Bureau, 2013.

Knight, Marian. "Historic Mount Adams." Cincinnati Museum Center, http://library.cincymuseum.org/topics/l/files/longworth/chsbull-v28-n1-his-027.pdf.

Kramer, John. "Norwood Homeowners Carl and Joy Gamble Announce Sale of Home." Institute for Justice, March 30, 2007, https://ij.org/press-release/norwood-oh-eminent-domain-release-3-30-2007/.

Kramer, Melissa. The Inclines of Cincinnati. Charleston, SC: Arcadia, 2009.

Kramer, Scott. "The Norwood, Ohio Eminent Domain Trial." Institute for Justice, June 2004, https://ij.org/ll/june-2004-volume-13-number-3/the-norwood-ohio-eminent-domain-trial/.

Kron, Karl. "The Hills of Kentucky." Outing and the Wheelmen: An Illustrated Monthly Magazine of Recreation, October 1883–March 1884.

"Kruckemeyer, Edward H." Architectural Foundation of Cincinnati, https://www.architecturecincy.org/programs/biographical-dictionary-of-cincinnati-architects/k/.

"Land Ordinance of 1785." Wikipedia, https://en.wikipedia.org/wiki/Land_Ordinance_of_1785.

Lee, Gary. "$20 Million Settlement Reached Between Nuclear Plant Workers, Energy Dept." Washington Post, July 27, 1994, https://www.washingtonpost.com/archive/politics/1994/07/27/20-million-settlement-reached-between-nuclear-plant-workers-energy-dept/e99368ac-7518-4cc2-a352-e778c4345308/.

Leighninger, Robert D., Jr. Long-Range Public Investment: The Forgotten Legacy of the New Deal. Columbia: University of South Carolina Press, 2007.

"Letter from H. C. Wright." Anti-Slavery Bugle (Lisbon, OH), September 13, 1851, 3.

Levine, Neil Ann Stucky, ed. Transplanted German Farmer: The Life and Times of Christian Iutzi...in His Own Words. Sugar Creek, OH: Carlisle Printing, 2009.

Linebaugh, Peter. Stop, Thief! The Commons, Enclosures, and Resistance. Oakland, CA: PM Press, 2014.

"Lisa Crawford." Fernald Living History Project Transcript, Tape FLHP0166, August 17, 1999, http://www.fernaldcommunityalliance.org/FLHPinterviews/CrawfordLisa.pdf.

"List of Jesuit Educational Institutions." *Wikipedia*, https://en.wikipedia.org/wiki/List_of_Jesuit_educational_institutions.

"Little Miami River." *Wikipedia*, https://en.wikipedia.org/wiki/Little_Miami_River.

Lloyd, James T. *Lloyd's Steamboat Directory, and Disasters on the Western Waters*. Cincinnati: James T. Lloyd & Co., 1856.

Locke, Ralph P., and Cyrilla Barr. *Cultivating Music in America: Women Patrons and Activists since 1860*. Berkeley: University of California Press, 1997.

de Chambrun, Clara Longworth. *The Making of Nicholas Longworth: Annals of an American Family*. New York: Ray Long and Richard R. Smith, 1933.

Lubken, Uwe, "Rivers and Risk in the City: The Urban Floodplain as a Contested Space." In *Urban Rivers: Remaking Rivers, Cities, and Space in Europe and North America*, edited by Stephane Castonguay and Matthew Evenden, 130–44. Pittsburgh: University of Pittsburgh Press, 2012.

"Lunken Airport's History." City of Cincinnati, https://www.cincinnati-oh.gov/dote/lunken-airport/history/.

"Lyman Beecher." Ohio History Central, https://ohiohistorycentral.org/w/Lyman_Beecher.

Lytle, William, "Personal Narrative of William Lytle." *Quarterly Publication of the Historical and Philosophical Society of Ohio* 1, no. 1 (January–March 1906).

Lytle, William Haines. *Poems of William Haines Lytle*. Edited by William Henry Venable. Cincinnati: Stewart and Kidd, 1912.

MacLean, J. P. "Origin, Rise, Progress, and Decline of the Whitewater Community of Shakers Located in Hamilton County, Ohio." *Ohio History*, January 1901.

———. *Shakers of Ohio*. Philadelphia: Porcupine Press, 1975.

Madison, James. *The Writings of James Madison*. Volume 3. Edited by Gallard Hunt. New York: G. P. Putnam's Sons, 1902.

Maher, Neil M. "Labor: Enrollee Work and the Body Politic." In *Nature's New Deal: The Civilian Conservation Corps and the Roots of the American Environmental Movement*, 77–113. Oxford: Oxford University Press, 2008.

"Major Canals Built in the 19th Century, American Northeast." Geography of Transportation Systems, https://transportgeography.org/?page_id=1128.

"Marie Curie and Lise Meitner." Institute of Physics, https://www.iop.org/resources/topic/archive/curie-meitner/page_65216.html#gref.

"Mariemont to be Model City." *Cincinnati Enquirer*, April 23, 1922, 15.

Martin, James Joseph. *Men against the State: The Expositors of Individualist Anarchism, 1827–1908*. Auburn, AL: Ludwig von Mises Institute, 2009.

Masson, Doug. "Bicentennial Installment 2: Indiana as a Young State." *A Citizen's Guide to Indiana* (blog), January 11, 2016, https://www.masson.us/blog/bicentennial-installment-2-indiana-as-a-young-state/.

Maxwell, Sidney D. "Glendale." In *The Suburbs of Cincinnati: Sketches Historical and Descriptive*. Cincinnati: George E. Stevens and Co., 1870.

McBride, John, *Symmes's Theory of Concentric Spheres: Demonstrating that the Earth is Hollow and Habitable Within, and Widely Open about the Poles.* Cincinnati: Morgan, Lodge, and Fisher, 1826, Reprinted by Nabu Public Domain Reprints, n.d.

McDonald, Sue. "Along the River," *Cincinnati Enquirer*, May 12, 1984, 9.

McFarlane, Robert. *The Old Ways: A Journey on Foot.* New York: Viking, 2012.

McNutt, Randy. "Bike Path to Link Ohio's North, South." *Cincinnati Enquirer*, March 14, 2001, 14.

———. "Life in Utopia." *Dennison Magazine*, https://denisonmagazine.com/opening_page/life-in-utopia/.

———. "New Richmond Marker Recalls Slavery Opposition," *Cincinnati Enquirer*, 8 February 2003, 13.

Mecklenborg, Jacob R. *Cincinnati's Incomplete Subway: The Complete Story.* Charleston, SC: History Press, 2010.

"Mennonites." *Wikipedia*, https://en.wikipedia.org/wiki/Mennonites.

"Miamisburg." *Cincinnati Commercial Gazette*, January 9, 1885, 3.

"Miamisburg Mound." Ohio History Connection, https://www.ohiohistory.org/visit/museum-and-site-locator/miamisburg-mound.

Michael, Thomas A. "Harry Andrews and His Castle: A Rhetorical Study." In *Personal Places: Perspectives on Informal Art Environments*, edited by Daniel Franklin Ward. Bowling Green, KY: Bowling Green State University Popular Press, 1984.

"The Mill Creek Alliance." https://www.themillcreekalliance.org.

Miller, James M. "An Early Criminal Case: Samuel Fields." *Indiana Magazine of History* 1, no. 4 (1905): 201–3.

Miller, Robert Earnest. "The War That Never Came: Civilian Defense in Cincinnati, Ohio, during World War II." *Queen City Heritage* 49, no. 4 (Winter 1991): 3–22.

Mills, Debbie, and Margo Warminski. *Greenhills.* Mount Pleasant, SC: Arcadia Publishing, 2013.

Millward, Evan. "Massive Mixed-Use Development in the Cards for Former Factory Site in Norwood." WCPO, June 10, 2020, https://www.wcpo.com/news/local-news/hamilton-county/norwood/massive-mixed-use-development-in-the-cards-for-former-factory-site-in-norwood.

Milner, Jim. "High Flying with Martha Lunken." *Cincinnati Magazine*, February 16, 2015, https://www.cincinnatimagazine.com/article/high-flying-martha-lunken/.

Morgan, Michael D. *Over-the-Rhine: When Beer Was King.* Charleston SC: History Press, 2010.

Morrow, Ann. "Shakers' Many Gifts," HistoryNet, https://www.historynet.com/shakers-many-gifts.htm.

Morrow, Jeremiah. "Address of Governor Morrow." In *Annual Report of the Superintendent of State House to the Governor of the State of Ohio for the Year 1863.* Columbus: Richard Nevins, 1864.

Morrow, Josiah. "Jeremiah Morrow." *"Old Northwest" Genealogical Quarterly*, January 1906, 1–254.

Motsinger, Carol. "Justice League Calls Cincinnati's Union Terminal Home." Cincin nati.com, December 5, 2016, https://www.cincinnati.com/story/entertainment/ 2016/12/05/union-terminal-inspires-another-superhero-hq/95004910/.

"Mount Washington Comprehensive Plan." Mount Washington Community Council, April 2007, 95, http://www.mwcc.org/wp-content/uploads/2017/02/2007_mt_wash ington_comprehensive_plan.pdf

"The 'Napoleon of Promoters' Was Early Fort Thomas Developer and Major Promoter." Fort Thomas Matters, February 28, 2017, http://www.fortthomasmatters.com/2017/ 02/the-napoleon-of-promoters-was-early.html.

"National Historic Landmark Nomination: Duck Creek Aqueduct." National Register of Historic Places, https://www.nps.gov/hdp/project/coveredbridges/nhls/DuckCreek .pdf.

"National Register of Historic Places Program: Landscape Architecture Month Feature 2013, Mount Airy Forest, Cincinnati, Ohio." National Park Service, https://www .nps.gov/NR/feature/landscape/2013/Mount_Airy.htm.

"Nature of the Contamination." Museum display panel at Fernald Preserve Visitors' Center, photographed March 28, 2018.

Neem, Johann N. *Democracy's Schools: The Rise of Public Education in America*. Baltimore, MD: Johns Hopkins University Press, 2007.

"Newport Barracks." Explore Kentucky History, https://explorekyhistory.ky.gov/items/ show/44.

News of the Courts." *Cincinnati Enquirer*, March 9, 1923, 5.

Niehaus, Mary. "University of Cincinnati Co-Op: 100 Years of Success." *UC Magazine*, https://magazine.uc.edu/issues/1205/success1.html.

"Nike Missile Locations Ohio." Military Standard, http://www.themilitarystandard .com/missile/nike/locationsoh.php.

Noble, Greg, and Lucy May. "Cincinnati's Rise and Fall as a Brewery Town: From Porko- polis to Beeropolis, How It All Began." WCPO, January 17, 2017, https://www.wcpo .com/entertainment/local-a-e/cincinnatis-rise-and-fall-as-a-brewery-town-part-1 -from-porkopolis-to-beeropolis-how-it-all-began.

Noble, Kenneth. "U.S., For Decades, Let Uranium Leak at Weapons Plant." *New York Times*, October 15, 1988, 1.

"Norwood Mayor Praised." *Cincinnati Enquirer*, September 19, 1922, 20.

"Norwood, OH Eminent Domain." Institute for Justice, https://ij.org/case/city-of -norwood-v-horney/.

"Norwood, Ohio." *Wikipedia*, https://en.wikipedia.org/wiki/Norwood,_Ohio.

*Norwood, Where Legends Were Born*. https://www.norwoodlegends.com.

"NOW Transcript." PBS, June 24, 2005, http://www.pbs.org/now/transcript/transcript NOW125_full.html.

Nyboer, Est, comp. "The Complete Bush Quotes: Oceans No Longer Protect Us." Quotes Headquarters, http://estnyboer.com/bush/oceans.htm.

"Officials in Quandary Due to Objections of Norwood Residents to Negro Colony." *Cincinnati Enquirer*, July 4, 1922, 24.

"Ohio in the American Civil War." *Wikipedia*, https://en.wikipedia.org/wiki/Ohio_in _the_American_Civil_War.

"Ohio River Basin." Ohio River Basin Consortium for Research and Education, https:// www.ohio.edu/orbcre/basin/index.html.

Ohio State Board of Agriculture. *Annual Report*. Volume 5. Columbus: S. Medary, 1850.

Olson, Andrew. "Mammoth Internal Improvements Act: The Bee Line Railroad Facing Dilemma: Loss of Local Control." *Indiana History Blog*, March 13, 2017, https://blog .history.in.gov/the-bee-line-railroad-financing-dilemma-loss-of-local-control/.

Osborne, Mike. "Former US Nuclear Weapons Plant Undergoes Amazing Transformation." VOA News, June 22, 1010, https://www.voanews.com/usa/former-us-nuc lear-weapons-plant-undergoes-amazing-transformation.

"OTR History." Over-the-Rhine Foundation, http://www.otrfoundation.org/OTR _History.htm.

"Our History." Cincinnati Observatory, https://www.cincinnatiobservatory.org/about/ our-history/.

Owen, Lorrie, ed. *Ohio Historic Places Dictionary*. Volume 2. St. Clair Shores, MI: Somerset Publishers, 1999.

Owens, Robert M. *Mr. Jefferson's Hammer: William Henry Harrison and the Origins of American Indian Policy*. Norman, OK: University of Oklahoma Press, 2007.

"P&G: A Company History." https://www.pg.com/translations/history_pdf/english _history.pdf.

Pace, Doris L., and Marie Johns. *The Amish Mennonite Settlement in Butler County, Ohio*. Trenton, OH: Trenton Historical Society, 1983.

Painter, Sue Ann, Alice Weston, and Beth Sullebarger. *Architecture in Cincinnati: An Illustrated History of Building and Designing an American City*. Athens: Ohio University Press, 2007.

"Paddy's Run." Historical Marker Database, https://www.hmdb.org/m.asp?m=23991.

"Park Is Solution of Puzzle." *Cincinnati Enquirer*, September 6, 1922, 20.

"Park to Be Located in Norwood to Prevent Threatened Formation of Negro Colony." *Cincinnati Enquirer*, July 18, 1922, 10.

Parker, John P. *His Promised Land*. Edited by Stuart Seely Sprague. New York: W. W. Norton, 1996.

"Pastor Enters Red Cross Work." *Daily Telegram* (Adrian, MI), June 29, 1942, 1.

Pennoyer, Peter, and Ann Walker. *The Architecture of Delano & Aldrich*. New York: W. W. Norton, 2003.

Pension File of Leroy Lee, National Archives and Records Administration. "Federal Military Pension Application, Civil War and Later Complete File." Application 463231, Certificate 513815.

Perlman, Bennard. *Robert Henri: His Life and Art*. New York: Dover, 1991.

Peters, Gershom. *The Master, Or, The Story of Stories Retold*. New York: Fleming H. Revell Co., 1911.

"Phalange." *Encyclopedia Britannica*, https://www.britannica.com/topic/phalange-gov ernment.

Phillipson, David. *My Life as an American Jew*. Cincinnati: J. G. Kidd and Son, Incorporated, 1941.

Polley, Daryl. "Bellevue." In *Encyclopedia of Northern Kentucky*, edited by Paul A. Tenkotte and James C. Claypool, 77–78. Lexington: University Press of Kentucky, 2009.

Pollitt, Bethany Marie. "The Antislavery Movement in Clermont County." Master's thesis, Wright State University, 2012.

"Population by Counties—1790–1870, Table 2. State of Ohio." U.S. Census, https://www2.census.gov/library/publications/decennial/1870/population/1870a-09.pdf#.

"Potter, Russell, S." Architectural Foundation of Cincinnati, https://www.architecture cincy.org/programs/biographical-dictionary-of-cincinnati-architects/p/.

Pregill, Philip, and Nancy Volkman. *Landscapes in History: Design and Urban Planning in the Eastern and Western Tradition*. New York: John Wiley and Sons, 1999.

"Public Schools." Ohio History Central, https://ohiohistorycentral.org/w/Public _Schools.

"The Queen's Crown Jewels: J. Fitzhugh Thornton Memorial." Queen City Survey, February 18, 2008, http://queencitysurvey.blogspot.com/2008/02/queens-crown -jewels.html.

"The Queen's Drink? Beer." *Cincinnati Magazine*, July 1980, 81.

Reilly, M. B. "UC Earns Four Top Spots on Amazing Architecture List, More Than Any Other School." UC News, April 24, 2012, https://www.uc.edu/news/articles/legacy/ enews/2012/04/e15669.html.

"Rev. M. H. Coers Arrives in Africa." *Indianapolis Star*, June 6, 1943, 6.

Robinson, Michael C. "History of Navigation of the Ohio River Basin." Institute for Water Resources, 1938.

Rogers, Millard F., Jr. *John Nolen and Mariemont*. Baltimore, MD: Johns Hopkins University Press, 2001.

———. *Rich in Good Works: Mary M. Emery of Cincinnati*. Akron, OH: University of Akron Press, 2001.

Rolfes, Steven J., and Douglas R. Weise. *Cincinnati Art Deco: Images of America*. Charleston, SC: Arcadia, 2014.

"Roman Catholic Church." Ohio History Central, https://ohiohistorycentral.org/w/ Roman_Catholic_Church.

Rutledge, Archibald. "Finding a Piece of Glory." *Syracuse Herald-American*, August 29, 1965, 20.

Sanders, Scott Russell. *Staying Put: Making a Home in a Restless World*. Boston: Beacon Press, 1993.

Sarna, Jonathan D. "'A Sort of Paradise for the Hebrews': The Lofty Vision of Cincinnati Jews." In *The Jews of Cincinnati*, edited by Jonathan D. Sarna and Nancy H. Klein, 1–18. Cincinnati: Center for the Study of the American Jewish Experience, Hebrew Union College, Jewish Institute of Religion, 1989.

Sarna, Jonathan D., and Nancy H. Klein, eds. *The Jews of Cincinnati*. Cincinnati: Center for the Study of the American Jewish Experience, Hebrew Union College, Jewish Institute of Religion, 1989.

Scamyhorn, Richard, and John Steinle, *Stockades in the Wilderness: The Frontier Defenses and Settlements of Southwestern Ohio*. Cincinnati: Commonwealth Book Company, 2015.

Schaefer, Walt. "Airport Murals Need Repair," *Cincinnati Enquirer*, June 19, 1999, 15.

Schapker, Holly. "Adsum: Contemporary Paintings on Ignatian Spirituality." Xavier University, https://www.xavier.edu/mission-identity/xaviers-mission/buildings-statues-and-beauty/adsum.

Schiffer, Thomas. "Walton's Camp Bean Ridge a CCC Camp." *Cincinnati Enquirer*, January 27, 2016, https://www.cincinnati.com/story/news/local/boone-county/2016/01/27/waltons-camp-bean-ridge-soil-conservation/78949710/.

Schiffer, Thomas D. *Peters and King*. Iola, WI: Krause Publications, 2002.

Schivelbusch, Wolfgang. "Railroad Space and Railroad Time." In *The Railway Journey: The Industrialization of Time and Space in the Nineteenth Century*, 33–44. Berkeley: University of California Press, 1977.

Schulte, Edward J. *The Lord Was My Client*. Cincinnati: privately printed, 1972.

"Searching out the 'Old Dexter Whiskey' Three." *Those Pre-Pro Whiskey Men!* (blog), November 26, 2015, http://pre-prowhiskeymen.blogspot.com/2015/11/searching-out-old-dexter-whiskey-three.html.

"Second Baptist Church." New Richmond on the Ohio Underground Railroad Tour, http://newrichmondugrrtour.weebly.com/about.html.

Selhub, Eva M., and Alan C. Logan. *Your Brain on Nature: The Science of Nature's Influence on Your Health, Happiness, and Vitality*. Mississauga, Ontario: John Wiley and Sons, 2012.

"Serpent Mound." History.com, August 21, 2018, https://www.history.com/topics/landmarks/serpent-mound.

Seward, Larry. "The Anderson Ferry Has an All-Female Crew for the First Time in 203 Years." WCPO, March 9, 2020, https://www.wcpo.com/news/local-news/the-anderson-ferry-has-an-all-female-crew-for-the-first-time-in-203-years.

"Shakers." New World Encyclopedia, https://www.newworldencyclopedia.org/entry/Shakers.

Shetler, Jan Bender. *Imagining Serengeti: A History of Landscape Memory from Earliest Times to the Present*. Athens: Ohio University Press, 2007.

"Shocking Murder of a School Teacher." *Portsmouth Enquirer* (Portsmouth, OH), January 20, 1851, 4.

"Silver Jubilee." *Darke County Democratic Advocate* (Greenville, OH), January 7, 1888, 1.

Silverberg, Robert. *The Mound Builders*. Greenwich, CT: New York Graphic Society, 1970.

Simon, Stephanie. "Special Report: Class Struggle: How Charter Schools Get the Students They Want." Reuters, February 23, 2013, https://www.reuters.com/article/us-usa-charters-admissions/special-report-class-struggle-how-charter-schools-get-students-they-want-idUSBRE91E0HF20130215.

Sinnema, Peter W. "10 April 1818: John Cleves Symmes's 'No. 1 Circular.'" BRANCH: Britain, Representation and Nineteenth-Century History, http://www.branchcollective.org/?ps_articles=peter-w-sinnema-10-april-1818-john-cleves-symmess-no-1-circular.

Smith, Rebecca. "Saving the Dust Bowl: 'Big Hugh' Bennett's Triumph over Tragedy." *Society for History Education* 41, no. 1 (November 2007): 65–95.

Smith, William Henry. *A Sketch of Governor Jeremiah Morrow, or, A Familiar Talk about Monarchists and Jacobins*. Cincinnati: Ohio Archaeological and Historical Society, 1888.

"Soil Conservation in the New Congress." History, Art & Archives, https://history.house.gov/Historical-Highlights/1901–1950/Soil-Conservation-in-the-New-Deal-Congress/.

"Spanish-American War." History.com, May 14, 2010, https://www.history.com/topics/early-20th-century-us/spanish-american-war.

"Spring Grove." *Cincinnati Commercial*, April 25, 1870, 7.

Stegman, Albert Vinton, Jr. "Samuel Bigstaff." In *History of Fort Thomas*. Fort Thomas, KY: Optimist Club, n.d.

Stein, Stephen J. *The Shaker Experience in America: A History of the United Society of Believers*. New Haven, CT: Yale University Press, 1992.

Stephens, Sarah. "The Times Star Building." *CityBeat*, August 15, 2007, https://www.citybeat.com/home/article/13025688/the-timesstar-building

Stevens, William R., comp. *Fort Thomas Military Reservation 1888–1964*. Fort Thomas, KY: Campbell County Historical Society, n.d.

Stewart, W. A. Campbell. "Punishment in Friends' Schools, 1779–1900." *Journal of the Friends' Historical Society* 42, no. 2 (1950), https://core.ac.uk/download/pdf/153659671.pdf.

Stille, Samuel Hardin. *Ohio Builds a Nation*. Lower Salem, OH: Arlendale Book House, 1939.

Stimson, George P. "River on a Rampage: An Account of the Ohio River Flood of 1937." *Bulletin of Cincinnati Historical Society* 22, no. 2 (April 1964): 91–109.

Stockton, Julia. *Verses and Sonnets*. London: Forgotten Books, 2015.

Stoker, Gerry. "City of Norwood, Ohio, U.S. Environmental Protection Agency Work Plan for Brownfields Assessment Grants." 2

"Storer, Maria Longworth Nichols." Theodore Roosevelt Center, https://www.theo dorerooseveltcenter.org/Learn-About-TR/TR-Encyclopedia/Family-and-Friends/ Maria-Storer.

Striker, Bridget B. *Lost River Towns of Boone, Kentucky*. Charleston, SC: History Press, 2007.

Suess, Jeff. "1836 Cincinnati Riots Couldn't Stop Anti-Slavery Newspaper." Cincinnati .com, May 11, 2017, https://www.cincinnati.com/story/news/2017/05/11/1836-cin cinnati-riots-couldnt-stop-anti-slavery-newspaper/101497562/.

———. "Anti-German Hysteria in City during WWI." Cincinnati.com, March 11, 2017, https://www.cincinnati.com/story/news/2017/03/11/anti-german-hysteria-city -during-wwi/98895422/.

———. "Inclines Helped the City Spread Out." *Cincinnati Enquirer*, March 3, 2017, https://www.cincinnati.com/story/news/2017/03/03/inclines-helped-city-spread -out/98577752/.

———. "William Henry Harrison's Presidential Campaign Changed Politics." Cincinnati.com, May 23, 2015, https://www.cincinnati.com/story/news/2015/05/22/ william-henry-harrisons-bid-presidency-changed-campaigns-run/27774087/.

Sugden, John. "The Treaty at Fort Finney, 1786." In *Blue Jacket, Warrior of the Shawnees*. Lincoln: University of Nebraska Press, 2000. https://shawnee-bluejacket.com/ uploads/3/4/8/4/34847868/treaty_at_fort_finney_2.pdf.

"A Surprising Fact about Feminism." *Chicago Tribune*, January 7, 2016, https://www .chicagotribune.com/redeye/redeye-a-surprising-fact-about-feminism-20160107 -story.html.

"Symmes Purchase." Ohio History Central, https://ohiohistorycentral.org/w/ Symmes_Purchase.

Tallmadge, John. *The Cincinnati Arch: Learning from Nature in the City*. Athens: University of Georgia Press, 2004.

Tate, Skip. "Patron Saint of Lost Causes." *Cincinnati Magazine*, September 1988, 64–67.

Teetor, Henry B. *The Past and Present of the Mill Creek Valley*. Cincinnati: Cohen and Co., 1882.

"The Terrace Plaza Hotel: Recognizing Greatness." *AEQAI*, March 3, 2019, http://aeqai .com/main/2019/03/the-terrace-plaza-hotel-recognizing-greatness/.

Thom, James Alexander. *Follow the River*. New York: Ballantine Books, 1981.

Thompson, Ann. "Pioneer Cemetery Is Clue to Cincinnati Founders." WVXU, August 27, 2013, https://www.wvxu.org/post/pioneer-cemetery-clue-cincinnati -founders#stream/0.

———. "Remembering Norwood's GM Plant 30 Years Later." WVXU, August 25, 2017, https://www.wvxu.org/post/remembering-norwoods-gm-plant-30-years-later #stream/0.

Tibbets, John Henry. "Reminiscences of Slavery Times." Tibbets Family Antislavery History, https://fordwebtech.com/tibbets-history/JohnTibbetsLetter.php.

Tolzmann, Don Heinrich. *John Hauck: Cincinnati's West End Beer Baron: The Man and His Brewery*. Cincinnati: Little Miami Publishing, 2017.

Traub, George, and Debra Mooney. "A Biography of St. Ignatius Loyola (1491–1556): The Founder of the Jesuits." Xavier University, https://www.xavier.edu/mission-iden tity/xaviers-mission/who-was-st-ignatius-loyola.php.

Triggs, Oscar Lovell. *Arts and Crafts Movement*. New York: Parkstone Press International, 2014.

Triplett, Boone. *Canals of Ohio: A History and Tour Guide*. Wadsworth, OH: Silver Sassafras Publications, 2011.

Trong, Quan. "City's Largest Park Celebrates 100 Years." *Cincinnati Enquirer*, June 4, 2011, S6–S7.

Turner, Harold W. *From Temple to Meeting House*. New York: Mouton Publishers, 1979.

Tweh, Bowdeya. "RockTenn Closing Oakley Plant, Laying off 63." *Cincinnati Enquirer*, October 24, 2014, https://www.cincinnati.com/story/money/2014/10/24/rocktenn -closing-cincinnati-facility/17843825/.

"Wilmington Ohio Main Street 1930." *Uibles Family Blog*, http://uible.blogspot.com/ search?q=Artemus.

"Underground Railroad: Fee Villa." *Breathless Adventurer* (blog), June 27, 2015, https:// breathlessadventurer.com/2015/06/27/ur-moscow/.

"Union Baptist Church." https://www.union-baptist.net/about-us/our-history/.

"United States Indian Wars, 1780s–1890s." FamilySearch, https://www.familysearch .org/wiki/en/United_States_Indian_Wars,_1780s-1890s.

"United States Playing Card Company, Cincinnati." Ohio History Collection, https:// www.ohiomemory.org/digital/collection/p267401coll34/id/7880.

"Uranus." Greek Mythology, https://www.greekmythology.com/Other_Gods/Uranus/ uranus.html.

"Uranus." Haggard Hawks: Obscure Words, Language, Facts & Etymology, February 10, 2016, https://www.haggardhawks.com/post/2016/02/10/Uranus.

"USS *Maine* (1889)." *Wikipedia*, https://en.wikipedia.org/wiki/USS_Maine_(1889).

"Utopia, Ohio." History Collection, https://historycollection.com/10-american-utopian -communities-rose-perfection-dramatically-collapse/5/.

Venable, William Henry. *Beginnings of Literary Culture in the Ohio Valley*. Cincinnati: Robert Clarke & Co., 1891.

"Verschiedenes" [Sundries]. *Tagliches Cincinnatier Volksblatt*, March 27, 1914, 5.

"Victorian Funeral Customs and Superstitions." Friends of Oak Grove Cemetery, https://friendsofoakgrovecemetery.org/victorian-funeral-customs-fears-and -superstitions/.

Wade, Richard C. *The Urban Frontier: The Rise of Western Cities, 1790–1830*. Urbana: University of Illinois Press, 1959.

Walker, Linda Smith. *Williamsburg and Batavia: Images of America*. Charleston, SC: Arcadia, 2012.

"Walking Tour & Pocket History, Netherland Plaza." Historic Hotels of America, https://www3.hilton.com/resources/media/hi/CVGNPHF/en_US/pdf/en_CVGNPHF_Walking-Tour-and-History_Dec2016.pdf.

"Walton CCC Camp Bean Ridge." Historical Marker Database, https://www.hmdb.org/m.asp?m=133269.

Warren, Josiah. *Equitable Commerce: A New Development of Principles*. Edited by Stephen P. Andrews. New York: Burt Franklin, 1852.

"Water Tower Completed." *Cincinnati Enquirer*, September 20, 1940, 24.

Weigley, Russell. *History of the United States Army*. New York: MacMillan, 1967.

White, Emerson E. "History of Public Education in Ohio for Fifty Years." *Ohio Educational Monthly*, August 1897.

White, Gerald, "Central Parkway 'Subway' Isn't One, U.S. Official Says." *Cincinnati Enquirer*, April 5, 1963, 1.

White, John H., Jr. "The Cincinnati Inclined Plane Railway Company: The Mount Auburn Incline and the Lookout House." Cincinnati Museum Center, http://library.cincymuseum.org/topics/i/files/inclines/chsbull-v27-n1-cin-007.pdf.

"Whitewater Canal." *Moment of Indiana History*, June 13, 2005, https://indianapublicmedia.org/momentofindianahistory/whitewater-canal/.

"Whitewater Colony of Shakers Soon Will Disappear." *Cincinnati Times Star*, October 17, 1916.

Whitford, Frederick, Andrew G. Martin, and Phyllis Mattheis. *The Queen of American Agriculture: A Biography of Virginia Claypool Meredith*. West Lafayette, IN: Purdue University Press, 2008.

"Why the Star City." City of Miamisburg, http://miamisburg200.com/history/.

Wilde, Renee. "WYSO Curious Investigates the Explosive History of Buildings along the Bike Path." WYSO, July 27, 2017, https://www.wyso.org/post/wyso-curious-investigates-explosive-history-buildings-along-bike-path.

"William Henry Harrison and the Cincinnati & Whitewater Canal." Historical Marker Database, https://www.hmdb.org/m.asp?m=78769.

Williams, Byron. *History of Clermont and Brown Counties, Ohio: From the Earliest Historical Times down to the Present*. Volume 2. Milford, OH: Hobart Publishing, 1913.

*Williams Hamilton County Directory for 1907–8*. Cincinnati: Williams Directory Co., 1908.

Wilson, Calvin Dill. *Glendale the Beautiful*. N.p., 1931.

Wise, Isaac Mayer. *The World of My Books*. Translated and with an introduction by Albert H. Friedlander. Cincinnati: American Jewish Archives, n.d.

Wohlfarth, Jenny. "What Lies beneath Fernald Preserve." *Cincinnati Magazine*, June 7, 2019, https://www.cincinnatimagazine.com/citywiseblog/what-lies-beneath-the-fernald-preserve/.

Wolberger, Ofer. "Cincinnati Starchitecture." *New York Times*, September 13, 2015, https://www.nytimes.com/slideshow/2015/09/13/magazine/university-of-cincinnati/s/cincinnati-university-slide-P1KC.html.

Wolff, Claude. "'Garden of Hope' Chapel Being Built in Kenton." *Courier-Journal* (Louisville, KY), August 8, 1956, 17.

Works Progress Administration. *Cincinnati: A Guide to the Queen City and Its Neighbors.* N.p.: US History Publishers, 1979.

"Would Enjoin Health Officer." *Cincinnati Enquirer*, March 27, 1914, 10.

Wright, Steven. "R. K. LeBlond's Legacy Lives On." *Cincinnati Business Courier*, March 9, 1998, https://www.bizjournals.com/cincinnati/stories/1998/03/09/focus3.html.

Zdrojewski, Ed. "Frederick Geier and the Cincinnati Mill." *Cutting Tool Engineering*, June 1993.

# LOCATION INDEX

Kathleen R. Smythe is an African historian with years of fieldwork experience in Tanzania, East Africa. She is the author of *Africa's Past, Our Future* (2015). She also teaches and writes about sustainability and has recently published *Whole Earth Living* (2020). She cares deeply about restoring humanity's interdependence with all other living beings and ecosystems. She finds great joy in doing small tasks alongside others that help to nourish a local food system and in walking and biking for short or long journeys. She is the mother of two grown children from whom she has already learned a great deal.

Chris Hanlin is a retired architect, longtime cyclist, local historian, and photographer. He loves historical research and loves a good story.